Thank you Damien

for all your relief.

Evelyn

FOR MICHAEL

Fig. 1

Natacha Rambova

"A questing, creative woman far ahead of her time – and truly exotic." [1]

---

1 *Kirkus Reviews*, review of *Madam Valentino, The Many Lives of Natacha Rambova,* by Michael Morris, August 1, 1991.

Published by:
Viale Industria Pubblicazioni
Torino, Italy – A.D. 2017
viplibri@libero.it
www.viplibri.net
Copyright 2017
Michael Morris and Evelyn Zumaya

In Deposito Legale presso SBN
http://www.sbn.it/opacsbn/opac/iccu/free.jsp

ISBN: 978-0-9987098-0-2

BEYOND VALENTINO

A *Madam Valentino* Addendum

by

Michael Morris

&

Evelyn Zumaya

TABLE OF CONTENTS

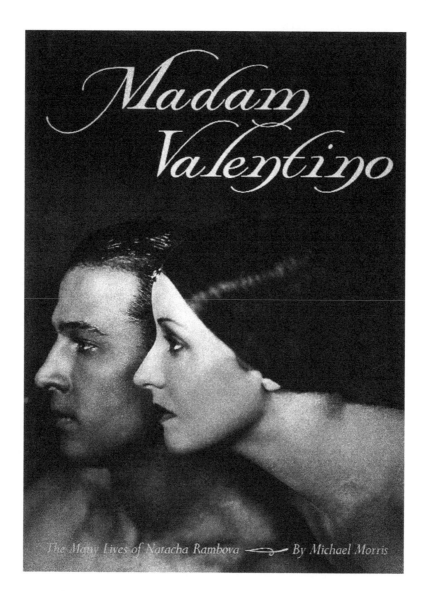

Fig. 2

Madam Valentino, by Michael Morris, published by Abbeville Press, 1991

A WORK IN HEAVENLY PROGRESS

An Introduction by Evelyn Zumaya

Ms. Flower Hujer sits before her vanity table mirror, an arc of light bulbs addressing her eighty-two-year-old face. The danseuse finesses; she is pleased with her makeup, hair and silken wardrobe.

Her kohl-lined eyes smolder and her blazing cheek bones leave no doubt. In the boudoir of her Astoria, New York home, this grande dame scrutinizes the final touches on an entrance she has been anticipating for months. Flower Hujer is about to meet Father Michael Morris in the Russian Tea Room on Fifty-Seventh Street in New York City, an historic restaurant where "defining cultural moments take place." [2]

It was November 2, 1989, when Michael Morris, a forty-year-old Dominican friar from Berkeley, California, escorted Flower Hujer to dinner in the Russian Tea Room. He chose his setting wisely; a grand, Russian Modernist venue near Carnegie Hall founded in 1927 by members of the Russian Imperial Ballet.

Michael Morris and Flower Hujer had been exchanging letters and phone calls for a few years but this dinner would be their only face-to-face meeting. Michael eagerly anticipated his coveted interview with a contemporary of Natacha Rambova; the subject of a biography he was then researching.

Flower Hujer was once a student in Theodore Kosloff's Imperial Russian Ballet School in Los Angeles. Natacha Rambova taught at Kosloff's school and was a prominent member of his retinue. Flower was but a ten-year-old when she began her ballet studies with Theodore Kosloff and Natacha Rambova, but by the fall of 1989, her memories of those days gone by were still vivid.

No photographs were taken during Ms. Hujer's Russian Tea Room dinner with Michael Morris but she seized the opportunity to present him with an autographed, black and white publicity photograph. The inscribed photograph was a recent portrait promoting her upcoming dance recitals. Despite her advanced age, a reviewer for the *New York Times* heralded her performances that year with the headline, "*Exotic Motions with a Jolt of Presence.*" [3]

By 1989, Michael Morris had been researching his Rambova biography for almost ten years and Ms. Hujer was not the only Natacha Rambova contemporary he cleverly located and impressed. The interviews he conducted with those who knew her personally were many and provided him with a substantial and unique archive of first-hand accounts. This wealth of discovery would form the foundation of his Rambova biography published in 1991, which he titled, *Madam Valentino*.

Michael Morris researched and wrote *Madam Valentino* throughout the 1980's, just prior to the advent of the internet. Consequently, a great deal of his research was conducted via handwritten letters. These letters included correspondence with two other members of Theodore Kosloff's ballet troupe, Vera Fredova and Agnes DeMille as well as Rambova's companion and secretary, Mark Hasselriis. Michael's correspondence with other notables including Los Angeles District Attorney James Idleman, Bollingen Foundation editor William McQuire, writer and activist Dorothy Norman and actress Patsy Ruth Miller, fill some one hundred folders in his unparalleled Rambova archive. Although Michael Morris published *Madam Valentino* in 1991 to rave reviews, he never ceased

---

2   http://www.russiantearoomnyc.com/
3   Dunning, Jennifer, *The Times Book Review*, April 18, 1990.

hoping for a way to share more of his archival materials. When I first met Michael in 2000, he was adamant that *Madam Valentino* was still a "work in progress".

Over the subsequent years since our first meeting, I completed my biography on Rudolph Valentino titled, *Affairs Valentino* with Michael's mentorship as he reiterated he felt a *Madam Valentino* addendum was imminent. Such an addendum he defined as being, *"ancillary material that supports our biographies, mine on Rambova and yours on Valentino."* [4] Michael's addendum remained a concept, a dream, until 2009 when he was invited to participate in the organization of an international conference on Rudolph Valentino sponsored by the Italian National Cinema Museum and the University of Turin.[5]

As a member of the conference's Scientific Organizing Committee, Michael encouraged me to submit a paper on my Valentino research. My work was accepted and I was invited to read the paper at the week-long conference in February. Michael was also scheduled to read a paper on Rambova.[6] It was while preparing his speech for the Valentino conference in Turin that Michael renewed his desire to publish more of his archive. Turin became the turning point in transforming *Beyond Valentino, The Madam Valentino Addendum*, from dream to reality.

From the onset of our friendship, Michael and I shared a mutual respect for each others work and collaborated on several projects, not only *Affairs Valentino* but Aurelio Miccoli's fine account of Rudolph Valentino's childhood years, *The Infancy of the Myth*. In this spirit we began a collaboration on *Beyond Valentino*. Michael was emphatic this book not be just another Natacha Rambova biography. His goal was to present a compendium of archival material, primarily photographs, along with introductory essays, sufficient to grant coherence to the project's overall presentation. Above all, he wished to focus on Rambova's scholarship and showcase her unpublished writing. He lamented that although he received permission to publish these works in 1991, his publisher felt the materials too lengthy to include in *Madam Valentino*.

Our initial efforts included the exchange of hundreds of e-mails as we debated how best to present the disparate elements, or miscellany, he wished to include. We designed several preliminary book covers, devised an outline and began to organize Michael's enormous archive of correspondence and photographs. Our work remained sporadic until the spring of 2016.

It was then Michael received a terminal diagnosis. He wrote to tell me the unthinkable news and without pause turned to the subject of the completion of this book with a, "Time's a'wasting!" Despite the obvious challenges, we resolved to work diligently depending on his physical well-being. By the end of June, this book was moving towards completion and due for publication by the end of 2016 in commemoration of the 25th anniversary of the publication of *Madam Valentino*. On July 8th, I sent Michael an e-mail with news I would soon forward a revised cover design. He responded with a brief e-mail saying, "Great! Wonderful!" Those were his last words to me.

Seven days later, on July 15th, Michael Morris passed away. I knew he was gravely ill, yet I expected some sort of recovery, extended treatment and a little more time. News of his sudden death hit hard and during the ensuing days of mourning, the fate of Michael's *Beyond Valentino* remained in question. In September, I traveled to Berkeley, California to meet with his family and his literary executor. They made the decision that I would complete Michael's last work. Shortly after this meeting, I received his entire, magnificent Rambova archive. It was then I realized Michael had left me the seeds with which to plant and nurture to fruition his beautiful garden that had been his dream for twenty-five years. As the contents of those unwieldy boxes of files unfolded, discoveries were made, new directions in research were required of me and unexpected twists and turns

4 E-mail sent on March 23, 2014 from Michael Morris to Evelyn Zumaya, "...I will say that we are presenting here..ancillary material ..."
5 Convegno Valentino, (Valentino Conference) *Rodolfo Valentino, La Seduzione Del Mito, Mostra, Film, Convegno, Seminari, Incontri, Omaggi, Recital*, Febbraio – Maggio, 2009.
6 Convegno Valentino, "*Intorno a Rodolfo Valentino*", February, 24, 2009.

rendered the task before me overwhelming.

As Michael had yet to write his introductory essays to each chapter, I created this text by incorporating his copious hand-written notes, transcripts of his lectures on Rambova and our fourteen years of e-mail exchange. The process of completing this work also required a great deal of research for me as Natacha Rambova was not my field of expertise. This said, she certainly became so.

The work was at times further complicated with the realization that I was completing my friend's posthumous work. How sad I often felt, realizing Michael did not live quite long enough to see his dream realize. I took heart in an e-mail he sent me shortly after he fell ill, *"My body may be breaking down but my mind is on fire and my creative juices are flowing. I am so blessed to have you as a dear friend and an artist aid me in this my last Rambova tribute!"* [7] I could never have envisioned when I read those words that I would finish this book without him.

In Flower Hujer's thank-you note to Michael Morris, dated December 15, 1989, she gushed over her evening in the Russian Tea Room, describing it as "wonderful." I bet it was! In fact, I am able to make such a definitive statement from personal experience.

For on the bitter cold, final night of our week-long stay in Turin for the Convegno Valentino in 2009, Michael Morris booked reservations for the two of us to dine at Del Cambio, the city's most historic restaurant. Del Cambio, on the Piazza Carignano, was founded in 1757. Then, the establishment was not only a restaurant but the end of the carriage line from Paris to Turin and a station where the teams of horses pulling carriages from Milan to Genoa were changed.

Once again, Michael Morris chose his setting wisely. The Del Cambio, just as the Russian Tea Room in New York City, has been the site of countless "defining cultural moments" with patrons including Casanova, Balzac, Nietzsche, Verde, Maria Callas, Audrey Hepburn and in 2009, Michael Morris and Evelyn Zumaya. It was during our Del Cambio feast, served under glittering chandeliers in the baroque dining room, where the *Madam Valentino Addendum* was finally born. As our private waiter poured us through two bottles of wine, Michael and I christened the new book *Beyond Valentino* and launched this project with all possible "In Vino Veritas" sincerity. As we flew out of Turin the following morning, gazing down at the snow-covered Alps, our minds were already churning about *Beyond Valentino*. Now it is an eventful eight years later and I am proud to say; Fait Accompli!

I sit today shivering on a stone bench on the Piazza Carignano, reflecting upon the completion of this book and doing so through a veil of melancholy. With Turin's Egyptian Museum on my left and the birthplace of this book, that bastion of fine dining, Del Cambio just before me, I recall the original vision of this book that once sparkled with the enthusiasm and wit of my friend Michael Morris.

Yet, I am sure Michael would have none of my despairing. He would be off to make reservations for a fabulous meal, ordering a round of martinis and regaling me with laughter. I take this to heart as I dedicate *Beyond Valentino* to him as a tribute to his devotion to Natacha Rambova's legacy and in memory of his gallantry and brilliance throughout the years he reigned as her sole biographer. I remain eternally grateful to him for sharing the creation of this book with me, for his seeing the beauty in this spirited project so long ago, for his vision in devising a means to share his Rambova archive in this ingenious design and for working so very hard to do so until his last day on earth.

A Cura di,
Evelyn Zumaya
Turin, February 2017

---

7 E-mail from Michael Morris to Evelyn Zumaya, excerpt, May 2016.

Fig. 3

Flower Hujer, 1989

"To Michael, with the greatest admiration for his beautiful project, Flower Hujer."

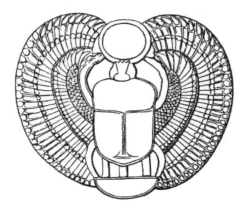

Fig. 4. Neb-Kheperu-Re

"Pictures invite the eye not to rush along, but to rest a while and dwell with them in the enjoyment of their revelation. In the fashioning of this book, therefore, my thought has been to let the spirit of the pictures rule and to arrange it so that the reader might enter into its pages at any turn they liked." [8]

8   Joseph Campell, *The Mythic Image*, (Princeton University Press, 1974) p. xi.

A Prelude
1897 - 1925

CHAPTER ONE

Fig. 5

Wink

"She was a stunning child." [1]

_____

1 M. Morris, *Madam Valentino*, Abbeville Press, 1991, p.31.

THE ARTIST AS A YOUNG GIRL

Natacha Rambova was born Winifred Shaughnessy in Salt Lake City, Utah in 1897. Natacha's mother, Winifred Kimbell, divorced her husband, Michael Shaughnessy, a Colonel and Civil War veteran, when their daughter was only three. Thereafter, the child's nuclear family was primarily female, constituted by her mother, an aunt and female cousins. This was not unusual, for her mother's family were Mormon pioneers. The custom of multiple wives creating community under the protection and governance of a distant patriarch had long been codified by religious tradition in Utah.

After Winifred Kimball's divorce from Colonel Michael Shaughnessy, she and her daughter moved to San Francisco where little Winifred, nicknamed "Wink", received her primary education. Her mother, nicknamed "Muzzie", then embarked upon a career in interior design, earning a fortune designing for her San Francisco clientele.

Muzzie re-married and took as her second husband Edgar DeWolfe, the brother of Elsie DeWolfe, the woman credited with having turned the art of interior design into big business. It was Aunt Elsie DeWolfe who suggested to her new sister-in-law, Muzzie that little Wink be educated in Europe. In 1905, at the age of eight years old, Wink was enrolled at Leatherhead Court, an exclusive school for girls on the outskirts of London.

Leatherhead Court provided a desolate childhood experience for Wink, one that scarred her emotionally even as her intellectual life thrived. She later recalled how she immersed herself in mythology and art history in order to assuage the loneliness of those years. *"My interest in mythology and legend began as a child,"* she declared, *"as I never read any other kind of book."* [2] Greek and Roman mythology, Nordic legends, Arabian tales, nothing escaped her attention as she sought to satisfy her insatiable need to lose herself in fantasy and fable.

Wink's summer vacations were spent in France under the watchful eye of Aunt Elsie DeWolfe, whose home, Villa Trianon in the city of Versailles, was a veritable salon for celebrated European dignitaries and artists. Wink devoted her time to drawing and studying ballet at the Paris Opera.

All the while she was being introduced to the leading luminaries in the world of art including Sarah Bernhardt, Henry Adams, Count Robert de Montesquieu, Bernard Berenson, Loie Fuller, Auguste Rodin and Paul Poiret. The early influence of Aunt Elsie and summers spent at the opulent Villa Trianon established a broad cultural reference and artistic vocabulary for Wink.

Elsie DeWolfe was well-known in London, Paris and New York, having been an actress before she turned her artistic and professional attentions to interior design. Rejecting the then popular Victorian interior decor style, Elsie DeWolfe preferred late 18th century furniture and design. Her elegantly appointed rooms were light with pastel colors and floral fabrics and appreciated as a breath of fresh air by her clients. Wink was not only influenced by Aunt Elsie's penchant for the theatrical and her 18th century interiors but also by her eccentric lifestyle which included morning yoga practice.

---

2 Undated letter from Natacha Rambova to Mary Mellon at the Bollingen Foundation, Library of Congress, Manuscript Division, Bollingen File.

Aunt Elsie was convinced of the mental and physical benefits of yoga and young Wink would rise at dawn during her summers at Villa Trianon to join in assuming the morning asanas, or yogic postures. Aunt Elsie was also fond of walking on her hands and adept at standing on her head for long periods of time.

Whether Wink continued such a discipline when she returned to Leatherhead Court for the school year is not known. However, the influence of Aunt Elsie's Hindi practices in the setting of her home's 18th century surrounds manifested artistically in Wink as she grew into womanhood. Her artistry and life would reflect all elements of her childhood summers at Villa Trianon.

"In the nearly nine years that Wink spent at Leatherhead Court, she was most enthusiastic about field trips to the museum and ballet. The British Museum was a veritable sanctuary of visual stimulation. It provided her with solid evidence of those mythic people she read about, from the wrapped mummies and decorated sarcophagi of the mysterious Egyptians to the marbled deities found in the Parthenon fragments of the ancient Greeks. And when the Russian Ballet visited London, Wink clamored to see that one idol who was a myth in her own day, Anna Pavlova.

The Russian prima ballerina made her English debut at the Palace Theatre in London in 1910, accompanied by her partner, Mikhail Mordkin. Starting with that engagement and Pavlova's two London appearances the following year, Wink faithfully stationed herself at the stage door after each performance in order that the legendary dancer might sign the ballet scrapbook she made with the pictures pasted in it of her favorite Russian stars: Tamara Karsavina, Vaslav Nijinsky and Mikhail Mordkin. In Wink's pantheon of Russian dancers there was one other, Theodore Kosloff. He had a brief debut appearance in London at the Coliseum Theatre, but the memory of that performance on a gray July day in 1909 would prove fateful for the young girl.

...At the Coliseum that day, there was coincidentally another woman in the audience for whom this performance would have its long-lasting effect. Her name was Winifred Edwards, and neither she nor Wink nor Theodore Kosloff had any idea then how their lives would be intimately connected to each other in the future. "[3]

---

3 *Madam Valentino*, p. 15 -17.

Fig. 6

Baby Wink, Utah, 1897

Fig. 7

Wink as young girl, San Francisco

Fig. 8

Wink's Father, "The Colonel" Michael Shaughnessy

"Her father was an Irish Catholic from New York who enlisted in the Union forces and became a noted fighter and Civil War hero. Afterward, he was appointed as U.S. Marshall of Mississippi where he fought an engaging duel or two - he was then transferred to the Utah Territory.

It is ironic that while he was stationed there to monitor the Mormons and make sure they didn't violate the anti-poligamy laws, he married a Mormon himself, made a fortune in mining interests and fathered one child. This child, Winifred Kimball Shaughnessy was nicknamed, "Wink" so as not to confuse her with her mother. The marriage did not work out, the Colonel was much older than his bride and so by the time Wink was three – she and her mother were on their own." [4]

---

4 M. Morris archival notes.

Fig. 9

Wink begins her schooling at Leatherhead Court

Fig. 10 – 11 Leatherhead Court

Fig. 12

Wink's Leatherhead Court school portrait, London

"It was Aunt Elsie DeWolfe who suggested that Wink be educated in Europe. The child didn't want to leave home and family but was scuttled off at the age of eight to Leatherhead Court, an exclusive girl's school outside of London. She was desperately lonely and lost herself in art, dance and mythology." [5]

---

5   M. Morris archival notes.

Fig. 13

A Studious Wink at Leatherhead Court

"Described in the *Leatherhead Directory* at that time as 'a high class school for young ladies' Leatherhead Court was situated on Randalls Road, on the outskirts of the town, in an area surrounded by park lands and meadows. The forty-year-old half-timbered and brick building was an eclectic pile, part Georgian and part Tudor, with a multitude of of leaded windows, gables and chimneys. To Wink it must have seemed a strange castle, where girls from all over the world were deposited by their wealthy parents, to be coddled and sternly corrected by headmistress, Miss Tullis."[6]

---

6 *Madam Valentino*, p. 34 – 35.

Fig. 14

Wink's favorite ballet instructor at the Paris Opera ballet school, Roseta Mauri y Segura, performing in wooden clogs in the ballet created for her, *La Korrigan* (The Goblin Maiden) by Francis Coppee in 1880

Fig. 15

Paris Opera school ballerina, Roseta Mauri y Segura,
painting by Lèon Comerre

Fig. 16 – 17 Aunt Elsie DeWolfe's Villa Trainon in Versailles

Fig. 18

Summer! Wink with Aunt Elsie DeWolfe at Villa Trianon

Fig. 19-21 Aunt Elsie DeWolfe

Fig. 22-23

Elsie DeWolfe's personal sitting room at the Villa Trianon

Fig. 24

Elsie DeWolfe, Lady Mendl, 1946

"Be pretty if you can, be witty if you must, but be gracious if it kills you." [7]

7   Elsie DeWolfe commentary

Fig. 25

"I'm going to make everything around me beautiful—that will be my life." [8]

---

8   Elsie DeWolfe commentary

Fig. 26

Wink in self-styled tutu

"She became a great fan of Pavlova and saw a rising Russian star, Theodore Kosloff, dance at the London Coliseum." [9]

---

9 M. Morris archival notes.

CHAPTER TWO

Fig. 27

"Kosloff told Wink that she had the potential of becoming a première danseuse under his tutelage, of course. But two things were necessary if she hoped to pursue a career in dance. First, she must never again wear shoes with heels; they destroyed a dancer's posture. Second, she must change her name.[1]

---

1 *Madam Valentino*, p.43

Dance & Design

During the outbreak of World War I, mother Muzzie brought her daughter Wink home to San Francisco. However, the seventeen-year-old had no interest in staying home and convinced her mother to allow her to study ballet in New York City. There she would live with her Aunt Teresa Werner and study with Theodore Kosloff, a Russian emigré and former member of Diaghilev's Ballet Russe. Kosloff had recently opened a dance studio in Manhattan.

Having studied ballet in Paris with Roseta Mauri, young Wink was already a dedicated ballet student. It was not long after arriving in New York City that she became Theodore Kosloff's favorite student and his constant companion. Succumbing to the Russian dance instructor's charms, she changed her name to Natacha Rambova and joined his ballet troupe.[2]

By 1916, Natacha was touring with Kosloff's Imperial Russian Ballet and had assumed a position of assistant instructor. Theodore and Natacha became romantically involved as he led her to believe she was his alone. Their affair took place while he supported his wife and child, living in a foreign country and while he treated the other members of his female staff as his private harem.

Theodore Kosloff's Imperial Russian Ballet Company was a success wherever it played. With music composed by Borodin and Stravinsky and costumes derived from designs by Bakst, the newspapers hailed their performances with stellar reviews. In their New York City engagement, the dance troupe broke box-office records once established by Sarah Bernhardt. When the company reached Los Angeles, they attracted the attention of the motion picture industry, most notably director Cecil B. DeMille, who offered Kosloff a lucrative movie contract.

During this time the world's attention was focused on South America where the ruins of Macchu Picchu had just been discovered. Subsequent cultural elements soon surfaced which had as their inspiration the ancient Indian civilizations of Central and South America. Frank Lloyd Wright launched his Mayan styled architecture in Los Angeles and Theodore Kosloff made his movie debut in DeMille's Aztec themed film titled, *The Woman That God Forgot* starring opera singer Geraldine Farrar. Yet unbeknownst to director DeMille, it was Natacha Rambova who designed Kosloff's elaborate costumes for the film.

The Imperial Russian Ballet began its second season in the fall of 1917, with a timely production number titled, "The Aztec Dance" performed pas de deux by Theodore Kosloff and Natacha Rambova. They portrayed themselves with exaggerated make-up, partial nudity, costumes of leather, metal plates and grommets, feathers and copper body paint. Their Aztec Dance was innovative and avant guard, incorporating the warlike with the ceremonial.

---

2 *The Ariavarta Journal, 2001.* Origin of the name Natacha Rambova explained by Michael Morris to Dr. Vladimir Rosov.

Meanwhile in Russia, the Bolshevik Revolution ruined Kosloff's financial investments there and he found himself forced to remain in Hollywood and work in DeMille's pictures in order to earn a living. Together with English ballerina, Winifred Edwards, (stage name, Vera Fredova), Theodore and Natacha opened a dance studio in Los Angeles to raise funds. The women took charge of the classes (among their pupils being Agnes DeMille and Flower Hujer) while Theodore acted in a string of DeMille movies.

During this time Natacha's considerable design talents were being utilized by both Kosloff and DeMille. She designed the fantasy sequence in a film based on the Cinderella myth titled, *Forbidden Fruit* (released in February of 1921) and fashioned the Fairy Godmother's costume after the prototype found in the Mater Dolorosa imagery of popular Spanish piety. Her innovative design produced a transformed heroine who wore a ball gown based on an 18th century court costume. However, in the film this costume was illuminated by and covered with tiny electric lights.

While Natacha grew increasingly disappointed by Theodore's infidelities, she found solace and inspiration in art and in designing the costumes and stage settings for the dance troupe. During this emotionally difficult time in her life, when she was described by others as withdrawn and weeping, she was counseled by Vera Fredova, who told her,

"Love comes and goes, my dear, but art endures forever." [3]

When not touring with Kosloff's Imperial Russian Ballet, Natacha engaged in disparate creative projects. She designed a coloring book for children using mythological figures to depict the embodiment of certain colors. For the color brown, she drew the god Vulcan with his anvil and in a pose similar to that used by

3   M. Morris, *Madam Valentino*, p. 50.

the artist Ingres in his famous 19th century painting, *Zeus and Thetis*. In the design she created for the color red, Natacha depicted the god of war, Mars, in a pose reminiscent of the *Apollo Belvedere* in the Vatican.

She drew upon her European art education and coupled this with her own fertile imagination to continue creating a series of striking costumes and sets. Even as Theodore betrayed her with other women, Natacha draped him in her exotic designs, accentuating his physique and enhancing his foreign allure. All the while he took full credit for her designs while befriending DeMille as the two men spent many weekends hunting and carousing on DeMille's country estate called Paradise, located in the mountains north of Los Angeles.

Natacha received no credit for her earliest screen design efforts as Theodore kept her role as designer hidden away at the dance studio where she taught and cooked while he basked in his Hollywood limelight. It was his fatal mistake to ask Natacha to deliver a series of her own design sketches to the Russian actress Alla Nazimova, who recently arrived in Hollywood from Broadway where she'd been a success interpreting Ibsen.

Alla Nazimova came to Hollywood with the intention of producing and starring in "high class" artistic films and she often asked Theodore Kosloff for design assistance. When Nazimova discovered Natacha's design talent she hired her on the spot, releasing her from the physical, psychological and artistic bondage Theodore imposed upon her.

When Natacha packed her belongings to leave, his response was to shoot her in the leg. One wonders whether Natacha learned any lesson about love from this violent and traumatizing event. It certainly can be surmised from this incident that she would be inclined to wonder if art and not *amour* would be her path to a life fulfilled.

While working as Nazimova's art director for such films as *Billions, Aphrodite, Camille* and *Salomé*, Natacha's knowledge of the latest developments in design blended effectively with her inventive twists on replicating images from the past.

She was well-acquainted with current European trends in fashion, architecture and design. For instance, the alcove featured so predominately in *Camille* was inspired by Emil-Jacques Ruhlmann's "Interior" (featured in L'Art Decoratif Français, c. 1920).

With her keen ability to analyze modern design trends and historical artistic masterpieces, Natacha successfully interpreted her compelling designs. Design, art, archetypes and myth became the essentials of her life.

It was while working as art director for Nazimova's production of *Camille,* that Natacha met Rudolph Valentino, the lead actor in the film. As Valentino's friend and business manager would recall:

"Natacha was then the art director for Alla Nazimova, and was designing gorgeous gowns for that eminent artist in Pierre Louy's 'Aphrodite'. Rudy (Rudolph Valentino) told me that he and Natacha did not speak the first time they saw each other, nor were they even introduced. Natacha, in her cool, detached way, calmly went about her business without so much as a glance in the direction of the proud young Valentino.

...Every strong personality in man or woman will understand that this aloofness could not fail to intrigue so intense an individual as Rudy. Possibly he himself did not realize this, but the fact remains that, from this time on, it was observed that Valentino made persistent efforts to be with Natacha in what was perhaps an unconscious but nevertheless determined attempt to break down her reserve." [4]

It was not long before Natacha's chill towards Valentino thawed and the two fell in love despite his being a married man at the time. It has subsequently been alleged Valentino's "marital woes" were complex yet they were remarkably simple; he married the actress, Jean Acker, who rejected him on their wedding night. When he fell in love with Natacha, he found the impetus to proceed with and secure his divorce from Jean Acker.

His marital status did not prevent him from living with Natacha during their engagement while they established their life together, both personally and professionally.

4 George Ullman, *The George Ullman Memoir*, p. 137.

Fig. 28 – 29

The youthful Theodore Kosloff

Fig. 30

Snapshot of the residence where Theodore Kosloff held his Los Angeles dance studio, 1917

Fig. 31

The Imperial Russian Ballet School, third from left standing in dark dress, Vera Fredova, to Kosloff's right & holding hands, Flower Hujer, Natacha Rambova, third from right standing, 1919

"...Kosloff was a dedicated and extraordinary teacher who developed students to their utmost degree. Unlike so many others, who taught only toe-work and classicism, he had an open mind. We did all sorts of character work and mime. He was more of an artist than a teacher of technique...."[5]

---

5   Flower Hujer, interviews with M. Morris.

Fig. 32

Vera Fredova in "Romances of a Russian Winter" with The Imperial Russian Ballet, 1917

Fig. 33

Theodore Kosloff

"...When Kosloff was mad at his students he would yell, 'Take your make-up and toe shoes and go to home!" [6]

_____

6 Flower Hujer, interviews with M. Morris.

Fig. 34

The Aztec Dance

"....The Aztec number was choreographed for the 1917 – 1918 (second tour) after Kosloff had completed the film "*The Woman That God Forgot*" with Geraldine Farrar..." [7]

---

7   Vera Fredova correspondence with M. Morris. On reverse of photograph Natacha wrote, "Look at me!"

Fig. 35

"...When Rambova went to Kosloff's studio as a pupil (with a chaperone) in New York, she was out of practice from her French ballet experience. Kosloff was furious with her and drove her. Yet she fell in love with him. He promised to stage an entire production around her (with her family paying of course). This never materialized..." [8]

---

8   Vera Fredova correspondence with M. Morris.

Fig. 36

Fig. 36A

Natacha Rambova costume sketches

Fig. 37   Fig. 37A

Coloring Book Designs by   Ruby Red
Natacha Rambova

Brown

Fig. 38

Theodore Kosloff, unknown dancer and Natacha Rambova

" Supreme grace is represented in the amazingly clever Russian dancers who interpret a repertoire of
new terpsichorean creations." [9]

---

9   Caption on back of photo.

Fig. 39

Natacha Rambova's costume & set designs for *Fool's Paradise,* the "skaters on ice" scene

"... Rambova was not so good at technical problems. Her designs on paper did not always translate easily to set. ..." [10]

---

10   Vera Fredova correspondence with M. Morris.

Fig. 40

Costume design for *Salome*, with Alla Nazimova

"Her designs for Salomé so closely ape the Bearsdley drawings that one can't tell what her aesthetic was." [11]

---

11 Letter from Mark Hasselriis to M. Morris, October 6, 1987.

Fig. 41

Natacha Rambova's set & costume designs for the dream sequence in *Billions*, 1919

Fig. 42

Natacha's costume sketch for the Cinderella ball gown in *Forbidden Fruit*

Fig. 43

The ball gown of electric lights designed by Natacha Rambova for *Forbidden Fruit*,
as worn by Agnes Ayes

Fig. 44

Theodore Kosloff in his later years

"...Kosloff was actually prudish. He did not like painted women. Girls of his troupe had to have a family escort to go out at night..." [12]

---

12 Vera Fredova correspondence with M. Morris.

CHAPTER THREE

Fig. 45

"She was gorgeous! Men fell on their faces when they saw her." [1]

---

1 Notes from M. Hasselriis interview with M. Morris.

THE CREATION
OF A
HOLLYWOOD ICON

Of all her lovers, Natacha Rambova exercised her greatest influence on silent film icon Rudolph Valentino. She would transform him from the mustachioed villain of his earliest films, prior to their meeting in 1920, into the pomaded leading man he became. Natacha's influence over Valentino catapulted him into the paragon of style and costumed elegance thereby defining his legacy and ensuring his role as a Hollywood icon.

Valentino's polished image and screen pageantry was also an inevitable consequence of his passionate relationship with Natacha Rambova. Cameraman and friend, Paul Ivano, who once shared an apartment with Natacha and "Rudy" on Sunset Boulevard recalled how Natacha would faint from the intensity of lovemaking. *"Rudy looks best in the nude,"* she once declared and then made sure he was photographed and filmed accordingly.

Images of Valentino in the nude appear during the first days of his relationship with Natacha. That she was responsible for this turn of events is apparent by the antiquarian and art historical intelligence of his poses. She positioned him to be photographed as the god Pan, an agrarian deity renowned for sexual prowess. She undoubtedly knew this motif as it was well-known previously in the world of art and dance.

In 1912, Diaghilev's Ballet Russe presented *The Afternoon of the Faun*, which took Europe by storm. Natacha adapted the costume Leon Bakst designed for its star, Vaslav Nijinsky, and interpreted it for Rudolph Valentino. The series of photographs of Valentino as Nijinsky in *The Afternoon of the Faun*, represent a first instance of "high brow art" intersecting the career of the Italian immigrant actor.

This exotic flavor conformed to what author Gaylyn Studlar claims characterized the American woman's emerging desires. What art historians have labeled "the male gaze", that is, male artists creating imagery focused on female nudity for the pleasure of male observers, is in this instance, reversed.

Here we have a female artist (Natacha Rambova) focusing upon the nudity of her husband (Valentino) and disseminating it for the pleasure of other female gazers. That the origin of this inspiration is also embedded in the homosexual milieu that bonded Diaghilev to Nijinsky generates some confusion, namely, whether the iconography connected with Valentino is the domain of the female heterosexual gaze or the male homosexual gaze, or both.

While it is easy to understand Natacha's coupling of her husband Rudy as model to an archetype inherited from the Greco-Roman past, it is more startling to see her fuse his physique to the cultural myth of the Wild West, the Native American. Such a pose allowed for ample nudity made palatable for the American public's taste. The image of the Native American warrior is as associated as much with nature in the United States as the image of Pan is to Europeans. That Natacha was born in the American West, that her family had been part of its colonization, underscores her rationale for choosing such a motif.

The explanation that the poses were supernaturally inspired by spirit guides who counseled the Valentinos, obfuscates the fact that art historical precedents exist which Natacha would have been aware of. She outfitted Rudy in an Indian loincloth and had him strike pose after pose based upon a sculpture titled *Appeal to the Great Spirit*, created by Utah-born artist Cyrus Dallin.

Dallin came from a Mormon pioneer family, as had Natacha. He also fashioned the statue of the Angel Moroni positioned atop the Salt Lake City Temple. Natacha's great-grandfather, Heber C. Kimball, laid the cornerstone to that Temple.

The sculpture of an American Indian praying was cast in Paris in 1909 and won a gold medal for its exhibition in the Paris Salon at the same time Natacha was then a ballet student at the Paris Opera. Likewise, the sculptor James Earle Fraser created the doleful image of an American Indian brave exhausted by his battle called *End of the Trail*. This was created for the 1915, Pan-Pacific International Exposition held in San Francisco. Natacha was living in that city with her mother at that time having returned home from Europe at the beginning of World War I.

Thus it is not surprising that her gaze, which in turn becomes the emergent female gaze in cinematic audiences of the 1920s, focuses upon Valentino's physical form in his movies where she exercised artistic control. The reporter Adela Rogers St. Johns supported this view when she said that, *"the lure of Valentino was wholly, entirely, obviously the lure of the flesh."* [2]

In Valentino's film, *The Young Rajah*, Natacha's set and costume designs afforded the spectators ample flesh when she draped her husband in little more than pearls. In his films *Monsieur Beaucaire* and *Blood and Sand* there are extensive dressing scenes showcasing Valentino's physique.

In one particular scene from *The Young Rajah*, Natacha again referenced art historical sources and recreated for the film an iconography celebrated in Hindu mythology. Rudy was posed as the deity Vishnu, one of the five primary forms of God in Hindu mythology. His consort Lakshmi accompanied him as they were filmed floating in a cobra-hooded boat.

That Natacha's artistry and taste dominated Valentino is evidenced especially in those inventive cases where her creation bordered upon the absurd. In one costume she designed for *The Young Rajah*, Valentino wore a turban decorated with an explosion of pearls emanating from the side of his head.

In instances like this, Natacha's miscalculation would be used against her by her critics. The movie *Monsieur Beaucaire* would eventually become her artistic Waterloo when some critics declared she had effeminized Valentino, hiding his masculinity underneath a wardrobe of satin costumes and powdered wigs.

The desire to embark upon *Monsieur Beaucaire*, a project that would invoke all things *dix-huitieme* was not solely Natacha's idea. Rudy, whose mother was French, loved to visit the grand villa on the French Riviera, the Chateau Juan les Pins, home of Natacha's adoptive father and Muzzie's third husband, cosmetics tycoon, Richard Hudnut.

The influences of Natacha's adolescence manifested in her *Monsieur Beaucaire* designs. The years she spent at Villa Trianon with her Aunt Elsie DeWolfe, whose favorite artist was Fragonard, cannot be overlooked for setting the artistic and thematic tone of *Monsieur Beaucaire*, a film that received almost universal acclaim when it was first released.

Natacha's artistic pride was wounded however whenever criticism was leveled against her lamenting, *"Some of the farmers of God's country have taken unkindly to the white wigs."* [3]

2 *Madam Valentino*, p. 152.

3 *Madam Valentino*, p. 152.

The elitism in her statement was repeated later when she complained about her husband being sent fan mail *"...from girls in Oshkosh and Kalamazoo."* The statement is also revelatory in regards to the the status of their marriage after *Monsieur Beaucaire.* Mr. and Mrs. Rudolph Valentino were portrayed through carefully-crafted articles in fan magazines, as living in exotic homes, enjoying European vacations and extravagant lifestyles while pursuing their interest in psychic and spiritual activities.

From as early as 1923, Rudy and Natacha were experimenting with automatic writing and increasingly heeding the advice of etheric beings, or "voices" they contacted via séances. Although the occult appears to have been a subject of more fascination to Natacha, it was an interest Rudy embraced.

"Rudy was extremely psychic in temperament and was a really very good medium himself. He used to have automatic writing sèances with Natacha, Aunt Tessy (Aunt Teresa Werner) and Mrs. Hudnut, during which many excellent messages were given." [4]

Rudolph Valentino's reliance upon the daily guidance of two "master guides", an American Indian spirit he called Black Feather and an ancient Egyptian he referred to as Mesolope became public knowledge. His open admittance to participating in various forms of occult activity did not shock his public.

With magician, illusionist and escape artist, Harry Houdini and Sir Arthur Conan Doyle, author of the Sherlock Holmes detective series collaborating to present spiritualism to their audiences as being valid and entertaining, Natacha and Rudolph Valentino contributed to the fashionably chic trend. The Valentinos were no less enticed by the paranormal than their peers of the day.

Whether mediums were deemed frauds or genuine, whether it was all hokum or real; these were topics being discussed by the mainstream population. With Doyle's publication of *The New Revelation* in 1922, his reputable stature as an author granted credibility to the subject of mediums, spiritualists and séances.

Rudolph Valentino and Natacha Rambova contributed to the legitimizing of paranormal trends as they admitted to consulting voices from beyond via mediums and utilizing automatic writing to seek advice in regards to their film projects as well as their personal lives.

Despite Natacha and Rudy's belief they were receiving psychic assistance, it would only be a few years before the public and the movie producers pried them apart.

Natacha likened her husband to a man-child, yet she besotted him. She mothered him, managed him and dressed him for his films until he reached a point in his career where he decided he could only advance professionally by signing a contract with United Artists excluding her from any creative involvement.

Natacha was not present for the signing of this controversial contract as she had been with his other contracts. In doing so, Rudolph Valentino was effectively destroying his marriage, for their marriage was based as much on art as it had been on physical attraction. Natacha consoled herself in the production of a movie she devised titled *What Price Beauty.* Her film would not have a debut for lack of a distributor. This while Rudy's career and his latest films made with United Artists continued to achieve positive review and acclaim.

Throughout, the Valentino's love lingered, even as their marriage further disintegrated. Pinkerton Police detectives, hired by Valentino, informed him of Natacha's infidelity with a studio official. Was this a deliberate attempt on the part of Natacha to measure Rudy's love for her through jealousy? If so, it further dented the wreckage of their marriage with anger, violence and desperate lovemaking.

As their marriage fell apart during the

4   Wehner, *A Curious Life,* p. 372.

summer of 1925, Natacha tried to convince Rudy that their end was near. Hollywood collector, William Self was in possession of letters Natacha wrote to Valentino at the end of their union. Two sentences from her correspondence stood out in all their anguish.

"With my arms around you, I give you my last kiss. You were my first real love and will be my last."

With a parting kiss at a train station in Los Angeles on August 15, 1925, staged for the benefit of the gathered press, Natacha and Rudolph Valentino separated and would never see each other again. Despite her bitterness, Natacha's creation of the archetype of Rudolph Valentino as the Latin Lover evolved as part of American film myth.

Fig. 46

Natacha Rambova & Rudolph Valentino with their German Shepard, "Sheik" and Pekingese puppy, "Little Chuckie" in Hollywood @ 1923

Fig. 47

The Valentino's Whitley Heights living room

"....It was a hillside house. You entered a hall which gave upon a floor with only two bedrooms and two baths. You had to go downstairs to find the living room with its black marble floor and cerise hangings. The color scheme of the bedrooms was canary and black, the exotic combinations of the entire house being the work of Natacha. It was oriental in the extreme and its violent contrasts of color were anything but restful." [5]

5   *The George Ullman Memoir*, p. 173.

Fig. 48

"During this period the Valentinos were living in the house on Whitley Heights which Rudy occupied as a bachelor. This was only about ten minutes' drive from the studio, they were able to run back and forth at will. From its windows you could see the hills which form the Hollywood Bowl, and the flaming cross which marked The Pilgrimage Play." [6]

---

6   *The George Ullman Memoir*, p. 173.

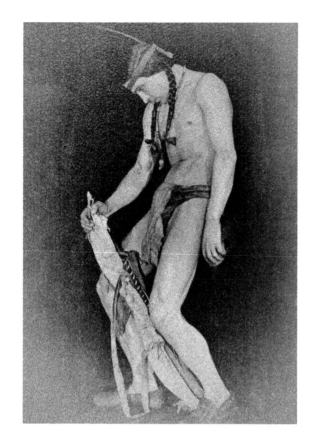

Fig. 49   Fig. 50

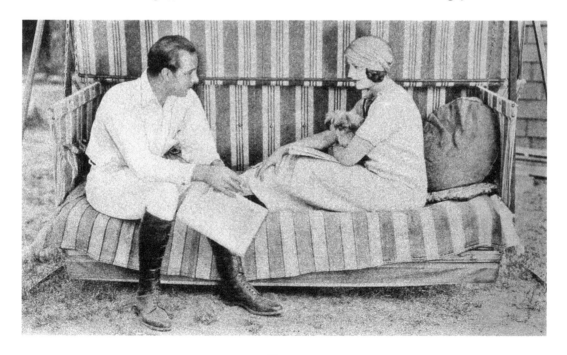

Fig. 51

Fig. 52

Fig. 52A

Valentino as Nijinsky by Helen MacGregor, 1923

"The photos of Valentino posing as Nijinsky's faun were basically Natacha Rambova's artistic manifesto to the film industry. Not only do they represent the wedding of his body to her highly cultivated mind, they were a challenge to Hollywood, where they were readily disseminated, to raise cinema from mere entertainment to fine art. Unfortunately, all her photos managed to do were to provoke (Valentino's first wife) Jean Acker's divorce lawyers who brought them to court in an effort to shock the judge with the impression that this is how Valentino spent his time with his mistress." [7]

---

7 M. Morris archival notes.

Fig. 53

Rudolph Valentino in *The Young Rajah* wearing Natacha Rambova's costume design

"Valentino's most popular movie roles were those in which he was either wounded or killed. Real death superseded the effect these films had upon the public psyche and launched the filmic hero into mythic immortality." [8]

---

8   M. Morris archival notes.

Fig. 54

Rudolph Valentino in *The Son of the Sheik*

"Rudy's heightened psychic senses made it possible for him to see many shadowy forms and snatches of scenes long ago, reflected in the Astral Light. But in this realized atmosphere of the Arabian Nights it was not difficult to imagine in these moonlit gardens the faint twang of some lute or the hushed laughter of some Moorish beauty with raven tresses." [9]

---

9 Natacha Rambova, *Rudy: An Intimate Portrait of Rudolph Valentino*, p. 121.

Fig. 55

Mr. & Mrs. Valentino

"Rudy and Natacha's story is Pygmalion in reverse. This is the only time in Hollywood history when a woman was responsible for fashioning a male movie star and establishing him as an idol. Mauritz Stiller created Garbo, Josef Von Sternberg created Dietrich. In a sense Rambova created Valentino, the Latin-lover, because it is a role that had its origins in their passionate, often turbulent love life." [10]

---

10 M. Morris archival notes.

Fig. 56

Rudolph Valentino

"I do not hesitate to assert that, while Natacha Rambova could never cause a world-worship such as Rudy achieved almost without effort, yet Natacha was the greater soul. And it is only fair to say that her culture, which she painstakingly but subtly communicated to her husband, was one which others recognized and which in my opinion put him forever in her debt. He was truly, and in the highest sense, elevated by his association with Natacha." [11]

---

11 *The George Ullman Memoir*, 184.

Fig. 57

Fig. 58 – 59
Monsieur Beaucaire, sets and costumes by Natacha Rambova

Fig. 60

Monsieur Beaucaire sets and costumes by Natacha Rambova

"Today, you read about women who have taken commanding roles in the production, design or direction of films and have to jump hurdles men have not had to. And when you look at Rambova back in the 1920's, it's remarkable what she was able to do." [12]

12 Michael Morris relates to Susannah Hunnewell, *The New York Times Book Review*, October 27, 1991.

Fig. 61

Lois Wilson in Natacha Rambova's ball gown design in *Monsieur Beaucaire*

Fig. 62

Rudolph Valentino as photographed by Edward Steichen, 1926

"Hollywood, which has made a fortune in concocting tragic love stories, had a real one in the love life of Rudy and Natacha. It was glamorous. It was passionate. It even had its moments of comedy and suspense – but ultimately it was ill-fated. They say that heroes must die young. Valentino died at the age of thirty-one from complications incurred from the fact that his muse, the love of his life, had left him. And when he went to his grave, he wore the platinum slave bracelet she had placed on his wrist." [13]

---

13   M. Morris archival notes.

Foxlair

The Richard Hudnut Estate, in the Adirondack Mountains. North Creek, New York

Fig. 63

The "Big House" on the Hudnut Foxlair estate

Cosmetics tycoon, Richard Hudnut was Muzzie's third husband. His twelve-hundred acre estate in a secluded valley in upstate New York became a luxurious family getaway which he refined, cultivated and decorated over twenty years. Calling his estate Foxlair, the nearest town was the North Creek, a small town located four hours north of New York City and an hour north of Saratoga Springs. Well-hidden in the Adirondack mountains, Foxlair provided a welcome retreat for Natacha Rambova during the summer of 1922, as she left her husband Rudolph Valentino in Hollywood to await a court's decision on the status of their marriage. When Valentino went on strike later that summer, he traveled to Foxlair to evade studio detectives and join Natacha.

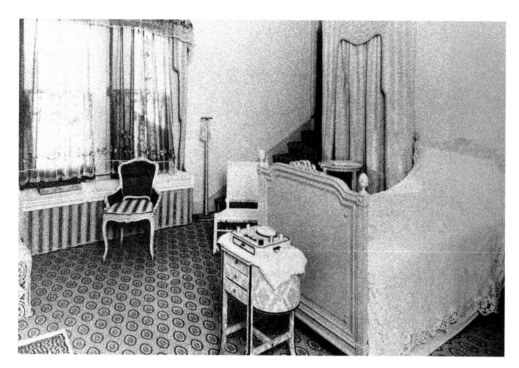

Fig. 64

Natacha's Foxlair Bedroom

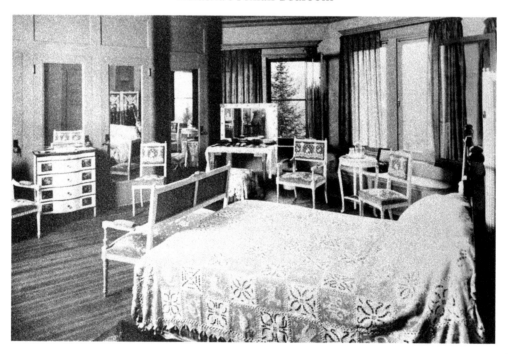

Fig. 65

Rudolph Valentino's Foxlair Bedroom

Fig. 66

The Foxlair Parlor

"Despite the fact that the prestigious home lacked electricity and telephone service, Richard Hudnut guaranteed the Foxlair experience rivaled any extravagant resort. He retained a retinue of overly qualified maids and butlers, a Swedish masseuse and a personal French chef. While the raccoons, woodchucks, porcupines, squirrels and an occasional bear carried on the outdoor business of Foxlair's wild acres, the indoor residents on the hill enjoyed luxuries unheard of in that neck of the woods...." [14]

---

14 E. Zumaya, *Affairs Valentino*, p. 130 – 131.

Fig. 67

An overcast day at Foxlair, view from the veranda

THE CHATEAU JUAN LES PINS

THE RICHARD HUDNUT RESIDENCE ON THE CÔTE D'AZUR, JUAN LES PINS, FRANCE

Fig. 68

"The Court of Palms"
The Doberman Kabar, Rudolph Valentino and Natacha Rambova

"The sun, sea and seclusion of Juan les Pins would provide an idyllic retreat for Rudy and Natacha. The stately environs became the perfect setting for Rudy to begin a smooth transformation into his next screen character; the aristocratic Monsieur Beaucaire. When photographer James Abbe arrived from Paris to visit the Valentinos, he captured some of the immediate effects of how life at the chateau was influencing Rudy. He had retired his Savile Row suits to sport casual white slacks, open shirts and a beret." [15]

---

15 *Affairs Valentino*, p. 195.

Fig. 69-70 Dining Room & Grand Living Room at the Chateau Juan les Pins

Fig. 71-72 A parlor & the paneled library at the Chateau Juan les Pins

Fig. 73-74 Muzzie's bedroom & a sitting room

Fig. 75

Natacha's Bedroom at the Chateau Juan les Pins

"The Hudnut chateau is filled with treasures; old Gobelin tapestries, collections of jade and ambers, and lovely old furniture upholstered in Saint Cyr needlepoint in mellowed colors, and there are enormous Savonerie rugs of great beauty of color and design. All of these things hallowed by the breath of time give forth a vibrational quality that makes for an unusually psychic atmosphere". [16]

16 Wehner, *A Curious Life*, p. 367-368.

Fig. 76

Paul Joanowitch, Austrian, *Richard Alexander Hudnut Portrait,* 1925, Oil on canvas. Gift of Mrs. Richard A. Hudnut, from the Permanent Collection of the Utah Museum of Fine Arts.

Fig. 77

Paul Joanowitch, Austrian, *Winifred Kimball Hudnut Portrait,* 1925, Oil on canvas. Gift of Mrs. Richard A. Hudnut, from the Permanent Collection of the Utah Museum of Fine Arts.

Fig. 78

Paul Joanowitch, Austrian, *Natacha Rambova,* 1925, Oil on canvas. Gift of Mrs. Richard A. Hudnut, from the Permanent Collection of the Utah Museum of Fine Arts.

Fig. 79

Natacha Rambova's sketch (1921) for a costume as it would appear in Valentino's film, *The Cobra*. She titled the sketch, "The Egyptian Woman" and gave it to Svetoslav Roerich. The sketch was recovered by Dr. Vladimir Rosov in the Nicholas Roerich Museum archives.

Fig. 80

Scene from *What Price Beauty* produced and directed by Natacha Rambova, with Myrna Loy on left

"... *What Price Beauty* ought to be called *The Divorce Picture* as the difficulties which arose from its inception to its close covered precisely the time of differences between the Valentino's..." [17]

---

17 *The George Ullman Memoir*, p. 183

Fig. 81

What Price Beauty with Nita Naldi

"....Upon our return to Hollywood, plans were at once set into motion for the production of Natacha's movie, *What Price Beauty*. This clever story Mrs. Valentino wrote herself. She was thoroughly familiar with her subject, being the step-daughter of the well-known perfumer and manufacturer of cosmetics, Richard Hudnut. In her picture she made clever fun of the agonies women undergo, the time and money they spend in beauty parlors..." [18]

---

18 *The George Ullman Memoir*, p. 168

Fig. 82

Federico Beltran-Masses painting Rudolph Valentino as the Caballero Jerezano

"During the first few weeks of July, Natacha's nocturnal absences from home became so frequent that house guest, Federico Beltran-Masses suggested his friend Rudy hire a private detective to follow her. In Spain, he said, that is exactly what any man in his position would do. When George heard Beltran-Masses' suggestion, he told Rudy in no uncertain terms that hiring a detective to trail Natacha would only result in disaster. But Rudy's mind was made up and George was dispatched to hire a detective. When Rudy received the detective agency's first report of his wife's covert activities, George's worst fears realized..." [19]

19 *Affairs Valentino*, p. 262

Fig. 83

"....The agenda for the remainder of that day included a carefully choreographed appearance by Rudy and Natacha at the train station where they would announce their marital vacation. Natacha would deliver a statement, as prepared by George, stating she was traveling to New York with her Aunt Teresa to seek a distributor for her film, *What Price Beauty* and then on to France to visit her mother. ....the entire plan would be carried out without a hitch. Early in the evening of August fifteenth, the Valentinos were chauffeuered from their Whitley Heights home to the train station in their Isotta-Fraschini town car. Before press and photographers they behaved as a couple embarking on a brief and amicable separation as they affectionately kissed each other good-bye. What was not known to the press or anyone present that day; this would be Rudy and Natacha's last kiss and they would never see each other again.." [20]

---

20 *Affairs Valentino*, p. 266.

Fig. 84

"Nevertheless, she was sped in her labor of love by the fact that inherently Rudy possessed a fineness and gentleness and chivalry which formed a superb foundation for her superstructure of culture. An example was his regret when the divorce occurred. I remember that he said to me:

'You know I bear Natacha no grudge, and I wish her all the success in the world. She'll get it too, for she is still young and has her life before her. I am glad that I did not rob her of the best years of her life. If the separation had to come, I am glad it came so quickly.'

I knew he felt himself deeply injured. I consider this a rather fine thing for him to say, especially as I realize that he meant it, and was not saying it for effect." [21]

21 *The George Ullman Memoir*, p.184.

MRS. VALENTINO ON GRAFT
by
Mrs. Rudolph Valentino

Movie Weekly on June 7, 1923
Republished in the Los Angeles Herald Examiner March 6, 1978

A movie, as the public sees it, presents to the average eye a simple story set in a series of more or less elaborate scenes, the why and wherefore of which it never occurs to the average screen patron even to wonder about. He or she sees the picture and that is all there is to it. They never so much as wonder as to the multitude of details that went into its construction, much less the illimitable sources of graft that each picture potentially contains.

In my experience as an art director I was able to observe much of the sources of graft that prevail in many studios and the methods that are employed to make them effective. If I can open the eyes of the public to ever so small an extent in this matter, I shall feel that I have been well repaid for the pains I have taken.

To begin with, the art director or the technical director of a studio has all to do with the properties that are used. By this I mean that he or she is in entire charge of ordering the costumes and designing the sets which, in the latter instance, extends to the selection of furniture. Right here is something I shall return to presently, as a particular form of graft in the production end of the movies.

The properties that are used in the scenes are rented from concerns that make a regular business of supplying such things to movie studios and, as I have said, it is the job of the art director to select his materials for various sets and scenes. Now, in some instances, a collusion is formed between the art directors and the firms that supply the materials, that results in the movie company, for which the art director works, being charged an excessive sum for materials that are worth, say, only half the amount,

For instance, if a certain piece of furniture were needed that could be rented from another store for $25, the art director, if he were so minded, could patronize the store with which an arrangement had been made, with the result that the furniture would be rented for $50. The difference of $25 would go into the pockets of those who were parties to the contract. Graft!

In another way the evil works a still greater detriment to the art of the screen. Frequently, the right thing cannot be procured from one of the stores with which an arrangement exists and, as a result, some other article must be substituted which is not artistically appropriate. Whenever this situation arises, it is usually dismissed by the director with the contemptuous remark, "Oh, the public doesn't know the difference anyway!"

And perhaps the public, which is not an art expert, does not know the difference. But what it does know is the price of the admission its pays, and the present high prices are often made necessary by the tremendous production costs that arise out of the graft situation that exists.

The matter of transportation is another thing that checks off a fresh item on the movies' ledger of graft. These contracts for transportation are given out by the heads of departments. In giving them, there is naturally existent the question of preferment, for its stands to reason that the head of a department can give his contract to whomever he chooses.

Usually, he chooses to give it to someone who, at the end of the year, will reward his kindness with a handsome automobile. The cost of this automobile, needless to say, appears ultimately on the company's bill, for business concerns have not yet grown so philanthropic as to give something for nothing. It appears on the company's bill and in all due course is blandly okayed by the grafter at the head of the department.

Do you see? And the way that this reacts upon the public is to make the production costs greater, the rentals to the exhibitors greater, and the admission prices that the exhibitor charges the public therefore greater than they would be did the graft not exists. This is why and how it interests YOU.

BEYOND VALENTINO
(1925-1966)

Chapter Four

Fig. 85

"The animal in her was tamed but not crushed." [1]

---

1   Letter from Mark Hasselriis to Michael Morris dated, August 6, 1987.

VENTURING SOLO

With Rudolph Valentino ensconced in his luxury bungalow on the United Artists' studio lot in Hollywood,[2] New York City's press pursued Natacha eager for details as to what went wrong in the marriage of Hollywood's most beautiful couple.

The rumor prevalent among Valentino fanatics and movie-goers blamed the separation on the possibility Natacha refused to bear children. The notion that Valentino had been unfaithful with one of his beautiful co-stars was also bandied about. Natacha avoided the onslaught of press, ignored the rumors and instead immersed herself in disparate endeavors.

Soon after her arrival in New York, she announced plans to write a tell-all book about her marriage to Rudolph Valentino. She emphasized her announcement by posing next to a table spread with an array of Rudy's love letters. To the disappointment of Valentino's fans and a few interested publishers, the Rudolph Valentino exposé never materialized.

While the New York press reported inanities such as the claim Natacha left Valentino because she did not want to cook his spaghetti dinners, she settled into single life in Manhattan. She was determined to prove to the American public that she was a capable artist and designer, with or without the name recognition of her famous husband.

She did not mourn her departure from Hollywood and felt she had never adapted to the Hollywood lifestyle. The criticism she received from Valentino's fans and the press was not debilitating for Natacha and instead it inspired her defiance. She exhibited no outward grief over her failed marriage and entered into an industrious phase in which she stretched her artistic range by writing, acting and designing. She was still Mrs. Rudolph Valentino and while regaling New York City with her name, beauty and talent, many doors opened.

Natacha told one interviewer at the time she was writing a novel while also covering the sensational Snyder-Gray murder trial as a reporter. [3] She was designing the wardrobe for an upcoming Broadway production titled, *Those Few Ashes*, and authoring a history of costume and decoration throughout the ages, commencing with the year 4000 B.C.

"I am illustrating the costume book too, so, all in all, I haven't much time to throw away." [4]

Despite her busy agenda, she attended regular week-end gatherings of spiritualists known as the "Bamberger Circle" or the "Saturday Nighters". The members of this group conducted séances and shared theosophical beliefs, (theosophy being a study of god and all religions based on mystical insights). The Bamberger Circle regulars included three mediums: Mrs. Alpha Gabriel, Miriam Epstein and George Wehner. [5]

In November, Natacha invited George Wehner, renowned celebrity medium, to her apartment at 9 West 81st Street, where she hosted a séance. Perhaps Wehner charmed Muzzie and Natacha because he was born on the founder of Theosophy, Helena Blavatsky's birthday. Wehner considered Blavatsky one of his several "spirit guides". With Muzzie and friend, singer Donna Shinn Russell in

---

2 E. Zumaya, *Affairs Valentino*, p.309.

3 Uncited newspaper article, *Rambova Sees Fight of Wits*, New York, April 23, 1926, M. Morris Collection.

4 *Rambova Busy with Theater and Writings*, *Portland Express*, March 26, 1927.

5 Wehner, *A Curious Life*, p. 360.

attendance, Wehner performed his initial séance so admirably that Natacha wept. According to Wehner,

"The important point of this séance was that it wrought a great change in the mind of Miss Rambova, upsetting many of her materialistic viewpoints and creating the desire in her for the more spiritual. There and then she decided to study seriously the great truths of spiritualism and theosophy." [6]

Natacha insisted Wehner devote all of his time to her and conduct séances only in her home. Wehner was not able initially to accommodate Natacha and convened with her gathering of friends twice a week where he channeled voices. He spoke through his many "master guides", not only Helena Blavatsky but an American Indian he called White Cloud. Natacha's affiliation with George Wehner began in the fall of 1925 and was encouraged by Muzzie, as she was also fond of the young psychic, believing his abilities to be genuine.

In addition to hosting regular séances, throughout that fall and into the spring of 1926, Natacha embarked upon a prolific artistic phase. Perhaps her angst, directed west towards Hollywood and Rudolph Valentino provided her with the necessary inspiration and energy. Or perhaps Wehner's "voices from beyond" provided her with the direction required for her new ventures to succeed.

She immersed herself in the study of "H. P. B." (Helena P. Blavatsky), theosophy and the "Wisdom Religions" while also taking center stage as an actress in several dramatic performances in Boston and New York.

In January of 1926, her divorce was granted in absentia, from Rudolph Valentino as she performed in Boston starring in a murder mystery, *The Triple Cross.* She was cast as Anne Dowling, a glamorous heiress distraught over the arrest of her fiancé who is charged with murder.

By the time the play opened at the

Empire Theater in New York on February 21, the script had undergone last minute rewrites, including a new title, *Set A Thief.* Natacha's performance was noted for its striking mannequin presence with one reviewer commenting how *"Natacha Rambova, easy to look upon and strikingly costumed as she was, did not have a part of any but stock value."* [7]

On February 7, 1926, Natacha debuted in a second play titled, *The Purple Vial,* which opened at B.F. Keith's Palace on Broadway and Forty-Seventh Street. The play was an adaption of the original play, or "sketch" by Andrew DeLorde. The plot revolved around a Russian General and was set within the context of suspense, intrigue and espionage.

"Natacha Rambova was surprisingly adequate as the girl outwitting the fiendish general. Playing with occasions and running gamuts that would have taxed some of our better known emotional actresses, she gave a performance that was a revelation from one coming out of silent drama for her first speaking role." [8]

In May, Natacha, Aunt Teresa and George Wehner sailed to France with five Pekingese puppies and a monkey, to visit the Hudnut Chateau Juan les Pins on the Riviera. Aboard the ship, Wehner continued to conduct his nightly séances and alleged several psychic experiences occurred during the crossing.

Natacha passed the summer of 1926 on the French Riviera in Juan les Pins with Wehner continuing séances in a room in the Chateau referred to as the "H. P. B. Room" in honor of Helena P. Blavatsky.

On August 16th, Natacha received a telegram from Rudolph Valentino's manager George Ullman in New York with news that Rudolph Valentino was gravely ill. During that evening's sèance, Wehner utilized his "voices"

---

6 Wehner, *A Curious Life,* p. 340.

7 *Variety,* "Mystery Play a Hit", 1927, undated.

8 *The New York Times,* Sunday, February 7, 1926 and February 10, 1926, *Variety,* review titled, *"Natacha Rambova and Co. The Purple Vial (Sketch).*

to inform the Hudnuts and Natacha that Valentino was about to pass away.

On August 23, Wehner's predictions manifested and Rudolph Valentino died at the age of thirty-one years.

That Natacha felt responsible for his untimely death is evidenced by her further and immediate immersion into spiritualism. In the weeks following Valentino's death, she alleged she transcribed the consoling words of Valentino's departed spirit as he shared his descriptions of heaven and the after-life. According to Natacha, he related elaborate revelations about the architecture and landscapes of the after-life and commented on famous people he met there. She also claimed he was able to hear and see events occurring on earth.

There was no doubt Valentino's death shocked the world, including Natacha. When she returned to New York she stunned Valentino's fans by sharing news that she was channeling his lengthy accounts of life after death while in a trance and in the company of her psychic, George Wehner.

She soon published a book, titled *Rudy: An Intimate Portrait by His Wife* as a more prudent account of her life with Valentino than the one she proposed to write immediately after their separation. Yet, she chose to include in this book, a section titled, "Revelations" as the official transcript of her séance transmissions from Valentino.

The death of Valentino brought more innuendo upon Natacha, as many of his grieving fans cast her into the role of villainess in his tragic death. Some believed he was so grief-stricken over their divorce that he drank himself into an early demise.

Natacha was not immune to the public's criticism although her bitterness would not be revealed publicly for decades. Unbeknownst to the press and Valentino's fans at the time, she penned her response in the form of a screenplay she titled, *All That Glitters.*

All That Glitters was never published during her lifetime nor has it ever been produced on stage. Natacha put it aside, only sharing it with her mother who was horrified and insisted every copy be destroyed.

The screenplay survived and today serves as the denouement in understanding of how Natacha truly felt inside that celebrity relationship. It is an authentic portrait of her life with Valentino as well as a lightweight comedy with a twist often staged in the 1920's and 1930's.

All That Glitters is a veiled satire of real people Natacha knew during her Hollywood years. In many ways, this piece of apparent stage fluff is in reality a wife's revenge as the catharsis of writing *All That Glitters* appeared to have put Natacha's resentment over her failed marriage to rest.

She moved into an apartment on 55th Street near 5th Avenue and there opened a dress shop in a store front below her apartment. While growing more deeply involved in the "Wisdom Religions", she launched a retail venture designing and selling custom dresses and gowns for wealthy patrons.

By July of 1928, the press reported Natacha Rambova's dress shop was so successful she was expanding into the wholesale market. In her statement issued to the press at the time, Natacha expressed her views on womens fashion.

"'Gowns by Rambova, are not,' announces the former wife of Rudolph Valentino, 'all cut on one pattern. Women are types, every woman has her own type.' This is the theory of Natacha Rambova, whose dress shop in New York has been so successful she plans to start a wholesale establishment, to be opened on July 26, her Hollywood friends learned yesterday." [9]

In addition to designing, managing her shop and issuing fashion commentary, Natacha's interest in spiritualism, ancient cultures, religion and symbolism intensified. It was during this time she began refining her

---

9   Uncited newspaper article, *"Gowns? Natacha's Best Bet!"*, June 28, 1928.

studies to focus on the unifying theories of religious symbols of all ancient civilizations.

By 1929, she had become a prominent member of a new age cultural illuminati movement in New York City whose members included author Talbot Mundy, singer Donna Shinn Russell, medium George Wehner and theosophist Alice Bailey. Natacha's own introduction to theosophy occurred a few years prior to her leaving Hollywood.

Muzzie first brought her daughter to the Theosophy Society of Point Loma near San Diego and it was there she introduced her to Talbot Mundy. Mundy, a widely-read adventure writer was a prominent member of the Theosophical Society. After he moved to New York, he and his wife, Dawn Allen became close friends with Natacha. The Mundys participated and hosted many of George Wehner's séances in their Greenwich Village home.

Initially Talbot Mundy acted as an articulate and knowledgeable literary voice for the theosophical movement and for a while he served as an advocate for Wehner's psychic abilities.

I, of my own knowledge, know that Mr. Wehner is a medium through whom, at times, such wisdom speaks as is not to be found in books. In circumstances under which no fraud was possible, while he was in a complete trance, in an apartment in which he had never previously been, such information came through him as could not possibly have been obtained by human agency; or by thought reading or thought transference in any ordinary meaning of those terms. [10]

By 1929, Natacha was exploiting her exotic beauty wisely, still on a stage of sorts, setting hair and wardrobe for her day's performance while being rewarded for maintaining the Hollywood image for which she was known.

However, her appearance began changing from the recognizable glamour of her days in Hollywood. The importance of sustaining a merciless perfection in her daily public appearances grew less important to her.

Additionally, her daily activities were changing and instead of movie stars, movie sets and studio lots, she moved in a community of artists, writers, poets, photographers, philosophers, scientists and spiritualists. Those she chose to include within her new inner circle considered themselves fortunate to be in her presence. Both men and women worshiped Natacha Rambova, and in some instances her effect rendered them sycophants.

It would not be long before her beauty and spiritual magnetism drew another love to her side. Eager to leave her Hollywood Valentino fiasco behind, she would discover a new world of esoteric exotica, high in the new twenty-seven story art-deco skyscraper at 310 Riverside Drive; The Roerich Society Master Building.

---

10 Wehner, George and Talbot Mundy, *A Curious Life*, p. 13.

Fig. 86

"She was not by any means a Pollyanna and could even be grim at times."[11]

11 Letter from Mark Hasselriis to M. Morris.

Fig. 87

*"Prefers a Career to Cooking Rudy's Meals, Says Mrs. Valentino", New York...*Photo shows Mrs. Rudolph Valentino, wife of noted film star, with Rudy's love letters to be used as a reference in writing her story of their life together. Mrs. Valentino has startled the film world by going on a marital vacation instead of the usual separation or divorce." [12]

---

12 *International Newsreel Photo* and caption, August 24, 1925.

Fig. 88

"Spaghetti Stifled Love, Says Mrs. Valentino – New York, ...'a dish of spaghetti is a grand thing', writes Mrs. Rudolph Valentino of her life as the wife of the noted film star. 'But', she adds, 'it is not artistic'. According to her story she became tired of being a housewife and answering his fan mail and finally solved the problem by suggesting a marital vacation, somewhere, where she would not have to cook spaghetti." [13]

---

13 *International Newsreel Photo* and press release, August, 24, 1925.

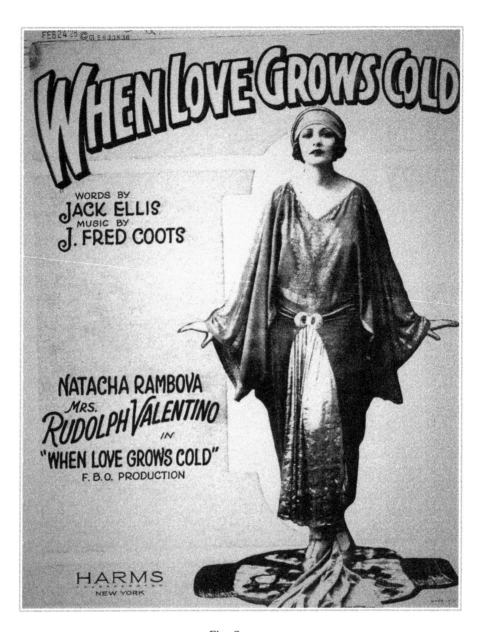

Fig. 89

"With the newspapers full of Natacha Rambova and her claims to psychic communications with her departed husband, Rudolph Valentino, comes the timely Hamilton Theater announcement that beginning Monday, this colorful wife of the departed screen lover will be seen in Laura Jean Libby's greatest novel, 'When Love Grows Cold'. Mrs. Rudolph Valentino, in this story of a white hot love is said to present a vibrant, sparkling woman and her love for a man who 'could never understand'." [14]

---

14 *Lancaster News*, March 20, 1927, "Miss Rambova in Hamilton Show, Valentino's First Wife Comes Here in *When Love Grows Cold*".

Fig. 90

"The beautiful mate of the World's famous Sheik, the Best Dressed Woman in the World. The story of love that wrung the hearts and souls of two continents – that thrilled – a million feminine hearts the earth over!" [15]

15   Uncited newspaper article in Michael Morris Collection.

Fig. 91

Natacha Rambova in *When Love Grows Cold*

Fig. 92

"To achieve her success, Mrs. Valentino obtained the services of some of the greatest geniuses of the profession; one and all, I saw these men pass under the spell of her personality and yield up to her the greatest treasures of their art. This brings me to the subject of this woman's amazing fascination. Not only was her taste in dress an eye-arresting thing, Oriental, exotic, sometimes bizarre, but her costumes invariably added to the almost sinister fascination she was able to exert whenever she chose." [16]

---

16 *The George Ullman Memoir*, p. 160.

Fig. 93
Rudolph Valentino's Bier in Campbell's Funeral Church, August 1926

Fig.94
News coverage of Valentino's death

Fig. 95

"Tuesday morning came cables verifying the séance prophecy. Dear Rudy, beloved of millions, had ended his earth-incarnation and had passed into that great Future which is so inexplicably always the Now.

Natacha was prostrated by the news. Those who fancy this much misunderstood child to be cold and indifferent should have seen her as I saw her then. Her genuine grief proved her great love for Rudy, and her remorse at their misunderstandings and mistakes was heart-breaking to see. I am convinced, from my closeness to the true facts surrounding these romantic figures, and regardless of what others may say, that Rudy was and ever will be the one real love of Natacha Rambova's earth-life.

I was happy that these two children of the limelight had been reconciled by their exchange of cables before death had stepped in. It made the final separation easier, and Rudy made the Great Change with Natacha's last cable under his pillow." [17]

17 Wehner, *A Curious Life*, p. 373

Fig. 96 – 97

The séance process and the role of the medium, (illustrative)

Fig. 98

Helena P. Blavatsky

Fig. 99

The Theosophical Society Seal

Fig. 100

Natacha Rambova clothing line label

"Rambova Boosters, New York City. As believers in fair play, we would like to thank *Photoplay* for its defense of Natacha Rambova in February's issue. Miss Rambova has been treated most unfairly by the majority of the reporters and interviewers. They have placed her in a ridiculous light and made her seem petty by twisting her words spoken for publication. We have commented among ourselves on the splendid, womanly manner in which Mrs. Valentino has conducted herself throughout the entire affair, and sincerely hope things will end satisfactorily for her through *Photoplay's* assistance. May we assure Mrs. Valentino of our moral support and best wishes for a successful career? Signed, The Bebe Daniels Girls Club, Dorothy Lubow, President." [18]

---

[18] *Photoplay Magazine*, April 1926, "Brickbats and Bouquets".

Fig. 101

Natacha Rambova Dinner Gown with Belt, 1928-1931, gold braid embroidery on silk velvet. Collection of Phoenix Art Museum, Gift of Mrs. Philip Markert. Photo by Ken Howie.

Fig. 102

Natacha Rambova Afternoon Ensemble, 1928-1931, printed silk chiffon and crepe. Collection of Phoenix Art Museum, Gift of Mrs. Philip Markert. Photo by Ken Howie and Natacha Rambova, American Afternoon Dress, 1928-1929, printed silk satin. Collection of Phoenix Art Museum, Gift of Mrs. Philip Markert. Photo by Ken Howie.

Fig. 103

Natacha Rambova Dress and Jacket, 1928-1931, silk velvet and brocade. Collection of Phoenix Art Museum, Gift of Mrs. Philip Markert. Photo by Ken Howie.

Natacha Rambova on Glamour

Excerpted from a letter from Mark Hasselriis to Michael Morris dated October 6, 1987 and postmarked, "Long Island, New York".

"Concluding thoughts (For this letter but never Forever!) :

Natacha was surrounded by glamour early in life and also by beauty. She often spoke of each, separately, and never failed to point out that glamour was illusory and a distortion of, better still, a 'false image'. She had doubtless had her fill of this in the world of movies. She called Hollywood 'Piscean' and by implication 'Neptunian'; a watery world of glistening dream images and make-believe which not only provided entertainment but also an unreal world for some of its participants with the occasional heartache and the strands of malice which later both she and the Hermetic texts say characterizes a fault associated symbolically with that astrological sign.

She told me that in its higher aspect 'Neptune' represented the lofty heights of spiritual vision and that subtle perfection the ancients held and which the end of the Great Cycle (the Zodiac) also symbolized. This too, she said, the best films rising to a height of excellence as art were more than mere entertainment, but she herself had no illusions about the general fare or product of the place; true quality is a manifestation.

Beauty, as distinct and opposed to glamour, Natacha held was the true image of 'Reality' – meaning of course not what is ugly in the world and which also is called reality, but what is a reflection of the world's basic essence before it has been misused or distorted. Even so, she once wrote that we can sometimes pay too much attention to beauty and therefore miss where it is our duty or work should lead us, or by paying too much attention to achieving it in life we neglect more important considerations.

I had never heard anyone else articulate such ideas with such clarity, and I know she was sincere in what she said, yet the glamour seemed to stick to her in the minds of others and yet I thought that perhaps even they were really in pursuit of beauty and a kind of perfection and that Natacha somehow represented it in some way.

Best wishes and good health until I write again, Mark "

Fig. 104

Natacha Rambova Evening Dress, 1928-1931, silk chiffon. Collection of Phoenix Art Museum, Gift of Mrs. Philip Markert. Photo by Ken Howie.

Fig. 105

Natacha Rambova, New York City, circa 1928

" ALL THAT GLITTERS "

A Play

in

Three Acts

-by-

NATACHA RAMBOVA

[Donna Russell - crossed out]

109

..."Natacha occupied her time writing a seriocomic play, a three-act thinly veiled indictment of Hollywood and her marriage to Rudolph Valentino. Titled *All That Glitters*, the work opened old wounds with such a merciless, surgical precision that Muzzie wept when she read it...*All That Glitters* was never produced on stage. It may have been too risky a venture in that so many of its characters were uncomplimentary depictions of powerful celebrities. Nevertheless, writing it was therapeutic for Natacha, who portrayed her marriage to Rudy as vindicated and saved - if only in the make-believe realm her own play attacked." [20]

20 *Madam Valentino*, p. 192-193.

ALL THAT GLITTERS

A Play
In
Three Acts

by

Natacha Rambova

This screenplay was originally deposited with the Library of Congress on July 22, 1927 with the title page revealing the play was co-authored by Natacha Rambova and Donna Russell. The name "Donna Russell" was crossed out. As the Library of Congress clerk could read the name through the marking, he penciled the name in for posterity.

According to William McQuire, Donna Shinn Russell was a singer and "a friend of Natacha Rambova's who also participated in séances."

CHARACTERS

HENRY WARWICK

ALICE WARWICK, his wife

WILLIAM KENDALL, a lawyer

MAX R. SCHWARTZ, a motion picture producer

FLORIS MacGILLACUDY, a scenario writer

MARCELLE MARSON, COUNTESS de LINSKY, a movie star

COUNT JEAN de LINSKY, her husband

MORRIS GOLDBERG, a publicity man

AGNES DRAKE

MARY ELIZABETH BINTER, a movie flapper

MRS. BINTER

"CURLY" PIKE, the western hero

EDMONDE RAYMONDE

PETE, the still man

BUCKLE, the valet

HODKINS, the butler

A CREDITOR

2 Footmen (policemen in Scene I)
2 Moving men (extras in Scene I)
4 Extra girls (movie fans)
Musicians (off stage)

ACT I

Scene I

SCENE: The lobby of the Coliseum Theatre, Hollywood. Entrance doors center. Both doors open and backed with black drop. Ticket rail and ticket box at center of rail. Two large columns down stage right and left masking with right and left returns. Above the double doors center is an electric sign that reads: MARCELLE MARSON in "HER TENTH LOVER." It is the occasion of the opening of the picture.

AT RISE: ALICE WARWICK, the head usherette of the theatre, is discovered just below the double doors center. She is a girl in her early twenties, beautiful in a severe way. She has a practical sensible air about her. HENRY WARWICK is discovered behind the ticket rail. He is dressed in the livery of the theatre. Henry is rather good-looking and has an air of boyish enthusiasm which greatly increases his attraction. It is evident that his mind is more on the excitement going on around him than on his business of taking in the tickets. PETE, the still man, is down stage left by the column with his camera. Camera focused upstage right. Just as the curtain rises Pete's voice is heard, "Already? Still!" MARCELLE MARSON, in private life the Countess of Linsky, and her husband, the Count of Linsky, are posing for publicity stills. Marcelle is a dark, exotic type, strikingly gowned and jeweled. The Count is an immaculately dressed foreigner, a bored aristocrat who has sold himself to be a prop, nothing more, and does it well. MORRIS, a live-wire press agent, is directing the taking of the stills and is standing right center just out of line of the camera. There is a policeman up left above the column. Three or four young girls are eagerly peering over his shoulder to see Marcelle and the Count. As the curtain is well up the cameraman's flashlight gun is set off. The Count and Countess relax from their pose and start to mover center.

MARCELLE
(affecting an English accent)

Thank goodness that's over!
Jean, hold my bag.

(Hands her rather large jeweled evening bag to the Count to hold while she adjusts her wrap. He takes it as though he were long since resigned to his role of playing lady's maid to Marcelle. The girls giggle and nudge each other. The policeman smiles and looks at the Count as though he were some sort of insect).

MORRIS
(stopping them)

Just a minute, Countess. I want one more.

MARCELLE

But you've already made – oh –well – just ONE more.

MORRIS

Fine.

(Morris goes over and pretends to pose Marcelle but takes the opportunity to speak in an undertone to the Count)

Count, for God's sake try to smile for once.

(Count smiles mechanically)

Fine! Hold it...How's this, Pete?

PETE

(with his head under the camera cloth)

Count, will you move in a little closer to the Countess?

(the Count moves slightly)

There that's it. Now already. Still!

(Before Pete can shoot the still AGNES DRAKE, CURLY PIKE and EDMONDE RAYMONDE enter from above the column right. AGNES to the discomfort of everyone, gets in the camera line before they can shoot.) AGNES is a movie comedienne who has seen starring days. She is beginning to fade and tries to make up in cheap jewelry and flashy clothes for what she lacks in freshness. She has sympathy and a certain breezy charm of her own. One of her noticeable characteristics is the impression she gives of always having had just one highball too many for perfect diction. CURLY is the Cowboy hero, a Tom Mix type. He is dressed in dinner clothes, but wears a large fawn colored sombrero, white buck gloves with fringe and carries over his arm a very loud checked evening coat. He also displays as much in jewelry as possible. EDMONDE is a typical Latin leading man – slick and seductive and thoroughly convinced of his irresistibility.

AGNES

Hello Marcelle. How's the little Countess tonight?

MORRIS
(irritably but gently)

Just a minute Ag. I'm taking a still of the Count and Countess.
This is the opening of the Countess' new picture you know.

AGNES

Do I know? What do you think we're here for?

(sees the sign above the door center, stops and reads aloud)

"Marcelle Marson in 'Her Tenth Lover' "
Why ten? Well, purity will out.

(turning to the Count)

And how have you been, Count?

CURLY

Ag, same here.

(Agnes obediently does as she is told)

MARCELLE
(furious but with great dignity)

Morris, please continue with the stills.

MORRIS

Come on now. Ready? Still!

(Before Pete can take the picture, MARY ELIZABETH BINTER enters, followed by MRS. BINTER. MARY ELIZABETH is the typical movie flapper with blond curls. Hers is the tragedy of those who can never grow up but must always remain sweet sixteen, although that milestone has already long since passed. MRS. BINTER is stout and determinedly efficient. They are in the camera line)

PETE

(exasperated – coming from under the camera cloth)

Oh for the love of Kelsey, get a cop to keep the movie stars out instead of the fans.

AGNES

My god! Pollyanna would!

(Marcelle boils with rage)

MRS. BINTER

Good evening, Marcelle....Isn't it fortunate we are just in time for the stills, Mary Elizabeth?

MORRIS
(coming down to them)

Just a minute.

MARY ELIZABETH

But mother –

MRS. BINTER

Why, you don't mind posing with the Count and Countess on this occasion, do you dear?

MARY ELIZABETH

No Mother, but -------

MRS. BINTER

And you don't mind, do you Marcelle?

(not waiting for an answer, goes right on pushing Mary Elizabeth up to the Count and Marcelle)

Of course not. Now, dear, you stand here on this side of the Count.
There now -----

MORRIS

But this is a picture of the opening, Mrs. Binter.
And the Count and Countess -----

PETE

My god!

MRS. BINTER

Mary Elizabeth and I wouldn't have missed the opening for the world. We are both great admirers of the Countess.

MORRIS
(hopelessly)

Oh, all right – come on Pete. Ready? Still!

MRS. BINTER
(interrupting before still can be made)

Mary Elizabeth!

(She points to her nose wildly. Pete comes from under the black cloth with an expression of disgust.)

PETE

What the -----

MARY ELIZABETH

What, Mother?

MRS.BINTER

Powder your nose.

MARY ELIZABETH

Yes, Mother.

(she takes out her vanity and powders her nose. While she is doing this Henry Warwick edges into the picture)

MORRIS
(pushing Henry back)

Get back, will you? This ain't a gang comedy.

(Henry steps back)

Ready! Still!

MRS. BINTER

Now let's have another one. Mary Elizabeth, you stand here and Marcelle, you-----

(Marcelle moves away indignantly)

MORRIS

We've had enough.

MRS. BINTER

But you didn't get Mary Elizabeth's best angle.

(FLORIS MacGILLACUDY and M.R. SCHWARTZ enter. FLORIS is an exotic looking blond, slightly passé, who has a splendid business head but disguises it by many affectations. She writes scenarios and is Schwartz's right-hand. Her complex is that she understands sex appeal. She dresses accordingly and wears one long earring. SCHWARTZ is the usual hard-boiled movie producer, not over-burdened with unnecessary culture).

MORRIS
(delighted)

Look who's here!

AGNES

All on the job!

FLORIS
(rushing up to Marcelle)

Oh, my dear --- you look divine tonight. Good evening Count.

(he bows)

MARCELLE
(human for the first time)

Oh, Floris, what a darling earring! Is it new? Hello M.R.

SCHWARTZ

Evening, Marcelle.

AGNES
(coming down stage to Schwartz)

Hello M. R.

(pointing to sign of "Her Tenth Lover" above center door, then confidentially)

Which one were you?

CURLY

Come on, Ag.

MRS. BINTER

Say good evening to Mr. Schwartz, Mary Elizabeth.

MARY ELIZABETH

Good Evening, Mr. Schwartz.

(he ignores her)

AGNES

Great box office title, "Her Tenth Lover!"

MRS. BINTER

I can't imagine why they called it "Her Tenth Lover."

AGNES
(meaningly)

No, nobody can.

MRS. BINTER

You mustn't say such things before Mary Elizabeth.

AGNES

Sorry, I forget. Poor little thing, just sweet sixteen and never been ---lifted.

CURLY

Come on, Ag.

MRS. BINTER

If I didn't keep Mary Elizabeth pure she wouldn't be able to play childrens' parts.

MORRIS

Just one more Countess.

MARCELLE

Only with M.R. I must have one with M.R.

SCHWARTZ

No, I don't want to be in this. That's what I pay actors for.

FLORIS

Now, M.R., just to please Marcelle.

SCHWARTZ

Oh, all right, but bring in the others and let's get it over with.

> (Morris pushes the Count into the background and places Schwartz next to Marcelle)

MORRIS

Come on, Curly, Ag.....

> (starts grouping them all but pays no attention to Mary Elizabeth)

MRS. BINTER

Now where do you want Mary Elizabeth to stand?

MORRIS

(exasperated, points to the background)

Back there with the Count.

(He places Edmonde on one side of Marcelle and Schwartz on the other. Mrs. Binter places Mary Elizabeth on the other side of Schwartz. Agnes is standing between Edmonde and Curly)

AGNES
(turning to Curly)

Now don't I take you out swell?

CURLY

Yeah, this is a hell of a party ----stand around all night in the parade outfit, and as a prize you get your picture took with royalty.

(Agnes turns to Edmonde as Mrs. Binter takes Curly by the arm and draws him back next to Mary Elizabeth. During this action Henry has gradually edged downstage to get a good look at Marcelle).

AGNES
(to Edmonde)

See! He doesn't appreciate it.......and what I had to promise him to leave the horse at home.....

(Henry is now standing where Curly was. During this speech Agnes reaches out and takes his arm, thinking it is Curly. Turning to Henry)

Never mind, Curly. I remember the pie throwing days even if Marcelle doesn't. Once a pal, always......

(sees Henry instead of Curly)

Hello, Bright-Eyes, what are you made up for, the Count's bodyguard?

(Henry in embarrassment goes back to the ticket box. Floris has been watching Henry attentively for some moments).

MORRIS

Come on, let's get this. Ready, Pete?

PETE

Let's shoot. Ready? Still!

MRS. BINTER
(frantically)

Mary Elizabeth.

(Mrs. Binter taps her nose significantly)

MARY ELIZABETH

Yes, Mother.

(starts to powder her nose. While she is powdering,
Pete shoots his still)

MRS. BINTER
(in despair)

But Mary Elizabeth was powdering her nose.

AGNES

Come on, Marcelle, start the parade. Your public is waiting for you inside.

MARCELLE
(to the Count)

Come, Jean.

(she takes the Count's arm and exits through center doors)

MRS.BINTER

Come, Mary Elizabeth.

(pushes her right in behind Marcelle and the Count)

PETE
(hopefully)

Is that all, Morris?

MORRIS

Yep, I guess so.

(Pete picks up camera and exits left above column. Morris exits into the theatre. Applause is heard – the music begins to play)

AGNES

(taking Curly and Edmonde by the arm and starting for center doors)

Come on, let's follow the Count and Countess. They might think Curly is a Duke.

(They exit. Henry goes to doors center and stands talking to Alice excitedly. Alice sees a spot on his uniform and tries to clean it by spitting on her handkerchief and rubbing it vigorously).

FLORIS
(catching Schwartz's arm)

Look at that boy over there. He's just the type for my new story, "Young America".

(Alice sends Henry back to the ticket box and exits into the theatre)

SCHWARTZ

We've already engaged Georgie Spelvia for that part.

FLORIS

That's easily arranged – Georgie hasn't the sex appeal that ----

SCHWARTZ
(disgusted)

Sex appeal! Where?

FLORIS

Now remember, you said the same thing about Harold Dunning when I picked him from that dancing contest last year. Today he's one of our best box office attractions. I understand better than you do the secret longings of our feminine public.

SCHWARTZ

All right. Try him out! Try him out!

FLORIS
(withering)

Why M.R., what do you mean?

SCHWARTZ

But how do you know he can act?

FLORIS

All he will have to do is be himself, and with a good director....

SCHWARTZ

I'll have to admit you've picked some winners.

(Calling to Henry)

Young man, come here.

HENRY
(coming down to Schwartz)

You mean me, sir?

SCHWARTZ

Can you act?

HENRY
(awkwardly)

How?

FLORIS

Now M.R. Let ME handle this.

(to Henry)

Mr. Schwartz means – would you like to become an actor?

HENRY

Who? Me?

FLORIS

Of course. Turn around please. I want to see your angles.

(Henry turns awkwardly)

Now a little to the left. See, I told you M.R. He has splendid angles, his profile is perfect for that part.

(Henry, not understanding, looks in embarrassment at his ankles)

And wonderful sex appeal.

(Henry looks startled, then smiles with boyish conceit)

Yes, and his height is good.....Can you fence?

HENRY

Huh?

FLORIS

I mean can you fight?

HENRY
(proudly)

Scrap? Sure, I used to fight down at the Legion. I was right up in the class too. I was being primed for a contender for the coast title, but Alice.....

FLORIS

Alice? Who is Alice?

HENRY

My wife. She's got no ambition. She wants me to start a business.

FLORIS

If you're a success in pictures, you can make more money than you could in fighting, and then you could buy a business.

HENRY

If I make good in pictures, what would I want with a business?

MORRIS
(enters from center door)

They are starting the picture.

SCHWARTZ

Come on.

FLORIS

What is your name?

HENRY

Henry Warwick.

FLORIS

Well Henry, you come to the studio in the morning. Ask for Miss MacGillacudy's office.

HENRY

Where?

FLORIS
(turns to Morris)

Give him the address Morris and tell him how to get there.

(as she exits with Schwartz)

Now M.R. you know I've never made a mistake.

MORRIS
(writing address on a card and handing it to Henry)

Gee, what a break you got.

HENRY

What? Why?

MORRIS

Don't you know who they are? That was M.R. Schwartz and Floris
MacGillacudy, the biggest producer and scenario writer in the business.

HENRY
(attempting to be nonchalant)

Yes?

MORRIS

She has picked all the big stars for the past six years – and some that weren't.

HENRY

Yes?

MORRIS

The men.

HENRY
(boastingly)

Well I bet she didn't pick a loser this time.

(applause from theatre inside)

See, that's what they'll be doin' to me.

MORRIS

With your modesty you ought to go far in pictures.

(he starts to exit)

Oh, by the way. A little tip, Floris collects jewelry.

(exits)

HENRY

(Alice enters center door and stands watching Henry.
Henry throws his shoulders back, looks himself over. Last of all his ankles)

They're not so bad.

(He struts around the lobby)

ALICE
(puzzled)

Henry –

HENRY

Hey, Alice, I'm going to be a movie star. Did you see the dame that went in there? Well she's Miss – Miss – er –Deefunny, and she writes the stories and picks all the stars, and the little fat guy with her is the one that makes all those pictures – and she picked me.

ALICE

But, Henry – why? ---

HENRY

Why? Because – well – she said I had splendid ankles – and wonderful sex appeal .

ALICE

Henry!

HENRY

And I'm just the right height –

ALICE

But Henry –

HENRY

She wanted to know if I could act. Act – well – watch me!

(He performs a bit of pantomime for her benefit. He imitates Curly)

Curly Pike!

(imitates the Count)

Count de Linsky!

(applause is heard inside the theatre. He bows.)

ALICE
(interrupting him)

But Henry, I don't think ----

HENRY

There you go pouring cold water on my ambitions again.
You didn't want me to fight and now ----

ALICE

I didn't say I didn't want you to – to go into the movies. It was all so sudden and --I was
wondering if you could do it.

HENRY

Do it? Say, I'm going to beat them all at this game. In a year I'll be a star.

(grabs her in his arms and swings her around)

You just wait sweetheart, I'm going to make money.

ALICE
(brightening up)

Then we'll be able to buy that business we've been saving for.

HENRY

Business! I'm going to be a movie star.....................

ALICE

And we'll be able to buy that little bungalow we saw.

HENRY

Bungalow? Say, we're going to have a real house with gardens and a fountain in it and - and we're going to have a car ---

ALICE

But it will take all we can save to buy that business. We won't be able to have a car at first.

HENRY

If we don't have a car, how am I going to get to and from the studio?

ALICE

Well, we might be able to buy a Ford --- and --- and then we could use it in the business for a delivery wagon.

HENRY

A movie star would look fine driving to his studio in a Ford delivery wagon wouldn't he? No, Alice, we're going to have a Rolls Royce like Marcelle Marson's! And you're going to have clothes like hers and diamonds ---

(pauses as he suddenly remembers something)

That reminds me.

(taps his pocket)

I bought you a little present this morning. I wasn't going to give it to you until we got home, but this is such a grand occasion ---

(takes a bracelet of brilliants out of his pocket and hands it to her)

ALICE

Oh Henry- how beautiful ----darling ----

(kisses him)

HENRY

It cost me all I had.

ALICE
(reproachfully)

Oh Henry --- ALL?

HENRY

Every bean – I didn't get my suit cleaned this week so's I could give it to you.

ALICE
(almost hopefully)

It can't be ----- real?

(they stand looking at it with their heads together as though fascinated)

HENRY

(takes it from her and holds it out, moving it in the light)

No, it isn't real – but God how it shines!

(as they stand looking at it--- fascinated)

CURTAIN

ACT I

Scene II

SCENE: The Living Room of THE MANSION, Hollywood, two years later. Center there is a circular arch with steps leading up to it. Through the arch can be seen a garden room with a fountain playing center. From the landing, steps lead up and off right and left to the next floor. On the right is a large arched doorway leading to the entrance hall. On the left is a high window overlooking the garden through which can be seen a cypress tree and a very blue sky. The set should give the impression of extreme height to dwarf the figures as much as possible. It is furnished in true DeMille style – bright colors and gold furniture to give the effect of the usual society living room as depicted in the movies. Table center, couches, chairs, lamps, etc., everything is there but the swimming pool.

AT RISE: ALICE is discovered talking to SCHWARTZ and FLORIS. She is dressed in sport clothes. She is not exactly untidy, but she looks more like a secretary than the wife of a motion picture star. The responsibility and strain of saving the irresponsible and child-like Henry from himself have told upon her. She looks nervous, worried and worn out. WILLIAM KENDALL, Henry's legal adviser and business manager, is standing just away from the group but is listening to the conversation. Kendall is a man in his early forties, tall, good-looking and with an air of refinement and intelligence.

SCHWARTZ
(angrily)

I tell you I won't stand for this another minute! Here we are right in the middle of this picture ----

FLORIS

Henry knew very well that today the long shots were going to be taken with all the extras.

138

SCHWARTZ

That mob is costing me over a thousand dollars an hour overhead and he has to go to a tea to meet a Spanish Duke. Bah!

ALICE
(smoothly)

I thought this publicity was valuable for Henry as Pickford and Fairbanks and all the others of importance will be there this afternoon. Henry understood that his double was to be used for the long shots.

SCHWARTZ
(furiously)

His double! We've used his double three days a week ever since we started on this picture. Does he think I'm just paying him for his closeups?

FLORIS

You know this director always takes his closeups in action continuity.

SCHWARTZ

Where the devil is he anyway? I want to talk to him.

ALICE
(soothingly)

He will be down in a few moments. He is dressing for the tea.

SCHWARTZ

Does it take him all day to dress for a tea?
We've been here for nearly an hour.

ALICE

You know, Mr. Schwartz, being the best dressed man on the screen, he has to be particular. His public expects it of him.

(the VALET enters with two or three suits over his arm)

Are you sending those suits to the cleaners, Buckle?

BUCKLE

Yes, Madame.

(Alice examines them carefully)

SCHWARTZ
(in an undertone to Floris)

I never saw so damn much cleaning in my life. I'll bet the graft that goes on in this house is nobody's business. More reasons why he hasn't any money.

ALICE

Is Mr. Warwick almost dressed, Buckle?

BUCKLE

He will be down presently, Madame.

(exits right)

SCHWARTZ

Presently! He has to come down here now. Does he think I have nothing else to do but wait for him? My time is valuable.

(Alice crosses and rings for the butler)

FLORIS

Alice, we have to get together on the story for his next picture. Henry is impossible. I can't talk to him.

SCHWARTZ

Well, who can?

FLORIS

Henry is determined to make it a costume picture. He wants to wear tights.

SCHWARTZ
(with disgust)

How could I sell a picture with him in tights?

KENDALL
(dryly)

I'd pay to see it.

HODKINS
(enters from right. Dressed theatrically)

ALICE

Hodkins, tell Mr. Warwick that Mr. Schwartz and Miss MacGillacudy have been waiting almost an hour to see him.

HODKINS
(bored)

Yes, Madame.

(exits upstairs center)

KENDALL

Mr. Schwartz, while we are waiting for Mr. Warwick there is a little matter I would like to discuss with you.

SCHWARTZ

About money I suppose?

KENDALL

Well, yes. Mr. Warwick dislikes to discuss business details. But as his lawyer and adviser I have to.

SCHWARTZ

He dislikes to discuss business. But I notice he doesn't mind spending the money.

HODKINS
(enters from the stairs center)

Mr. Warwick will be down directly.

MORRIS

(enters from right followed by Pete with still camera and paraphernalia)

(to Hodkins)

You run up there and tell him his PUBLICITY man is here with Pete.

HODKINS
(looks at Alice. She nods consent)

Yes, sir.

(exits upstairs)

142

ALICE

Why Morris, What are you doing here? Mr. Warwick is going out.

MORRIS

No, He isn't! I've got to get some new publicity stuff.

ALICE

But he is going out to tea to meet ---

MORRIS

Yes, but not until later. I made this appointment with him yesterday.

HENRY

(Rushes downstairs dressed in L.A.A.C. track suit. He carries dumb-bells and boxing gloves. Henry has lost none of his charm. Being a star – to him – is a delightful game in which work doesn't enter. He is living in a fool's paradise and getting a great kick out of it)

Sorry I kept you waiting, Wow.

(turns to others)

Hello.
(to Morris)

Now, where do you want me, Moe?

SCHWARTZ
(angrily)

See here, I have been waiting to talk to you for nearly an hour, do you realize-

HENRY

Alice, you talk to W.R. - Now Moe, do you want the boxing gloves first or the dumb-bells?

ALICE
(significantly)

The dumb-bells.

MORRIS

All right. The dumb-bells.

HENRY
(poses with the dumb-bells)

How's this?

SCHWARTZ
(furiously)

That can wait! Listen to me!

(Henry turns to Schwartz)

Why weren't you at the studio this morning?

HENRY

You tell him, Alice.

SCHWARTZ

I'm talking to YOU. We've been held up enough on this picture with your foolishness.

HENRY
(indignantly)

Foolishness? Do you think it is fun for me to train all morning to be in condition to take these still for your publicity department? Moe has landed a big story with *Physical Culture* and all the other magazines and asking for new stuff.

SCHWARTZ

I could buy the whole damn magazine for what that mob has cost me today.

HENRY
(pleadingly)

You talk to him, Alice.

(strikes a pose)

All right Moe, how's this? Ready, Pete? Make it snappy.

PETE

Great – every pose a picture. Right. Still!

(Pete shoots the still. Henry changes his position. Kendall watches this with amusement while Schwartz furiously talks to Floris in an undertone.)

HENRY

Now get this one.

(He poses)

MORRIS

Great!

ALICE

Henry, that's your bad angle.

145

HENRY

Oh, yes.

(turns a little to the right)

Ready, Pete?

ALICE

Henry ----

HENRY

Yes?

ALICE

Your diaphragm.

(points to Henry's slouched position)

HENRY

Oh.

(Henry stands very erect and pulls his stomach in to give athletic appearance. Gives Alice a questioning look. She nods.)

PETE
(Pete shoots still)

Right!

HENRY

One more.

(changes his position. Pete takes it and Henry starts for stairs)

SCHWARTZ

Just a minute. You've got to listen to me -----

HENRY
(goes over quickly to M. R., smiles and pats him on the back)

If it's art M.R., talk to Alice, if it's money, talk to Kendall.

(rushes upstairs and exits)

(Morris and Pete are in earnest conversation down left)

ALICE

But Henry –

SCHWARTZ

I've handled a lot of them, from soda fountain clerks to college professors, but Henry is the God damndest idiot I've ever met yet.

ALICE

Now, M. R., he is only trying to do what he thinks is important.

SCHWARTZ

I hire him to act, not to think.

FLORIS

This next story must be decided on.

SCHWARTZ

Wait till we get this one finished first --- will you?

FLORIS

But it must be settled. If it's a costume picture it will take a lot of preparation.

SCHWARTZ

Well it won't be.

ALICE

But the fans want to see him as Cellini.

KENDALL

Cellini with a profile like that!

SCHWARTZ

Who the hell is Cellini?

FLORIS

Why, M.R., you know. The great artist who made cups for the cardinals.

SCHWARTZ

That ought to make a great picture. Henry making cups!

FLORIS

But he was also noted for his love affairs.

SCHWARTZ

Then he ought to do it well.

FLORIS

Henry wants Marcelle to co-star with him.

(with a meaningful look at Alice)

SCHWARTZ

What? Have those two in the same picture?

FLORIS
(glancing at Alice catily)

With Marcelle in the picture I'm sure he would never miss a day at the studio.

ALICE
(calmly)

With their two names together you could make a big special. I should think it would be a good business move M.R.

SCHWARTZ

But I thought that football story was settled on.

FLORIS

But Henry doesn't want to do the football story. He wants to be romantic.

SCHWARTZ

Yes, especially where Marcelle is concerned.

> (Kendall moves forward to interrupt as if he would save Alice from this situation. Schwartz stops him and goes on)

And that's another thing I came here to talk about.

FLORIS
(warningly)

Now, M.R. ---

SCHWARTZ

Oh, I can talk to Alice, she has good common sense.

ALICE

Of course you can talk to me. But it is utterly ridiculous. There is nothing more to it than their mutual interest in this picture, and the public wants to see them play together.

SCHWARTZ

Yes, but not in private.

ALICE
(indignantly)

They don't!

SCHWARTZ

Now there is no use trying to kid me, Alice. You know everyone is talking about it, and I'm not going to let that young fool kill himself on the screen if I can help it. I've got too much involved.

ALICE

But M.R., it is too silly to speak of. Henry and Marcelle -----

SCHWARTZ

No it isn't. With the women's clubs on the rampage, we can't have any scandal and run the risk of having his pictures stopped.

ALICE

Aren't you making a lot out of nothing?

SCHWARTZ

You'd be surprised what they can make out of ----- nothing.

FLORIS
(Hastily)

Where there is smoke, you know there is generally fire.

SCHWARTZ
(to Floris)

Yes, and you wanted to put them both in the same picture.

MORRIS
(aside to Pete)

Yes and in this business familiarity generally breeds contempt.

SCHWARTZ

Now listen here Alice, you've got to keep Henry away from Marcelle.

ALICE

M.R., don't you think you are exaggerating?

SCHWARTZ

No, and if you won't talk to him, I will.

HENRY

(Rushes downstairs dressed in a riding habit, very extreme in cut and with patent leather boots. He carries a picture of the Prince of Wales)

All ready, Moe?

MORRIS

Come on, Pete.

PETE

Right.

SCHWARTZ

Henry, come here.

HENRY

Huh?

(with slight annoyance that they are still there)

SCHWARTZ

There is something I must talk to you about.

HENRY

Talk it over with Alice. She attends to all the details.

SCHWARTZ

This is no detail.

HENRY
(to Alice)

Alice, here is that picture of the Prince of Wales. Will you pose me just like it. Come here Morris, this is the pose.

(Henry takes same pose as the picture)

All right, Alice?

ALICE

Yes dear, it's all right.

SCHWARTZ

Good God!

MORRIS

Ready, Pete?

PETE

Right. Still!

ALICE
(with preoccupied air)

Henry.

(Taps her own diaphragm. Henry immediately pulls up straight and draws in his stomach)

PETE

Still!

(shoots the still)

HENRY

Now get this one.

(takes another pose, then remembering something, turns quickly to Alice)

Oh, Alice, did my new handkerchiefs with our crest on them arrive?

FLORIS

Your crest?

HENRY

Yes, the Warwick coat of arms. That man, the Count sent me to, has traced my ancestry back to the war of the Roses.

ALICE
(with embarrassment)

Oh, Henry, please -------

HENRY

Well, he did, didn't he?

SCHWARTZ
(sarcastically)

I suppose when you go to England you will stop with your cousin, the Prince of Wales.

HENRY

No, we were mortal enemies. His family fought for the wrong rose.

SCHWARTZ
(turning away)

Oh god!

KENDALL

Maybe you can overlook that. You know all of the pillars of the industry have to meet the Prince.

MORRIS

Come on, We've got to get this other shot.

HENRY
(takes poses)

All right.

MORRIS

Ready, Pete?

HENRY

Wait a minute. Alice, is this all right?

ALICE
(without turning)

Yes, dear.

HENRY
(crossly)

How do you know it is? You didn't look.

ALICE
(turns to him and then in a preoccupied manner)

Oh, yes dear. A little to your left.

HENRY
(turns and says petulantly)

You're a big help, you are.

PETE

Still!

(shoots the still)

MORRIS

How about one with your wife? That would be different.

HENRY
(looks Alice over disapprovingly)

Oh, Alice isn't dressed for stills ---

(looks at his wrist watch)

And besides I'll be late.

(starts for the stairs).

SCHWARTZ

Say, are you going to listen to me or not?

HENRY

I can't. I'll be late for the tea!

SCHWARTZ

To hell with the tea! That can wait!

HENRY

But the Spanish Duke won't and when I go to Europe this summer he is going to get me presented to the King of Spain.

SCHWARTZ

And I suppose the King will pay your salary if this picture flops?

HENRY

Oh what's the use of talking to you? You've no head for business. Think of the publicity.

(exits upstairs)

MORRIS
(calls after Henry)

Hey, we've got to get the rest of those stills.

SCHWARTZ

Anymore stills you take will be taken at the studio. Get that damned paraphernalia out of here and no more publicity stunts without my O.K. Do you hear? Come on Floris.

(Pete and Morris take camera and light and exit right)

FLORIS

But, M.R., we have to decide about that costume picture.

SCHWARTZ

There'll be no costume picture. He will do that football story – and without Marcelle.

ALICE

M.R. ----please -----

SCHWARTZ

And if YOU don't break this up between Henry and Marcelle – I will! She'll make pictures in the Eastern Studio.

KENDALL

Mr. Schwartz, when can I see you at your office? Anytime tomorrow will do.

SCHWARTZ

If it's about anther advance for Henry, you can save yourself the trip. He doesn't get another cent. Come on Floris. Goodbye Alice.

(Schwartz exits. Floris turns to Alice as she is leaving)

FLORIS

Well, Alice, I did the best I could.

(exits after Schwartz)

(Alice watches them off. She avoids looking at Kendall. There is an awkward pause.)

KENDALL

Alice. You must do something. Things can't go on like this.

ALICE
(wearily)

Things have been going on this way for over a year now.
I don't see how they can very well be changed.

KENDALL

How can you stand it? Now it's Marcelle. Before Marcelle it was someone else, and before that it was someone else.

ALICE

I didn't mean that. I was thinking of the business. These little flirtations don't mean anything. He is just carried away with the glamour. They're never serious.

KENDALL

No? Are you sure?

ALICE

Yes. You see, I know Henry.

KENDALL

You knew him two years ago Alice. He is a very different man now.

ALICE

No he isn't. Henry is just the same enthusiastic boy I married four years ago. Only then it was the prize ring because he liked the excitement, the applause and the spotlight. He has just changed toys, that's all.

KENDALL

That may be true, but Marcelle is a damned dangerous toy.

ALICE

Why will you keep talking about Marcelle? I tell you that doesn't amount to anything. They are both too selfish and spoiled to put up with each other long. They will find each other out soon enough – then as usual he will come back to me.

KENDALL

And as usual you will be waiting with sympathy and understanding.

ALICE

Oh! Let's not talk about it – it's all so ridiculous – What we need to worry about are his pictures. All these idiotic publicity stunts when he should be working at the studio and always pretending to be something he isn't. For instance, this last notion about his family tree and having his crest put on everything..

KENDALL

Yes, he already has it on all of the automobiles. I suppose it will be on the footman next. Alice, how much longer are you going to put up with it?

ALICE

Can't you see he is just a child?

KENDALL

Yes and a damned spoiled one at that.

ALICE

Now Kendall -----

KENDALL

And you aren't helping matters a bit. No matter how big a damn fool he makes of himself, you always find excuses for him. What he needs are some good hard knocks to take the conceit out of him.

ALICE

Kendall, if he ever lost his conceit and found out what people really think of him, he would lose his one real asset --- his boyish self-confidence and enthusiasm – and then he would be through on the screen.

KENDALL

If he doesn't quit playing and get down to work, he will be through anyway.

ALICE

Oh, it hasn't reach that point yet.

KENDALL

Alice, you've got to face facts. Henry has been a star for over a year. He has made a lot of money but what has he to show for it? This house, four foreign automobiles and none of them paid for. He is head over heels in debt and drawn ahead on his salary. Schwartz is good and sore. When he said Henry couldn't have another advance on his salary, he meant it. Henry's pictures aren't going as they did and he'll play safe. Now, you have got to decide where you go from here.

ALICE

What do you mean?

KENDALL

I mean what are you going to do with Henry? He has to be made to realize what his position is. His last picture wasn't so good, and from what I can see of the way he is working now this one will be worse.

ALICE

Henry is a better actor than you give him credit for, and he has done all he could with this weak story.

KENDALL

Yes, and who picked the story? Still alibi-ing for him, aren't you, Alice? Even YOU can't handle him anymore.

ALICE

I can't? Why Henry depends on me for everything.

KENDALL

That's just it. He lets you do all of the work and then goes his own sweet playful way while you are doing it – free from all responsibility.

ALICE

But I like to attend to business.

KENDALL

Yes, it takes your mind off the other things that might have been. Alice, you deserve to be happy – and you're not. You are not a wife. You are just a combination mother, nursemaid and private secretary.

ALICE
(smiling)

What are you trying to do Kendall? Make me feel sorry for myself?

KENDALL

Well, by God, I'm sorry for you!

ALICE

Well, you can save your sympathy. I am perfectly happy.

KENDALL

Apart from your other accomplishments, Alice, you also seem to be the actor in the family.

HODKINS
(enters from left)

Madame la Countess de Linksy.

ALICE
(surprised)

Marcelle?

(turns to Hodkins)

Oh, show her in Hodkins.

(Hodkins exits left. Alice is taken off her guard. She is obviously disturbed at Marcelle's unexpected arrival. She turns and finds Kendall watching her. She avoids his glance and turns with her usual calm poise to greet Marcelle as Hodkins announces her.)

HODKINS

Madame la Countess.

(smiles behind her back as she enters the room)

MARCELLE
(gushingly)

Oh, Alice darling.

(pecks a kiss on her cheek)

You look too sweet for words. Is Henry ready?

ALICE

Ready?

MARCELLE

Yes, he is taking me to the tea this afternoon. Aren't you coming?

ALICE

No, I have some business to go over with Kendall ---
What perfectly beautiful pearls Marcelle ---are they new?

MARCELLE

These – oh these are just sport beads.

(to Kendall)

Spending the afternoon talking business under such pleasant circumstances won't make
you angry, will it Billy?

KENDALL

I'm a lawyer, Marcelle, not an actor.

MARCELLE
(sweetly)

Oh, I've met a few lawyers.

KENDALL

Yes, I know some of them.

MARCELLE

You see even lawyers can be useful at times.

KENDALL

Even though they have no family tree?

MARCELLE

Are you trying to be funny or merely crude?

KENDALL

I'm afraid humor isn't much in my line.

HENRY
(rushes down the stairs dressed in perfect afternoon attire –carries a walking stick)

Hello Marcelle, sorry if I kept you waiting.

MARCELLE

Oh, that's all right. Kendall has been very entertaining.

HENRY

Oh.

(gives a quick glance at Kendall)
(then turns to Alice)

Alice, will you ring for Hodkins?

KENDALL
(looking at watch)

Henry, you had better hurry – you mustn't keep the Duke waiting.

HENRY

We'll make it all right.

KENDALL

Of course, he won't mind waiting if he knows he is going to meet Madame la Countess.

(bows with mock gallantry)

HENRY

Yes, and he wanted to meet me too.

HODKINS
(enters, awaiting orders)

HENRY

Hodkins, tell Blake we will use the Hispano-Suiza.

HODKINS

Sorry, sir, the Hispano is in the shop, sir, but Blake said –

HENRY

Have him bring the Rolls, then.

HODKINS

Sorry, Sir, but the Rolls is also in the shop, sir, but Blake said –

HENRY
(with annoyance)

Then we will have to use the Minerva town car.

HODKINS

Sorry, sir, but the town car is in the paint shop having the coat of arms put on the door, but Blake said -

HENRY

What did he say?

HODKINS

Blake said, sir, that the only cars in running order, sir, are Mrs. Warwick's Dodge or the servants' Buick, sir.

ALICE

The only cars that ever run are my Dodge and the Buick.

HENRY

Oh, damn!

MARCELLE

Never mind, Henry! My Rolls is outside.

HENRY

Then we had better hurry along. Goodbye Kendall.

> (picks up stick and hat from the table where he has laid them to
> put on his gloves)

MARCELLE
(seeing his cane)

I see you are using the new cane I gave you Henry.

HENRY

Yes, did you see it Alice?

ALICE

No.

> (looks at stick)

KENDALL

Is the coat of arms on it?

HENRY

Yes, look.

> (shows cane to Kendall)

KENDALL
(looking at the stick)

Hmmm. Perfect. Did the Count have this done for you?

MARCELLE

Come on, Henry.

HENRY
(moving with Marcelle to the door)

I wish the Hispano was working. It looks great since the crest has been put on the doors.

(At the door Henry stops and as an after thought turns and rushes back to Alice, kissing her quickly. To Kendall)

Can we give you a lift, Kendall?

KENDALL
(smiling)

No, Alice and I must work so that you can play.

(A shadow crosses Henry's face but disappears at once as he hurries back to Marcelle at the door. As they start out Henry, suddenly remembering, turns again to Alice and says)

HENRY

Oh, Alice, see that Buckle gets my clothes back from the cleaners, will you?

(turns to Marcelle and speaks as they exit)

You know, no matter what suit I want to wear it's always at the cleaners.

(they exit)

(Alice starts to sort out the work on the table nervously. The scripts one place, the publicity stories another, etc. She is hurt and

furious, but is trying hard to conceal it. Kendall is watching her
and after a short pause he speaks)

KENDALL

Well, Alice, we had better get down to work. We have to go over the accounts and check
over these bills.

(Kendall opens a portfolio on the tables and takes out a large pile
of bills. He very methodically starts to sort them out. Alice is so
angry and hurt that the tears come to her eyes. Kendall, appearing
to notice nothing, turns to her)

Here, Alice, will you go over these -----

ALICE
(glances at the bills a moment – then pushes them away from her)

Oh, what's the use?

KENDALL

We have got to figure some way of getting Henry out of this.

ALICE

Yes, that is all I do. Try to figure some way out, but it's hopeless.

KENDALL

Well, Henry doesn't realize ---

ALICE
(speaking firmly for the first time)

Then it is time he did, for I'm not going to do this any longer.

(she gives the scripts and bills a shove)

KENDALL

Someone has to do it.

ALICE

Someone --- someone.

(growing more indignant each second)

Well, it's not going to be me.

KENDALL
(secretly pleased)

But Alice ---

ALICE

I've played nursemaid and secretary so long that I look like one --- He doesn't even want me to pose in a still with him......all I'm good for is to read scripts, pay the bills and worry – worry – worry. What time have I got for dressmakers, hairdressers and manicurists, and I look it.....I look like hell.

KENDALL
(amused as this is just what he has been waiting for)

Now, Alice, you mustn't -----

ALICE

No one ever expects ME to go to teas or anywhere else. I have to stay at home and read scripts for him, and now for Marcelle....while they go off to see a Duke....

(picks up a script)

Here's a script with a wonderful part for Marcelle.

(she tears it in half and throws it back on the table)

That's the last script I'm ever going to read.

KENDALL

Really Alice -----

ALICE

And these bills -- nothing but credit – credit – credit. We haven't a cent in the world! Henry signs his name to anything they give him to sign as long as he can get the cash – and I have to do the worrying! I don't even know what he's signing half the time – until they come to me to collect –If he's not careful he's going to get into a lot of trouble one of these days --- I'm through --- through explaining --- promising --- arranging matters.

(she takes up the bills as though she were about to tear then up)

KENDALL

Here, Alice, don't ----

ALICE

Don't worry, I'm not going to tear them up. You give them to Henry.

KENDALL

He doesn't know a bill from a tennis racquet.

ALICE

Then it's time he found out....time he learned how to worry. You give him these bills and tell him for me that they're nothing to the ones he's going to get for me....

KENDALL

Alice, are you mad?

172

ALICE

No, I've been mad all along, but now I'm sane. I've been a fool. It's about time I grew up too. Henry denies himself nothing, so I guess he can pay for the clothes and jewels I'm going to buy to live up to his Rolls Royces and his family trees.

KENDALL

But Alice, you can't ----

ALICE

Oh, can't I? Well, you watch me. From now on, I'm going to be just his WIFE.....and a DAMNED EXPENSIVE ONE.

CURTAIN

ACT II

SCENE.

The Living Room of the Warwick Mansion three months later. A party has been arranged to celebrate the opening of Henry's latest picture, the one upon which he was working in Scene 2nd, Act 1st. Great preparations have been made for the event.

AT RISE.

Agnes is seated on the couch at the left. Curly and Edmonde stand around drinking cocktails and highballs. A tray is on a table nearby containing empty glasses. A jazz band is playing in the next room.

AGNES

My god! What a flop!

EDMONDE

Ghastly...

(Conceitedly)

When my pictures are released there's always a terrific mob----wait -----

AGNES
(sarcastically)

Stops the traffic, doesn't it, Orchid?

CURLY

It's a good thing Alice wasn't at the opening tonight as she'd have passed out!

EDMONDE

By the way, why WASN'T she there?

AGNES

Look here, both of you, don't haul out the family skeleton. We've had enough disaster for
one evening.

CURLY

Where did Henry go? I thought I saw him in the hall when we came in.

AGNES

Oh, I guess he's shedding a few tears in secret.

CURLY

Better be tasteful. Let's pretend it was great.

AGNES

And add insult to injury....For God's sake, ring for Buttons and have him bring in some
more drinks. There's nothing in this house but style and orange juice....

(sentimentally)

I used to live on a farm near Kansas City-----

CURLY

You've had enough, Ag.

AGNES

I've only had five cocktails since I came. I know my capacity better'n you do.

CURLY

Speaking of Alice, I haven't seen her at the studio for a coon's age. She used to be down there –and now ---

AGNES

God! You're smart! And they say men never gossip!

CURLY

Everyone was just wondering ----

AGNES

That's how all the divorce dirt starts – by people just wondering.

EDMONDE

You never married, did you Ag?

AGNES

Not on paper! I wasn't going to take any chances on having a lot of cheap divorce publicity. Not me! I wasn't going to have MY fans say I was immoral!

EDMONDE

What became of him?

AGNES

Are you trying to be funny? Well, I guess I only cared for one of 'em really.....

(Sentimentally)

God! But he was a grand guy! I'd have done anything for that kid!

EDMONDE

Did he die?

AGNES

No! He went to jail for life – the poor fish!

CURLY

Ag will land a millionaire yet!

AGNES

Me?....Don't be funny! I wouldn't have a millionaire even if he was rich. I ain't trying to land anything except my little old ranch near Kansas City...Say, you ought to see my hen-coops and the house. It's the old farm I'm buying back – it ought to be paid up by next year! It's got six rooms and the porch is going to be lousy with roses! That's what I've been spending your money on showing Hollywood what great guys you are! I'm going to have a hammock where I can lie and look up at the sky and I'm going to get acquainted with the stars – real stars. And I'm going to get fat. No more pineapple and lamb chops for me! God! I'd hate to look a lamb in the face!.... That was the life, when I used to live down on the farm near Kansas City -----

CURLY

She's off again!

AGNES

But I got tired of the exterior and went to town. Ain't it strange how cows and chickens and the family pump don't register with you until you've had your fill of life's swill?

CURLY

Let Edmonde tell us about that soda fountain in Chicago, Ag.

AGNES

When I left the farm the first job I got was as a waitress in a one-arm lunch room in Kansas City....just a hole where they jerked beans and where there was no future for a kid like me. A girl never gets anywhere slinging hash, so when a burlesque troupe hit town and the owner of the show dropped in one night, I saw my chance and grabbed it. That guy said if I'd be affable he'd get me a job as a hoofer in the back row of a chorus....I got the job.

No, HE wasn't the one I loved!....At last I was New York and I joined a company playing on the East Side. Then my figure and a rich guy got me into the Follies. No money, but lots of fun. I used to live at the Vanderbilt on a dollar a day with tips.

On to the races...Then a movie producer's "yeoman" discovered me and he said I was just the type for pictures. Along with the job he gave me a Park Avenue apartment and a charge account and the use of a Packard. When you consider that a girl can't have everything without losing her self respect, it wasn't such a bad bargain.

CURLY

Now, Ag................

EDMONDE

How long have you been in pictures, Ag?

AGNES

Ten years! Hell, I'm only twenty-eight, ain't I Curly?

CURLY

Sure.

EDMONDE

That's rather young to retire.

AGNES

Another year of this artificial life and I wouldn't be able to die a natural death....There's only two things I could do after MY hectic career ----

CURLY

What are they, Ag?

AGNES

I guess no decent people would want to associate with me anymore. All I could do would be to marry some rich guy and go into society, or settle down on a farm. I guess I prefer the farm. That's why I'm going to buy back the old ranch near Kansas City. I'm going to have a runabout, a wringing machine and a husband – all self-starters. I can afford to get married then, as scandal won't hurt me. And I'm going to have a couple kids, and a dog....

(Henry appears in the doorway)

My god! Here comes Henry! He looks like he's been put through a washing machine and all the colors running.

CURLY
(slapping Henry on the back)

The picture was great!

EDMONDE

Wonderful!!

AGNES
(sympathetically)

Don't listen to them Henry! It wasn't so bad!
I've seen worse. Buck up!

HENRY
(on the defensive)

I don't know what you're all talking about!

HODKINS
(announcing)

Miss MacGillacudy, Mr. Schwartz and Mr. Kendall

AGNES
(catching a glimpse of Schwartz's expression)

Well, you're about to hear!....But for God's sake ring for the butler and have him bring in some more drinks before the fun begins. We'll all need 'em.

HENRY

I'm sorry, Ag. Alice looks after those things as a rule. She'll be down in a minute.

AGNES

Can't you press a button yourself – for once?

(Henry rings. He is disconcerted – worried – but continues to bluff as usual)

SCHWARTZ
(striding forward)

Well, Warwick ----

AGNES
(her fingers in her ears)

Tell me when the shot 'as gone off!

SCHWARTZ

What have you got to say for yourself?

HENRY

What on earth could anyone expect with such a story? How could ANYONE make anything out of a part like that? We had little enough story to begin with and none when we got through.

FLORIS
(furiously)

Really, Henry ----------

AGNES

Yes, ain't it queer how nine reels of film can make no story.

CURLY

Ag –come here.

(she obeys)

SCHWARTZ

See here, young man, after all we've put up with from you on this picture, you'd better not try and alibi yourself out on the story.

FLORIS

Who insisted upon playing the part? Who chose the story? If you had played a part suited to you instead of trying to be a Romeo.

HENRY

Why shouldn't I be a Romeo?

SCHWARTZ

Oh God! Listen to him!

FLORIS

It's a pity you can't see yourself as others see you! With your mind on everything but your work, you don't expect to be every incarnation of Edwin Booth!

HODKINS
(announcing)

Mrs. Binter and Miss Mary Elizabeth Binter.

MRS. BINTER
(rushing forward)

Oh Henry, allow me to congratulate you on your triumph! It was just too marvelous! Mary Elizabeth, tell Henry how wonderful you though the picture was! The poor child was simply overcome!

AGNES

We all were!

MARY ELIZABETH
(to Henry)

You were just too wonderful! I never enjoyed anything so much before.

(everyone exchanges glances of disgust)

AGNES

She WOULD!

MRS.BINTER

I suppose you were simply mobbed after the picture.

HENRY
(uncomfortably)

Not so much.

MRS.BINTER

I just thought I'd never get Mary Elizabeth away alive. She was literally torn to pieces by her fans.

MARY ELIZABETH

Now, mother ---

MRS.BINTER

Where is Alice? We didn't see her at the opening tonight.

HENRY
(embarrassed)

She – she was ill – I mean she had a headache.

MRS. BINTER

Oh, I am sorry! I haven't seen her at the studio lately and I thought ---

HENRY

She'll be down in a minute.

MRS. BINTER
(gushingly)

Good evening everybody. Mary Elizabeth, can't you say good evening to Mr. Schwartz.

MARY ELIZABETH

Good Evening, Mr. Schwartz.

SCHWARTZ

So you liked the picture?

MARY ELIZABETH

Oh yes! Oh, yes! It was so full of spontaneity.

AGNES

If we don't get some refreshments soon ---

(sees Hodkins coming with the tray)

Thank God! Here he comes!

HENRY
(to Hodkins)

Please tell Mrs. Warwick to hurry down. We are all waiting for her. Put the tray down on the table; we'll help ourselves.

HODKINS
(placing tray on table)

Very good, sir.

(exits upstairs center)

AGNES
(going over to table)

Come on, let's have a drink. Here, Mary, you'll need one after watching all that spontaneity and fighting your mob of admirers.

EDMONDE
(picking up bottle)

Haig and Haig. Three loud British cheers for the winning tram.

(pours out drink and passes it to Mary Elizabeth)

MARY ELIZABETH

No, thank you. I don't drink.

AGNES

Oh Lord, still pure and innocent. Or innocent at least.

FOOTMAN
(enters from left doorway and announces)

Madame la Countess de Linsky. Monsieur le Count de Linsky.

(All turn to the doorway. Henry rushes forward to meet Marcelle. Just as Marcelle enters with the Count, Alice enters down the stairs center. She is beautifully gowned, is wearing some marvelous pearls and other jewels and is carrying a large fan. There is a moment's pause – a silence at this startling picture of a new Alice. She has not only succeeded in overshadowing Marcelle but everyone else in the room as well. Henry looks in amazement at Alice.

AGNES

My God! All she needs is a COUNT!

MRS. BINTER
(amazed)

Henry said you were ill, but ------

ALICE
(smiling sweetly)

Ill? I'm never ill!

MRS. BINTER

We looked everywhere for you at the opening of Henry's picture tonight.

ALICE
(without any of Marcelle's affectations)

Wasn't there. I went to the opera to see Mary Garden.

AGNES

How was Mary? She didn't let her veils conceal her art say, did she? From what I hear they wouldn't even interfere with a camera.

ALICE

I enjoyed it very much. EVERYBODY was there.

HENRY
(nervously)

You see, Alice had already seen the picture in the projection room and as this was her last chance to hear Mary Garden ----

SCHWARTZ

You didn't miss anything by not being at the opening, Alice. It was a terrible flop.

ALICE
(indifferently)

I'm sorry.

(Kendall advances towards Alice and holds out his arm)

KENDALL

This is OUR dance, isn't it?

(Kendall leads Alice off with an air of proprietorship which upsets Henry)

AGNES
(loudly)

In our old days, Marcelle, this is where you'd throw the pie! Henry, you don't seem to realize that royalty has slipped in!

CURLY

Ag ----

HENRY
(absently)

Oh, good evening Marcelle. I didn't see you come in.

MARCELLE
(icily)

So I perceive.

(to the Count)

Jean, shall we dance?

(she takes the Count's arm with great dignity and they go
off through the arch into the ballroom)

AGNES

Come on everybody. After all this, we need warming up!

MRS. BINTER

Mary Elizabeth just loves to dance!

(they all exit except Schwartz, Floris and Henry)

SCHWARTZ

Now, let's talk business.

HENRY

I don't want to talk business. We're having a party ----

SCHWARTZ

This is one hell of a party! This is!

FLORIS

Come on, M.R., let's go. What's the use of arguing with HIM!

HENRY

Come around tomorrow and talk to Alice – She'll ---

FLORIS

Alice doesn't want to talk about your work anymore.

SCHWARTZ

You're dead right, she doesn't! She hasn't been coming to the studio lately at all. Had she been there to attend to things, this picture wouldn't have been such a failure.

FLORIS

She wasn't at the opening either, and from all appearances the only person in whom she is the least bit interested in is --- Mr. Kendall.

HENRY
(furiously)

What do you mean?

FLORIS

There are none so blind as those who refuse to see. If you hadn't been so full of yourself these last three months ----

SCHWARTZ

If Alice hadn't gone off the rails with Kendall, maybe things might have been different. She sort of keeps things together. NOW ----

HENRY
(beside himself with rage)

You'd think I was two years old by the way you talk! You'd think I couldn't MOVE without Alice....And let me tell you, M.R., that you're not the only producer in the world! ....I've had offers from three other companies. I won't allow anyone to interfere with my private life and I don't need any advice from you or Floris. I'm through with both of you!

SCHWARTZ
(secretly pleased but pretending fury)

Do I understand that you want to break your contract with me?

HENRY

I certainly do!

SCHWARTZ

Very well, that settles it!

(to Floris)

You heard that, Floris?

FLORIS

Yes.

SCHWARTZ
(to Henry)

Goodnight.

HENRY

GOODNIGHT!

FLORIS

Well, I've seen a FEW in my time, but Henry you're the ACE of FOOLS!

SCHWARTZ

You're flattering him again, Floris.

> (Schwartz and Floris go out. Henry drinks three cocktails, one after the other, then disappears into the ballroom)

HODKINS

(entering with another tray of cocktails and highballs, followed by Buckle with sandwiches)

This is about all I do lately. Make cocktails and highballs!

BUCKLE

You're lucky! All I do is to brush clothes and shine shoes. If the Prince of Wales has a hundred suits, Mr. Warwick has three thousand. He's got an outfit for every minute of the hour!

HODKINS

In that case, you'll have a wardrobe yourself by the time you leave here. He ain't MY size.

BUCKLE

Madame's careful, she knows the age and pedigree of every suit he's got.

HODKINS

They've got what THEY call royalty here tonight.

BUCKLE

Yes, I feel sort of sorry for the Count.

HODKINS

He's entirely out of his element here.....Say, why don't we ask him to come and have a drink of champagne with us in the pantry?

BUCKLE

Why not?

HODKINS

There's nothing like English hospitality.

BUCKLE
(taking cards from his pockets)

Say, old man, just put these cards in the pockets of the coats in the hall.

HODKINS

What are they?

BUCKLE

Eureka Cleaning and Dyeing Company.

HODKINS

Why do you bother about it?

BUCKLE

I've got an interest in the business.

HODKINS

That's different. You might leave a few on the table, too.

(Buckle does so)

When I was with the Duke of Manchester, I had more time to myself and I could speculate a bit.

BUCKLE

This ain't any easy life by no means. Mr. Warwick is a clairvoyant! He sees spots in his clothes before they're there! He wants everything spic and span. He even wants his shoes to look NEW. I tell him it ain't proper for a gentleman to wear new shoes but he wouldn't change his opinions about it unless the Prince of Wales wrote him a letter about the matter himself.

(the Count enters)

THE COUNT
(pleasantly)

Good Evening.

HODKINS

Good Evening, sir.

BUCKLE

Good Evening, sir. Thank you sir.

HODKINS

We were just speaking about you sir.

THE COUNT

Indeed?

HODKINS

If you wouldn't think it unusual, sir, we were thinking of offering you a glass of champagne in the pantry, sir.

THE COUNT

Unusual? It would certainly be usual to have a glass of champagne! But as far as taking it in the pantry is concerned, it would be the most natural thing in the world. Aren't we all in the movies now?

BUCKLE

Exactly sir.

HODKINS

If you will follow me, we'll open a bottle of 1906 Mumm and drink to each others health, sir.

THE COUNT

Nothing would give me more pleasure.

(they get out together)

(Henry re-enters and takes another drink. Marcelle, boiling with wounded pride, enters)

MARCELLE

(Exaggerating her English accent in order to show Henry what a worm he is – patronizingly)

I should like to talk to you about the picture we about to make together.

HENRY

It's off.

MARCELLE

What DO you mean?

HENRY

I've broken my contract with Schwartz.

MARCELLE
(amazed and furious)

You've broken your contract with Schwartz – without ---without consulting ME!!

HENRY

I can't see why you should mind whether I break my contract or not.

MARCELLE

(forgetting her English accent completely)

So – that's the way you talk to me, is it? After all I've done for you.

HENRY

Look here, Marcelle ----

MARCELLE

My God! Broken your contract! After all the trouble I took to persuade Schwartz to accept the Sixteenth Century picture for me! You're the damndest quitter I've ever met!

HENRY

He got sore about this flop and blamed Alice for it and I blew up and told him to go to hell.

MARCELLE

What has Alice got to do with OUR affairs?

HENRY

He made some remarks I didn't like about Alice and Kendall ---

MARCELLE

What of it! Why the hell should YOU care? Everyone knows –

HENRY

Go easy. I've had about all I can swallow tonight on that score.

MARCELLE

I should think you'd be delighted to get rid of her. It's about time you wore the pants of the family.

HENRY

You mind your own damn business, Marcelle. As far as wearing the pants of this family is concerned I do wear them. I'm easy-going and maybe a bit lazy, and I let Alice attend to a few details because I'm too busy to do it all – but I can fight like hell when I have to. I'm sick of having everyone say I'm an irresponsible child. From now on everybody's going to know I'm boss in my own house, and you and Schwartz and Floris and everybody else ----

(the Count re-enters, wiping his lips with his handkerchief)

MARCELLE

Jean! Jean! I'm being insulted!

THE COUNT
(indifferently)

Yes?

MARCELLE
(indignantly)

I tell you I'm being insulted by Mr. Warwick.

THE COUNT

What do you wish me to do about it?

MARCELLE
(sputtering)

Do? Do? Why –why --- defend me!

THE COUNT
(bored)

What did Mr. Warwick say to you?

MARCELLE

He said ---he told me to mind my own damn business!

THE COUNT
(lighting a cigarette)

That's very good advice to anyone.

MARCELLE
(taken aback)

You don't understand, Jean. He said – he said ---he said ---

(she ends desperately)

THE COUNT
(pretending to be serious)

That's very grave indeed! I'm amazed at him!

(Henry, sensing a domestic storm, exits)

MARCELLE

There's only one thing left to do and that is to fight a duel – with -

THE COUNT

When I sold my title to you, there was nothing in the contract about duels......I don't mind being used as atmosphere, or carrying your dogs about, or being used as a sort of lady's maid ---I suppose I MUST do SOMETHING – but if I begin to fight duels for your –er – honor – I'd be the busiest man in Hollywood.

MARCELLE

YOU'RE insulting me now.

THE COUNT

I'm sorry. But don't you think I get bored with all this vulgarity?

MARCELLE

Jean!

THE COUNT

Look at this dreadful house! It looks like one of the things they put on wedding cakes! It's all made of frosting and preserved cherries! It isn't real at all. It's just a set for a moving picture. And you and all your friends are like a lot of puppets, trying to imitate the people you read about. Warwick and his crest! Mon Dieu! C'est trop fort!

MARCELLE
(furiously)

I've never heard you talk so much before!

THE COUNT

I never have anyone to talk to.

MARCELLE

What about ME?

THE COUNT

You're all right until you open your mouth!

MARCELLE
(hysterically)

There's no chivalry in the WORLD anymore. No gentlemen -----

THE COUNT

Perhaps that's because there are so few ladies in -----

MARCELLE

You mean that for ME! I've never been so humiliated before in my life!

THE COUNT

Good! Now you know how I feel ALL THE TIME!

MARCELLE

I'm going home!

THE COUNT
(yawning)

There's no place else to go – unfortunately.

> (They advance towards the door just as Kendall and Alice enter. Marcelle takes the Count's arm as though nothing had happened, for the benefit of those who might be looking on. They go out.)

KENDALL

Thank heaven they have gone!

ALICE

Without saying goodbye to their hostess, too.

KENDALL

Your gown was too much for the Countess.

ALICE

Is there a glass there for me?

KENDALL
(handing her a cocktail)

I thought you never drank.

ALICE

I need a bit of something to help me along tonight.

KENDALL

We all do.

ALICE

From all appearances the picture was worse than I expected.

KENDALL

They say it was terrible......

(seating himself next to her)

I wonder if you realize what the real defect in Henry's picture is?

ALICE

Yes. I've known it all along.

(A little catch in her breath)

It's – it's his NOSE.

KENDALL

Exactly. If he had stuck to the schoolboy type of part –the type he played in his first films - he might had had a career in pictures, but quite frankly, he simply can't play anything romantic with THAT profile.

ALICE

I have no illusions about Henry's career. The schoolboy parts would have lasted for about two more pictures and then he'd have been out. Anyway, that's what happens to a lot of them. It takes more than one swallow to make a summer, and one film doesn't make anything but a shooting-star.

KENDALL

He couldn't have lasted anyway with HIS disposition.

ALICE

There's nothing the matter with Henry's disposition. He's just a young fool who has been placed in a ridiculous position by a silly female – I mean, Floris, of course! And the whole thing would be funny if it weren't so ---so --- sad.

KENDALL
(surprised)

You're sorry for him?

ALICE

No! I'm not the least sorry for him. It's the best thing that could have happened.

(adding a little bitterly)

-----as far as I'm concerned.

KENDALL

Are you going to stay and go down with the sinking ship, Alice?

ALICE

Certainly, NOT!

KENDALL

You look ravishing tonight.

ALICE
(gently)

Don't begin again.

(Henry enters, looking like a thundercloud)

Where is Mr. Schwartz and Floris?

HENRY

They're gone.

ALICE

So early? Are they coming back?

HENRY

They've gone for good.

ALICE

Wasn't that rather unusual?

HENRY

No.......We had a row and I told them what I thought of him.

ALICE

As bad as that?

HENRY
(throwing back his shoulders to show her what strong character he has)

Worse. I've cancelled my contract with him.

KENDALL

What! You have broken your contract with him! Didn't you know you had him hooked for thousands?

ALICE
(insinuatingly)

You forgot that EVERYONE wants Henry.

KENDALL

You've cancelled your contract! That is just what he HOPED you'd do! .....Now, all your creditors will close down on you! God knows it has been hard enough to stall them off as it is!

HENRY
(his voice trembling boyishly)

I've had about enough of your butting into my affairs, Kendall.

KENDALL

Isn't that what you pay me for?

HENRY

There are limits......You see too much of MY WIFE.

ALICE

Henry!

KENDALL

You won't talk business with me, so I have to consult her.

HENRY

It seems to me you're doing it too damn thoroughly.

ALICE

You forget yourself, Henry!

HENRY

Between the extravagances of the two of you, I'm pretty well cleaned out! Her clothes, her jewels, and YOUR bills ----

ALICE

Why shouldn't I have nice clothes and jewels? I'm YOUR WIFE! Heaven knows you have everything YOU desire, from imported cars to a swimming pool! I have only a miserable Dodge, and up until three months ago I wore practically nothing but kitchen aprons! Why, when I was usherette at the theatre, earning ten per week, I had better clothes than I had here for two years as the wife of a star! And as for Mr. Kendall, he has a right to be paid for his services. You're utterly childish!

HENRY

Childish!.......I'm a MAN!.....And what's more I'm not BLIND! I see what has been going on here for three months behind my back! I see -----

> (Agnes, Curly, Mrs. Binter, Mary Elizabeth and Edmonde all enter together. Henry, trying to control himself, turns upon his heel and leaves the room)

(The following conversations are all carried on simultaneously)

EDMONDE
(To Mrs. Binter and Mary Elizabeth)

When I opened in "The Slim Prince" I was completely taken off my feet by the fans, and when I left the theatre ---

MRS. BINTER

And until Mary Elizabeth went bathing in the surf no one would believe her hair was real.

CURLY
(to Agnes)

Did you see the way I took that hill in the last part of "Hold 'em Jim"? The *Hollywood Magazine* said -----

EDMONDE

You should have seen my legs in that costume.

AGNES
(at the top of her voice doing a solo part)

....when Marcelle tore her dress I told her to take off what was left and pretend to be a statue. I said anyone would stand for a statue as long as it didn't get into a bathtub!

(glancing at Alice and Kendall)

My God! We've come in on the wrong cue!

CURLY

Wait for me, Ag!

EDMONDE

If I were you, I'd tell Curly to leave me alone.

AGNES

I like Curly bossing me around. It makes me feel important. I'm sort of fond of him in a way. He's like a police dog, hairy and rough and I like to play with him. Gimme a drink quick!

(Alice rises and crosses the room. Kendall takes a drink and stands talking to Edmonde)

MRS. BINTER

You mustn't overdo, Mary Elizabeth. Remember, you have to be made up at the studio tomorrow morning at nine.

MARY ELIZABETH

Yes, Mother.

MRS. BINTER

In a couple of years Mary Elizabeth will be old enough to play grownup parts.

AGNES
(in an aside to Curly)

That's what she said ten years ago.

(Curly puts his hand over Agnes' mouth)

MRS. BINTER

I want her to get some education in the meantime.

AGNES

Education! You don't get education. It just naturally GETS YOU!

MRS. BINTER

I think MIND is very important in pictures.

AGNES

MIND! The only important mind I know in pictures is MIND your own business.

CURLY

Now, Ag ----

AGNES
(Taking up the cards Buckle laid down)

(Reading)

Eureka Cleaning and Dyeing Company.

CURLY
(in an aside)

Just some more graft among the servants.

AGNES
(to Edmonde)

Say Orchid, have you heard the latest about Marcelle....
She was going to play in "The Captive".

EDMONDE

I thought the picture had been banned because the lead is a Lesbian.

MRS. BINTER
(innocently)

Couldn't they make her an American?

AGNES
(convulsed)

EDUCATION!......You might suggest that to Mr. Schwartz, Mrs. Binter. He always
appreciates suggestions....Then I lived on a farm near Kansas City -----

CURLY

She's off again! Ag ------

EDMONDE

Here, Ag, have another drink and get to the Follies quickly.

CURLY

Give her three more and she'll forget she's had a past.

(the music starts again)

AGNES
(rising)

Come on, Orchid, this is our dance.

MRS. BINTER

Just one more dance Mary Elizabeth and we must go.

MARY ELIZABETH

Yes, mother.

(They all go out, leaving Alice and Kendall alone)

ALICE

I wish they'd all go home! The strain is terrible.

KENDALL

The time has come to make some sort of decision, Alice. You've had your revenge on Henry.

ALICE
(surprised)

My revenge?

KENDALL

That's what you've been trying to do, isn't it?

ALICE
(nervously)

Well yes, in a way.

KENDALL

You wanted to break him, and now that he has canceled his contract, the flop is complete.

ALICE

Practically complete.

KENDALL

There's no good hanging around any longer. It's time to clear out.

ALICE

Yes, It's time to clear out.

KENDALL

I've booked passage on the Olympic for the 10th of this month. Will you come with me?

ALICE
(gazing into space dreamily)

Europe? Europe would be wonderful after all this discord.

KENDALL

We could go to Monte Carlo for a few weeks.

ALICE
(mechanically)

Monte Carlo?

KENDALL

Or if you preferred, we could visit Egypt. I've always wanted to see Egypt.

ALICE
(in the same tone)

Egypt!

KENDALL

I'd make you happy, Alice.

ALICE

Happy? I wonder if I shall ever be happy again?

KENDALL
(He leans very near to her)

Of course you will, in a few weeks you'll for get this nightmare. As soon as you're my wife.

ALICE
(pushing him away)

Don't ----

KENDALL

Why do you always repulse me? I've tried so hard to be patient all these weeks. I love you so.

ALICE

This is a poor moment to speak of love. Everything here is so false ---just glamour and show and such madness underneath. Oh, I want to get away from it all!

KENDALL
(almost taking her into his arms)

Darling -----

(He makes a swift movement, as though he were going to embrace her. She puts up her hand to ward him off, but to Henry – who enters the room at that moment, it looks as though Kendall had kissed Alice.)

HENRY
(striding towards them –enraged)

Alice – the time has come for me to avenge my family honor! ---
Kendall, you're a sneaking coward.

(Kendall gets up to close the doors so that the dancers will not hear them. As he does this the saxophone outside is heard to laugh. All through this scene the jazz band is heard through the now closed doors)

ALICE

I warn you to be careful what you say, Henry.

HENRY

I'm going to say anything I like!

KENDALL
(returning)

I suppose it's all right for you to have a dozen women hanging around you at one time, while Alice -----

HENRY

That's a lie. Alice knows I didn't love anyone but her. We were perfectly happy until you butted in.

ALICE

You mean you were happy - For God's sake, be quiet. They'll all hear you!

HENRY

I don't care who hears me! .....A good thing too! The Warwick name has been dragged into the mud! Everyone is talking about you and Kendall! Do you think I'm going to sit back and let people think I'm a weakling! Tonight you didn't come to my opening! You two went to the opera together! If my picture was a flop, it was because I was so worried about you lately that I couldn't work. If I broke my contract with Schwartz it was your fault. I wasn't going to have him say that I didn't wear the pants in the family and that the reason my picture was no good was because YOU hadn't been to the studio, and all such rot! You've made everyone think I'm an irresponsible child and that I can't even smoke a cigarette unless you light the match for me. And now this love-making is the last straw – You never used to dress up for ME. You only bought fine clothes and jewels when you started to vamp Kendall. With MY money too! And just now in MY house you allow him to kiss you!

ALICE

Henry, will you stop?

HENRY

It's the most cold-blooded thing I ever heard of!

ALICE

Henry!

213

HENRY

I saw you, MY WIFE -----

(he breaks off)

KENDALL

You don't deserve such a wife.

HENRY

What have I done? I bought her a house and cars and everything a woman could wish, didn't I?

KENDALL

On credit. Anyone could do that.

HENRY

I'm a movie star and I make good money.

KENDALL

You spend ten times more than you make.

HENRY

That's my business!

KENDALL

Perhaps it is. But I love Alice and I am going to protect her from a crazy, irresponsible fool who hasn't the faintest notion of how to treat her.

HENRY

I won't stand any more of your insults.

(he begins to search in the drawers of his desk)

ALICE

Calm yourself, Henry. Don't speak so loudly.

HENRY

Calm myself. I'll calm HIM! Wait until I find my revolver. It will speak loud enough for EVERYONE to hear!

(he searches frantically for the revolver, but without success)

KENDALL

Don't be alarmed, Alice. I can handle this -----

HENRY

You just wait! I guess it's upstairs.

(he leaps up the stairs)

KENDALL

Here's your opportunity to come away with me. You can't stay here tonight. He might do you some harm.

ALICE

I'm not afraid of him....Leave me. I'll manage somehow tonight and tomorrow -

KENDALL

But darling, I can't leave you like this.

ALICE

I wish you would go. Please ---I'll be all right. I'll get rid of the party somehow. Tomorrow.

KENDALL

Are you sure you want me to go?

(Alice nods)

Tomorrow then, Goodnight.

ALICE

Goodnight.

(Alice sits looking into space, an inscrutable expression upon her face. Henry rushes half way down the center stairs, poking his head around the corner of the doorway)

HENRY
(petulantly)

Alice ---where's my revolver?

(The music continues in the ballroom)

CURTAIN

ACT III

SCENE: Same, a month later.

AT RISE: Henry is found slumped in an armchair, looking the picture of
                misery. Even the room has an air of gloom. There are no flowers
                in the vases and all the small personal objects have been removed.
                Buckle enters. He is no longer in livery.

BUCKLE

Mr. Goldberg has come, sir.

HENRY
(brightening up a little)

Show him in.....er.....Have you a cigarette handy, Buckle?

BUCKLE
(turns and opening a smart cigarette case offers it to Henry)

Help yourself, sir.

                (Henry takes a few cigarettes from the case, hands it back to
                Buckle, who goes out. After hunting a moment for a match,
                Henry lights a cigarette, throws back his shoulders and prepares
                to make an impression on Morris)

MORRIS
(sweeping into the room breezily)

What's the big idea, calling me up and asking me to come here?

HENRY
(still pathetically trying to bluff)

I've got some new ideas for publicity that I thought you'd like to hear.

MORRIS

They'd have to be good to let you on the front page again.

HENRY

I thought you might like to come with me on a new job.

MORRIS

What job? I work for pay, you know.

HENRY
(with attempted nonchalance)

I've got several offers.

MORRIS

Who had the courage!

HENRY
(with a show of pride)

One was from F.B.O.......

MORRIS

When?

HENRY
(a little uncomfortable)

Well, three months ago......

MORRIS

Just as I thought! While you were still with Schwartz you were still on the map – but now---

HENRY
(losing ground gradually)

I had another offer from.......

MORRIS

Poverty Row, I suppose, where they make five reelers in three days. Might as well call in the undertaker at once, and be done with it!

HENRY
(hopefully)

If I could get some good publicity just now, it might start something.

MORRIS

Say – if you called me up for that you'd better have another brainstorm. You can't pull dumb-bells at this stage of your game, and get away with it!...... When you were dripping sex appeal from your eyes two years ago, you could do a "Movie Star's quiet evening at home with his books" and all the other bromides, but not now.....God! New publicity stuff! Even a contract with the Metropolitan Opera Company as a lead tenor wouldn't get a break.

HENRY
(a bit humbly)

I thought I might take up aviation.

MORRIS
(sarcastically)

Aviation! Now, that's a bright idea! That is! That's new! That's an inspiration! See here, after Lindy's stunt you'd have to loop the loop from here to China to get a paragraph. Aviation! Ah Hell!

BUCKLE
(entering)

There's a moving van outside, sir. The men say they've come for the furniture.

HENRY

Send them away!

BUCKLE

They say they have an order to begin at once, sir.

HENRY

Stall them off! Tell them I won't see them.

BUCKLE

I can't, sir.

HENRY

Tell them they can't have the furniture until Mrs. Warwick comes back.

BUCKLE

No use, sir. I told them everything already, except that there's a death in the house!

HENRY

Then tell them, THAT!

BUCKLE

By the manner of them, sir, they'd certainly ask to see the corpse.

HENRY

Oh, well, tell them to come and get the filthy stuff. I never liked it anyhow.

(Buckle goes out)

MORRIS
(suddenly trying to catch Henry off his guard)

......Where's Alice anyway?

HENRY
(trying to hide his discomfort and appear natural)

Why, she went to New York for a trip – to buy some new clothes - -and - -to see the theaters!

MORRIS

Yes, I know all about that, but it sounds fishy to me – when you're broke...When's she coming back?

HENRY
(uncomfortable –but still trying to bluff it out)

In a few weeks ---I guess.

MORRIS

Then she's not back?

HENRY

What do you mean?

MORRIS

Well, I saw her in the station at Los Angeles three days ago.

HENRY
(eagerly forgetting his caution in his anxiety for news)

You did?

MORRIS

Yes – she had her suitcases with her.

HENRY
(excitedly)

What train did she take? -----was she leaving or coming in?

MORRIS

How should I know? I was there taking some stills of Marcelle and the Count who were leaving for Europe.

HENRY

Was -----was Alice alone?

MORRIS

Sure! .....

        (suddenly changing after a side glance at Henry)

No.....Kendall was there talking to her.....

HENRY
(despondently)

God! Then they've gone away together.

MORRIS
(enthusiastically)

Great!

HENRY
(indignantly)

Great? What do you mean?

MORRIS

Sure! Now that's a story you could get printed.

HENRY

No. It may not be true. It can't be true!

        (turning on Morris)

And even if it is, it's the one thing you can't use.

MORRIS
(on the job)

We'll soon find out if it's true or not! I'll phone Kendall's office and see if he's in town...

HENRY
(eagerly)

Yes, phone and see.

MORRIS

You might have thought of that before.

HENRY
(turning away to hid his emotion)

I did. But I was afraid to....to.....

MORRIS

Is the phone still connected?

HENRY

It was the day before yesterday.

(Morris goes to the phone and calls number. The movers enter and begin taking out the furniture. Henry walks up and down nervously)

MORRIS
(at the phone)

Hello! Kendall's office?

(surprised)

You don't say so? ..... Good. Thanks.

(turning to Henry)

Kendall has gone for New York.

HENRY
(sinking into his chair again)

Then.....it's true!

MORRIS

It's the best thing that could have happened to you! Think of the sympathy you'll get!

HENRY
(pathetically – almost to himself)

But Kendall won't make her happy. He couldn't make ANY woman happy.

(During this scene the movers come and go. Whenever they enter, Henry and Morris drop their conversation until they exit again; then quickly pick it up)

MORRIS

How do you know? You weren't such a hell of a success as a husband yourself.

HENRY
(starting up furiously)

You get out of here! When I want your opinion, I'll ask for it.

MORRIS

You're a fool if you don't hit back at Alice, and at the same time get a new break for yourself. This story is a scoop for any paper.

HENRY
(furiously)

A scoop! You're not a reporter any more, you're working for this industry and if you ever did anything so rotten as to spill inside stuff you'd be out of the studio for good. Nobody would trust you around any more. And if you ever did such a thing to Alice – I'd beat the hell out of you!

MORRIS
(sarcastically)

Is that so?

HENRY

Yes, that's so ---and you ---you-----GET OUT!

MORRIS

All right! All right! But don't expect any flowers from me at your funeral!

(he goes out)

(After Morris leaves, Henry again sinks into his chair, his head in his hands – more despondent than ever. He is face to face with facts as they are and no one to turn to. The movers entering pay no attention to him, but go about their work, which in this room is almost complete)

FIRST MOVER

There ain't much difference, Hank, between the moving and the movie business. After they've got started at the bottom --- we move 'em up – and when they've got to the top --- we move 'em out!

SECOND MOVER

This is the third moving picture I've directed this week, and they were all nine reel dramas with all star casts.

(They exit, their voices trailing off –leaving the stage absolutely quiet. Henry doesn't move. After a few moments their voices are heard again as they come back for the last pieces of furniture – Henry's armchair)

SECOND MOVER
(hears off stage as they come toward the door)

And did you see his last picture ---it was punk! Too slow! Nuthin' happened.

FIRST MOVER
(goes up to Henry ---shakes his shoulder)

Hey ---we gotta take this too ----

(He pulls the chair out from under Henry unceremoniously. Henry goes over wearily to the window and stands with his back to the door, looking out)

SECOND MOVER

Gee --- and can you imagine getting' paid real money for makin' love to a dame like that – if I couldn't do better'n that --- without pay ------ I'd----

FIRST MOVER

Ah, shut up, will ya ---- what do you think you are --- an expert on love making – -anyone would think to hear you talk – that you was Elinor Glynn.

(As they come toward the door, Agnes enters and stands in the doorway. She announces herself, imitating the butler)

AGNES

Miss Agnes Drake to see you, sir.

(she enters gaily. Henry turns)

Well, Henry, everything but the kitchen stove!

FIRST MOVER

Yeah ---we'll get that before we go.

(they exit)

AGNES

Cheer up, kid, the worst is yet to happen! I was passing the mansion, and I saw the radio going out, so I thought it looked kind of serious.

HENRY
(despondently)

It's all over, Ag.

AGNES

Oh, dry up ----it's only beginning!

HENRY

It couldn't be worse! I'm finished ---through.

AGNES

GOOD! Now there's hope.

HENRY

Oh, you talk like a fool, Ag!

AGNES

Sure I do! That's why everything I say has some sense to it! Only fools ever get anywhere, Henry. That's why you've got a future!

HENRY

Stop kidding me! This isn't the moment to be funny.

AGNES

I mean it!....You'd think you were having a funeral! Why, kid, you're just being BORN! ....Got anything to drink?

228

HENRY

No.

AGNES
(pulling a flask from her coat pocket)

Here, take some. You need it.

HENRY

No thanks. I only drink when I'm happy.

AGNES

You're going to be happy! Take a drop. Things are going to look different to you in a minute.

HENRY

Nothing but poison could help me out of my troubles NOW.

AGNES

I see Hodkins has gone.

HENRY
(nods pathetically)

All of them except Buckle. He sticks for some ungodly reason. I can't get rid of him and I owe him three month's salary I believe.

AGNES

Oh, it's just English, I suppose. God! But you look like the frost on the pumpkin!

HENRY

Don't try to be funny, Ag. I can't bear it!

(He buries his face in his hands)

AGNES

Now, look here, this won't do at all. Sit down and let's have a nice cozy little chat.

HENRY
(glancing at the bare room)

Cozy!

AGNES
(sitting crosswise on the floor and warming her hands at an imaginary blaze in the grate)

Sit down! Who cares if you get a bit dusty now.

(he sits)

Now listen to me! You ought to be the happiest man alive! You're getting out of the movie business while the getting's good! There's nothing in it, honey, but debts, heartaches and lonesome old age!

HENRY
(stubbornly)

But others succeed.

AGNES

So do they? It all depends upon what you call success. A lot of show! And it don't last! Look at Mary Elizabeth. She's got to stay sweet sixteen because she can't do anything but childrens' parts, and she's a lot nearer forty. Its just one continuous damn fight with something that's got to lick her in the end. Then what? What's she ever had out of life ---nothing real --- just a lot of make-believe --- we're all so busy making believe that we haven't time to be real until it's too late ---- and by then we've forgotten how. Look at Marcelle. She gets my goat sometimes with all her airs --- but she's pathetic too. She's always afraid --- lives in mortal terror that some day her public will find out she's human

230

instead of being an animated fashion plate. We're all afraid of reality --- and it's waiting around the corner for all of us. Then there's Edmonde --- just living on flattery and hot air --- and when THAT bubble breaks --- And look at me ---another one of the tragedies that hang around this town.

HENRY

I guess you're right Ag, but --- but what was wrong with ME?

AGNES

Don't you know, kid?

HENRY

No.

AGNES

Well, I guess someone's got to tell you. Can you stand it? Sure you won't get hurt?

HENRY

I've stood so much already, I don't think there's anything left that could hurt anymore.

AGNES

Well ----

HENRY
(trying to smile)

Is it -----as bad as all that?

AGNES

It's ----it's your nose.

HENRY

My ----my nose?

AGNES

Don't you ever take a look at yourself in the glass, Henry? "Be it ever so homely there's no mug like your own" – say, kid, I think I've got Gloria Swanson beat a mile, but look at me! All I'm good for is to be a clown! Yet I'd give my soul to play "CAMILLE", I think I could do it, too. Say, I could cough into the camera until I gave everyone the croup looking at me. You see, nobody sees himself as he is, Henry. Don't think that I mean that you aren't good-looking. You are. But your nose --- just wasn't built for --- Romance!

HENRY
(brokenly)

I never realized it ---I ---

AGNES

Of course you didn't! God just naturally fixed us like that --- made us blind except when we looked at others. I guess we'd all commit suicide if we could see ourselves as we ARE – before we'd learned enough to be able to stand it. I'm beginning to get snap shots of the real Ag ---- now and then, that's why I'm going to have a ranch where I can be myself without either being laughed at or arrested.

HENRY

There's nothing wrong with you, Ag.

AGNES

I'd be a riot in a love scene with John Gilbert, wouldn't I? No, I've got to stay where I fit --- and that's throwing pies. But you've been lucky. You've had all the damn nonsense knocked out of you before it was too late. You and Alice have a chance of happiness now.

(at the mention of Alice's name Henry nearly breaks down)

You've learned that Hollywood looks everything what it ain't. The real things - no one can see them for all the gold dust that's flying around blinding us all. It's all grand at first, but

232

after awhile it's a case of being all dressed up and no where to go. Now with you and Alice it's different. Alice is all wool and a yard wide. Hollywood is no place for a woman like her. I couldn't have stuck it if I didn't drink like hell to stop thinking....You know you was much happier when you were punching tickets and Alice was usherette. Oh, I know you can't go back to that now.....

(pauses, trying to think how she can help them, then suddenly)

Henry, I've got an idea.

(he looks up)

I told you about buying back the old home near Kansas City, didn't I?

(Henry nods)

Well, in six months the place will be mine. I thought that maybe you and Alice could go there for a spell to get your spunk back, and if you liked it I'd make you the manager of the place. I'll finance the trip and pay you a salary to run the farm. I'd thought of marrying some rough neck who liked chickens and eggs --- someone who'd think I was grand. But I ain't picked anyone yet and if I did later on we could arrange matters differently....

(tenderly)

Say, Henry, did you ever see little pigs --- just hatched, God! But they're the cutest little critters. And baby chickens, as they come out of the shell, all soft and fluffy, with their little hearts beating like time when you hold 'em in your hand....And then there's the lark. He's been there ever since I was a kid. It's the same lark because I recognized his song.... In them days the old woman...God! Henry when I think of how I treated the old woman, I could just crawl into a hole and die. I was so mean....and wasn't well. I remember she used to cough even then. Funny how I never seemed to hear that cough until after I went away....She died when I was in the Follies....the old man was alone for ten years after she died---- and I never went back once!....When I was a kid he used to take me on his lap, and hold me close to him...

(Agnes wipes away a tear with the back of her hand. Henry has his head down, with everything gone, this is about more than he can stand)

He's gone too. I guess all the real people on my map of the world are dead now....If I could only go back again when I was a kid – just for a minute – just to see the old woman and tell her I had heard her cough....But maybe somehow she knows....Sometimes she used to sing....She only knew one song. And how it got on my nerves....Oh, God! If I could hear her voice NOW!

(Agnes begins to sing "The Swanee River." She ends at "Far From the Old Folks at Home," then chokes)

You see, Henry, the old woman ran away from her home to marry the old man and she never saw her folks again. And I know what she felt when she was singing that song.

HENRY
(deeply moved)
(but trying to cheer Ag up)

You're a hell of a help, you are!

AGNES

It gets me sometimes, and it does me good to get it off my chest. As I was saying before, you and Alice could go to the ranch ----

HENRY
(brokenly)

Don't ---Ag ----

AGNES

Don't you want to?

HENRY

Yes, but it's impossible.

AGNES

I said I'd finance the trip, didn't I?

HENRY

It isn't that ......Ag-----Alice has left me for good.

AGNES
(incredulously)

Go on!

HENRY

It's TRUE! Do you remember the party here after the opening of my last picture?

AGNES

Do I? ----I'll never forget that party.

HENRY

Well, that night I found out that Alice loved Kendall.

AGNES

That lemon ice cream soda!

HENRY
(getting a little excited as he thinks about Kendall)

I wanted to kill him right then. But he sneaked away like a coward before I could find my revolver....The next day Alice left....She didn't take her trunks...so I hoped she was coming back...but I guess she left them because I hurt her pride....all the rotten things I said that night. She never came back. That was a month ago.

AGNES

Then her trip to New York is........

HENRY
(despairingly)

I just made that up. I didn't know what else to say to stop people asking questions. I don't know where she is. Morris said he saw her talking to Kendall three days ago at the station in Los Angeles. That's the first news I've had of her.

AGNES

Well, you poor kid.

(hopefully)

But maybe she's coming back.

HENRY

No, she won't come back. And it's all my fault. I know it now, I've had time to do a lot of thinking in the last few weeks.

AGNES

I'd never have believed it of Alice. To quit just because of the crash!

HENRY

Alice didn't quit because of that. She must have loved Kendall. God knows why....I don't see what she ever could have seen in him....But I don't blame her for leaving me. I'm --- I'm no good either.

AGNES
(offers him the flask again)

Have a swallow, Henry.

HENRY

No thanks.

AGNES
(taking some herself)

What are you going to do?

HENRY
(hopelessly)

I don't know.

AGNES

There's the ranch, if you wouldn't be too lonesome.

HENRY

You're great, Ag. Thanks just the same but ----

(An officer – followed by an excited little man –enters, pushing
the indignant Buckle aside roughly)

BUCKLE

I tell you Mr. Warwick isn't home!

CREDITOR
(pointing to Henry)

Yes he is ---there he is there.

OFFICER
(to Henry)

Mr. Warwick?

AGNES
(to officer)

You got a nerve forcing your way into a man's house. What's the big idea?

OFFICER
(ignoring Alice)

Are you Mr. Warwick?

AGNES

What's the matter with you --- too highbrow to go to the movies? Have another look. Don't you recognize him? He's Douglas Fairbanks and I'm Mary Pickford! TAKE OFF YOUR HAT!

OFFICER
(to Henry, still ignoring Agnes)

I've got ---
                    (takes papers from his pocket)

HENRY

I can't talk to you now. This is my busy day.

OFFICER

You can tell that to the judge. I've got a warrant for your arrest.

AGNES

Ain't he cute? You ought to be on the editorial staff of the Goldwyn Company with an imagination like that.

                    (the officer shows his warrant)

AGNES

(realizing how serious it is)

Have a drop Captain?

                    (she offers him her flask)

OFFICER
(threateningly)

You'd better look out young lady or -----
AGNES
(looks at him coyly)

Young lady! Flatterer!

(holding the flask upside down)

Gosh! – It's empty!

OFFICER

Come on Mr. Warwick, there's no use stalling.

HENRY
(recklessly)

You can't make ME any trouble.

OFFICER

Oh, can't I?

HENRY

No. I couldn't have any more than I've got already.

OFFICER

Come on. Step lively! I've got to pick up a couple of others on my way.

AGNES

Never mind, kid. I'll bail you out. Buck up! this is only the end of a nightmare. You'll wake up in a minute. When things get as bad as this, something always happens.

(Alice enters, dressed in a traveling suit and carrying a suitcase)

Look who's here!

HENRY
(crying out)

ALICE!

AGNES

What did I tell you!

OFFICER
(to Henry)

Come on. This isn't a tea party.

ALICE
(calmly)

What's the matter Henry? Where are you going?

OFFICER

He has given a bad check and he's got to come down and explain it to the judge.

ALICE
(to officer)

I'm Mrs. Warwick. I assume you there is some mistake. If you……

OFFICER
(pointing to the creditor)

You tell it to him. I'm only serving the warrant.

ALICE
(turning to the creditor and smiling reassuringly)

I can explain everything. Now, if you will put that check through again tomorrow you'll find that you will have no further trouble.

> (She takes him by the arm and leads him gently but firmly
> to the door, talking to him persuasively as they walk)

CREDITOR
(to Alice as they leave the room)

How do I know this isn't another stall? I've been waiting for my money for months and this check.......

ALICE

If you wish any further guarantee......

> (her voice dies away)

AGNES

My God! What a break! Say kid, what did you do that for?

HENRY
(childishly)

Well, he would keep pestering me – and I didn't know how else to shut him up so I gave him a check; I had plenty in the check book.

AGNES

With your idea of business, Henry, you should -----

CURLY
(appearing in the doorway)

Come on, Ag ---- If you hang around here much longer, you'll be pinched too. I just saw a cop outside.

AGNES

That's my cue! Goodbye Henry! Tell Alice about the ranch.

(Alice, having apparently rid herself of the office and the creditor, returns to the room as Agnes and Curly go out)

HENRY

Alice ---did you come back for your trunks?

ALICE
(a bit strained)

Yes.

HENRY

I packed them for you.

ALICE

That was good of you.

HENRY
(uncomfortable, and having so much to say that he doesn't know how to begin)

Are you going to leave Hollywood for good?

ALICE

Yes.

HENRY

When?

ALICE

Just as soon as I can settle a few things.

HENRY
(uncomfortably)

Alice --- I don't know how to thank you for --- for bailing me out of that mess just now --- I don't know how you did it or what to say --- except that ---

(smiles pathetically)

--- that I guess all I've ever done is to get into trouble for you to get me out of. I don't blame you a bit for leaving me.

(desperately going on with his confession which is doubly difficult because of Alice's silence)

I want you to know before you go that I realize now how rotten I was to you. You were wonderful to have put up with me as long as you did.....

(Alice watches him without showing any emotion)

I know I let you take all the responsibility – while I was playing around at being a movie star. That's why it made me sore when they said you wore the pants of the family – It's no good trying to bluff anymore. I knew all along that I was to blame ---that's --- that's why it hurts me so much.

(pauses and looks at Alice pathetically. She is still standing motionless, looking down at the floor. He goes on desperately)

I thought you ought to be happy because I was happy – but I guess you were having nothing but worry all the time.

(turns away)

I know it doesn't matter to you now – it's too late, but I just wanted you to know how sorry I am for what I said that night....about it being your fault that we had spent so much money ----- I don't know what made me say it ---- I was mad and hurt because you had dressed for him and not for ME – but it was my fault! I guess I didn't realize what you had on until that night ----I was too blinded by the glitter of it all to see the real thing I had --- until --- -it was too late!

(He pulls the little imitation bracelet which he had given her in the first act, out of his pocket)

I found this in your room, Alice --- I suppose that all I've ever seen is the imitation...even a long time ago ----

(holds out the bracelet)

See –- it lost all it's glitter now!

ALICE

(When she sees the little bracelet, she turns her head away for an instant! Then sits down on her suitcase)

Yes - Henry --- you've learned that cheap imitations only glitter when they're new.

HENRY

Yes, I have ---- but it's too late!

(kneeling beside her)

Alice ---I know I didn't make you happy ---but I want you to be happy – I want you to have everything ---I want you to be happy more than anything in the world ---and if --- if ---Kendall can make you happy ---well I hope you will be.

(he takes her hand and holds it to his cheek)

 I want you to be happy ---

(suddenly breaks down and buries his head in her lap)

Oh, Alice, don't leave me ---don't leave me ----I can't go on without you ---I'll ---I'll do ---anything ----

ALICE

(putting her arms around him and holding him close; tears filling her eyes.)

I'm not going to leave you – my darling ---ever ---

HENRY

(Slowly stops sobbing as he comes to the realization of what her words mean; then slowly raises his head and looks at her)

You mean --- you mean you're not going away ----you won't leave me-

ALICE
(taking his face in her hands)

No ----my darling.

HENRY

Then you've come back ----to stay!

ALICE

I've come back for you.

HENRY
(becoming more excited)

Then ---you don't love Kendall?

ALICE

No ---I never did.

HENRY
(puzzled as he tried to understand)

But if you weren't going to leave me – why did you go away a month ago?

ALICE
(speaking tenderly)

Because Henry – I knew that we couldn't go on ---until you realized....The crash had to come ---so the quicker it came and was over, the better ---dear ---, I went away because it was the only way to make you realize ---you had to find things out for yourself ---

(softly)

You see, dear, you WERE just a child ---and (looking down at him and smiling to herself) you had to go through all this to make you a man ---the MAN you are now.

245

HENRY
(straightening up a little – almost imperceptibly squaring his shoulders)

Yes –maybe I was ---irresponsible – at times

(pauses, thinking)

Alice ---did you ----did you know ---about my WORK?

ALICE
(smiling)

Yes, dear.

HENRY

(He buries his head in her lap for a moment, then slowly
                    straightens up as other thoughts run through his mind)

Alice, then where have you been all month ---in -----

ALICE

In San Francisco.

HENRY

But Morris said he saw you with Kendall ---three days ago ----

ALICE
(smiling)

Yes ---I came back three days ago -----to straighten out your affairs before Kendall went
East ----

HENRY

      (As he begins to understand his face lights up. At this moment Buckle enters, carrying several suits of clothes. When he sees Buckle he quickly gets to his feet – his boyish self-assurance reasserting itself)

BUCKLE

Shall I pack these, Madame?

ALICE

Yes, Buckle.

HENRY

More things from the cleaners! It's a wonder to me they left them without the bill being paid. Gosh – I wish we had all the money we've paid to that cleaner!

ALICE

We have.

HENRY
(not understanding)

What do you mean – we – have?

ALICE

We are EUREKA CLEANERS.

HENRY
(flabbergasted)

What?

ALICE

Yes – and Buckle is part of the firm.

HENRY

So – that's why I couldn't get rid of him!

ALICE
(gently)

Yes – someone had to remain here to look after you –and to keep me posted –

(smiles at Buckle who exits with importance)

HENRY

But the Eureka Cleaning Company is the biggest cleaners in Hollywood ----All the studios use ----

ALICE

Of course, it is! ----and now we have a branch in San Francisco. That's where our headquarters are going to be.

HENRY

Oh, that was what you were doing in San Francisco!

(suddenly thinking)

And that's how you were able to square that check ---we've got money now! ---But where did you get the money to start the business?

ALICE
(laughing)

I earned it from you.

HENRY

Earned it?

ALICE

You see, Henry, I always wanted a business. Don't you remember how I dreamed about it in the old days?....Well, when I saw how much you were spending in cleaning bills, it gave me an idea. I thought that, with you as my client, it would be cheaper to go into the business, and at the same time build up a future for us when the crash came....The business grew in spite of myself. God knows I haven't much business ability.

HENRY

Business ability! You're wonderful!

ALICE
(smiling)

Nonsense! I only made a success of the cleaning business because you were such a good client.....If you had been managing the business instead of me, we'd have ten branches today instead of two! With your personality and enthusiasm (and charm crossed out), there's no limit to what you could so as a business man!

HENRY
(beginning to strut around as he did in the old days)

You're right, Alice. I guess I was cut out for a business man! After all I'm glad I have a turned-up nose! If I'd had another kind of nose I might never have known the truth about myself.....

(Alice watches him with great tenderness)

And, say, this moving picture experience wasn't such a bad thing for me after all! Look at what I've learned! Look what I've learned about PUBLICITY! I've got ideas about advertising this business which will make it heard of from coast to coast. We'll have branches all over the country.

(Walking up and down)

Publicity! ....There's no reason why we can't have two branches in Hollywood and three in San Francisco – maybe four....And we'll have Buick delivery cars! Within a year the Eureka Cleaning Company will have its stores on all main streets of the different cities!....They'll make all the other cleaning establishments look like poverty row joints in comparison...I've got some new ideas about new methods of cleaning and .....

(The curtain goes down slowly on him telling what he is going to so with the cleaning business. Alice smiles happily at him all the while)

CURTAIN

Michael Morris and Evelyn Zumaya Discuss
All That Glitters

Zumaya:

I kept thinking as I read the play that Rambova was bitter. Bitter over everything and after all, why not be?

Morris:

I think Rambova was driven to write this play as if she was still trying to explain to the public what her role in the marriage was. She must have felt vilified to keep on trying to clear her name.

Zumaya:

The play is rife with her bitterness. And the dynamic between Alice, Henry and Kendall is revealing in that it is constructed to portray her actual life as she felt wedged between Rudy and George Ullman. For me it is interesting to read between her lines; to notice her adjectives. On several occasions she describes Henry's actions as "pathetic". Although she refers to him as childish and foolish, her use of "pathetic" exhibits scorn. It is obvious reading the play that she was angry over how she was being portrayed in her divorce from Valentino.

Morris:

In regards to the characters, I think it is safe to say that Rambova's William Kendall represents Valentino's business manager, George Ullman. Buckle the valet would be the Valentino's handyman, Lou Mahoney. In describing the Count, I think she is referring to her type of lover as as being an "immaculately dressed, bored aristocratic who has sold himself to be a prop."

And Marcelle Marson ("the dark exotic type") is obviously a combination of Nita Naldi (whom Rambova should have mistrusted alone with her husband) and either Gloria Swanson or Pola Negri.

Zumaya:

I was intrigued by the character Agnes' farm tales. Would Agnes be Marion Davies? Was Rambova pining for a country life that she found to some degree living in Mallorca? Minus the baby pigs?

Morris:

Yes, now that I review the play's dialogue it DOES seem that Agnes Drake is Marion Davies, the life of the party who knows everyone, the comedienne! You are spot on!

Zumaya:

I think the only character in the play that is probably spot on is that of Henry as Rudy. Even the character of Alice...his dear wife, does not feel like Rambova at times.

Morris:

Oh, I think Rambova is Alice, but it is a groundedness that seemed only to exist in her Mormon roots where practicality was prized and pretensions despised. It is a rural, feet on the ground, realism that she inherited from her ancestors but turned her back on (as did her mother) as the allure of glamour and celebrity and wealth beguiled her. I think she is chucking all that off in this play, but it is also a defense against her critics who felt her own pretensions killed Valentino.

Zumaya:

It is a good point to make as many people thought Rambova's pretensions impacted Valentino's career. Yet in his first memoir written in 1926, George Ullman says Rambova elevated Rudy and without her, he would have been nothing.

Morris:

And Marcelle, is she Pola Negri or Mae Murray or a combo of both? They both married Mdvani Counts. Kendall may be in Ullman's position but her extra-martial romance was not with Ullman. Perhaps by insinuating it was with the character that was occupied by Ullman, in real life it was a barb directed at him.

Zumaya:

The Countess could be Mae Murray.

Morris:

I don't think so. Mae Murray sued Rambova over a dress she made and thus would NOT be in the play. And yes, I think what Ullman says is true, but that was an observation made behind the scenes. The fans weren't aware of it.

Zumaya:

I saw the character of Agnes as Marion because of the spunkiness and comedic personality Rambova gave her. Also because of her role as a sisterly adviser to Henry. I think Marion held that role with many people in her world...everyone but Mr. Hearst!

Morris:

Oh I think Hearst appreciated her spunkiness and that's why she was such a good hostess at San Simeon. I don't see Rambova and Davies getting along together while in Hollywood. Marion was cheery and Rambova was deadpan and took herself too seriously. That's why she adopted Nita Naldi, another strange creation (from Irish and convent schooled young lady to treacherous vamp) as her best friend. But Rudy loved Marion.

Zumaya:

One of the most interesting aspects of this play is the mention of the dry cleaning business. When I was researching *Affairs Valentino*, I discovered the history of this company which actually existed as Ritz Cleaners. In Lou Mahoney's interview with *Movie Classics* magazine in 1973, he stated that he never had anything to do with that dry cleaning business which Valentino owned. When I discovered the court records of Valentino's estate settlement, I found Ullman sold the business to Lou Mahoney along with a company truck for two hundred dollars. He subsequently ran the business for several years.

Morris:

In *All That Glitters*, did Rambova reveal that Mahoney was running the business out of their home before it became Valentino's business? Was the graft she referred to in an article she wrote in 1923, a revelation? What other reason would Natacha have to include this odd element to her story line?

Zumaya:

Rambova's hatred for Hollywood is apparent as she consistently sets herself above those in Hollywood in the play. She does so by referring to the "vulgarity" and lack of taste of the people in the play. This is revealed especially through the character of the Count.

Morris:

I see it as a work that will convince others that she did NOT wear the pants in the family. That comes up again and again in the play. I noticed how many details are based on true incidents in their lives. And many of the references are destined barbs for particular people. Like the whole NOSE thing. Valentino's own nose provided a great profile, but any reference to a nose NOT being romantic was meant as an insult to his brother Alberto.

Zumaya:

I am sure Rambova wrote alot of the play as getting even but I think it is risky to take it all literally...I believe she was mostly getting back at Hollywood.

Morris:

One of the characters, Morris Goldberg is most probably Robert Florey or even Morris Gest who was an agent and publicity man when Rambova was dancing with Kosloff's troupe. He betrayed her to her mother in letting Mrs. Hudnut know that Natacha was engaged in an affair and that triggered her disappearance for a year. Yes, I think that Natacha certainly wrote this play to get even with some of the people in her past.

Zumaya:

I think it should be considered that Rambova was young when she penned this screenplay and this was her first and last attempt. I believe this was a cathartic exercise in which she could very well have written Alice in the first person. She seemed ready to tell the world in some way that she made Valentino who he was, nursed him through it and then when he became lost in the limelight, she was cast aside. This said, in her fairy tale ending, which of course did not happen to Rambova and Valentino, she rescues him one last time through her business savvy and stealth.

Morris:

Yes, I think Natacha had a brush with seriously wanting to be a screenplay writer and as many people do...they write about what they know at the time. If anything I think it is her trying to construct some legacy where she was the long suffering wife of a philandering husband who worked hard to keep it all together...and ultimately failed. How fascinating the politics of their love!

CHAPTER FIVE

Fig. 106

Madonna Oriflamma by Nicholas Roerich, 1932

"Throughout this century of wars and national struggles, the yearning of the public for ways of achieving peace has been great; the ideas of the (Roerich) Pact and the Banner provide a welcome answer to those yearnings." [1]

1   Roerich.org

A MUSEUM OF RELIGION AND PHILOSOPHY

Contrary to Natacha's heartfelt words to Rudolph Valentino in the final letters she wrote to him in 1925, he would not remain her last love for long. She soon found love beyond Valentino.

From 1929 to 1931, Natacha Rambova was engaged to be married to the third love of her life, Svetoslav Roerich.[2] It is little wonder Natacha found the handsome Russian artist irresistible. Svetoslav seemed to compensate for those characteristics she found ultimately lacking in Valentino. The educated, charismatic and world-traveled Svetoslav was seven years her junior, yet she did not find him childlike as she found Rudy to be.

Svetoslav Roerich was born in 1904 in St. Petersburg, Russia to Helena and Nicholas Roerich. He and his older brother George enjoyed exceptional childhoods with all academic and cultural advantage bestowed upon them by their worldly parents.

Father Nicholas Roerich first gained fame in his homeland as a set and costume designer for Sergei Diaghilev's Ballet Russe. As a member of the Russian modernist movement, Nicholas Roerich made influential friends and his oil paintings were exhibited and valued as master works of art. He would marry Helena Shaposhnikov, an intellectual woman, author and pianist.

In 1920, Nicholas and Helena Roerich came to America where he continued with his work in theatrical design and studio painting while she pursued her writing. They were both also known for their theosophical pursuits and interests in culture, philosophy and archaeology. In 1921, they founded the Master Institute of United Arts in New York City; a venture wherein Nicholas and Helena Roerich expanded their cultural campaign for world peace and unity to include all artistic media. They would utilize these avenues to purport the theosophical "Divine Principle" as being the source of all religion.

The Master Institute of United Arts was an ambitious undertaking as it was founded upon all religious and philosophical constructs including Buddhism, Theosophy as well as spiritualism and Judeo-Christian principles. This unique religious synthesis, presented at a time of world political turmoil held great appeal and resulted in Nicholas Roerich being nominated for the Nobel Peace Prize.

By 1929, when his son Svetoslav asked Natacha Rambova to marry him, Nicholas Roerich was internationally renowned for his esoteric writings, spiritual and religious paintings, his Central Asiatic expeditions and for his establishment of a Society devoted to world peace and the protection of cultural treasures. His Roerich Society was protected by their own flag, or banner, "The Banner of Peace" or the "Red Cross of Culture."

Yet, when Natacha Rambova became involved with the Roerich's Master Institute of United Arts in New York, it was Svetoslav Roerich who was excelling at art; following in his father's footsteps. In the late 1920's, Nicholas moved his family to Kulu, India,

---

2 Dr. Vladimir Rosov, "Based on the following facts that in 1929-1931 Natacha Rambova was living in the Master Building (Nicholas Roerich Museum), and so was Svetoslav Roerich up to 1931 (and they were officially engaged)".

located remotely in the lower Himalayas, where he founded a Himalayan Institute. He left Svetoslav in America to manage the family's business interests in New York. Svetoslav resided in the penthouse of the family-owned skyscraper, known as "The Master Building".

As the home of the Roerich Museum and the Master Institute of United Arts, the Master Building was occupied by artists, theosophists, spiritualists and was a center for all creative and artistic pursuits sponsored by the Roerich Society.

Several members of the theosophic Bamberger Circle embraced the Roerich philosophies and goals and moved into the Master Building, including Talbot Mundy and his wife Dawn Allen who leased an apartment on the 18th floor. Natacha Rambova and her psychic George Wehner, lived on the 20th and 21st floors. Wehner's weekly séances as hosted by Natacha and the Mundys continued after their move into the Master Building.

"Séances would typically begin with a recitation of the Lord's Prayer and the singing of hymns, until Wehner dozed off and went into the trance state. Entering the trance, the medium would seem to fall asleep, his abdomen would swell, and he might bang his head uncontrollably on the chair." [3]

When Talbot Mundy moved into the Roerich Master Building, he was a respected member of the Theosophical Society and addressed psychic experiences in two of his books, *Om* and *The Devil's Guard*. Although the séances Wehner conducted were initially regular events in the Master Building, Mundy was soon directing the séance participants towards a more credible and esoteric direction in the spiritualist movement. A cooling of interest in Wehner's communications with the dead came about after a falling-out between Talbot Mundy, Dawn Allen and George Wehner.

Wehner often related music he alleged to be channeling from deceased musicians. Dawn Allen, being a musician, transcribed Wehner's musical transmissions and with Natacha's assistance, a recital was organized. With Dawn Allen playing the piano and Donna Shinn Russell singing, Wehner was credited for the music. However, he grew irate claiming his music was being appropriated without his permission. This caused an irrevocable split between Talbot Mundy and George Wehner with Natacha and Dawn Allen following suit.

The séances grew fewer as Wehner grew increasingly unstable. Additionally, Talbot Mundy, Dawn Allen and Natacha were growing aware of the popularization of spiritual activities and the charlatans exploiting the trend.

Composite drawings appearing in newspapers represented séances with ghosts spinning in the air and mediums spewing gas and unidentified matter called "ectoplasm". It seemed prudent for the Bamberger Circle members to turn towards a more sophisticated venue to satisfy their study and interest in spiritualism. In this regard the Roerich Society's Master Institute of United Arts provided more respectable esoteric intrigue.

With Svetoslav Roerich's good looks and gentlemanly demeanor, his artistic abilities and a foundation in theosophy, (his mother Helena translated *The Secret Doctrine* by Helena Blavatsky into Russian), he charmed the Master Building's residents with little effort, especially Natacha Rambova.

He had studied architecture in England and art and architecture at New York's Columbia University, attended Harvard and won the Grand Prize of the Sesquicentennial Exposition in Philadelphia in 1926. His academic artistic training and expertise with oils, color and composition was reflected in his hyper-realistic portraiture and landscapes.

It is interesting to note that Svetoslav Roerich was photographed posing in various guises made famous by Rudolph Valentino. He

---

3   Brian Taves, *Talbot Mundy, Philosopher of Adventure, A Critical Biography*, p. 175.

was photographed as Valentino's signature role of the Sheik the same year the movie premiered and years before he met Natacha. He would also pose as a turbaned Rajah, although he lived in India where his parents established their home in Kulu.

Svetoslav posed in Chinese garb in Darjeeling, India in 1924, the same year a publicity photo was released by Valentino in a similar costume. What he perceived in himself vis-à-vis Valentino is difficult to interpret. It would seem these costumes were more authentic to Svetoslav whose family traversed Central Asia and planted lasting roots there, than they ever were to Rudolph Valentino.

Natacha found Svetoslav a compelling partner and her role in his life and his family's society was made known in August of 1929. It was then she was elected to serve as an officer of the Society of Friends of the Roerich Museum along with Dr. Forest Grant, Mary Siegrist, Nettie S. Horch, Henry Judson, Dr. Charles Fleischer and Edward E. Spitzer. [4]

While continuing to occasionally consult Wehner via his mediumship, Natacha divested her field of study, pursuing the Roerich philosophies of a unified cultural movement based on all religions and media.

"Natacha took the theosophical perspective as the basis for her own studies in Oriental and ancient philosophies and myths from Tibet, India and Egypt." [5]

As Natacha and Svetoslav were planning their life together, they were also actively involved in the planning of a museum they called, "The Museum of Religion and Philosophy". Their museum would be housed in the Master Building and would combine all aspects of the arts and include all quests for the Divine.

In a booklet advertising the proposed museum, Svetoslav was identified as the institution's president and "Director of Ancient Arts" while Natacha was appointed as secretary-treasurer and "Director of Drama". Talbot Mundy was appointed as "Director of Literature".

The program planned to include concerts, recitals, exhibitions, lectures, dramatic performances, radio broadcasts and even the production of motion pictures.

All faiths would be included under the Museum of Religion and Philosophy's programs and these programs were extended to esoteric groups as well. The paranormal, even secret societies such as the Knights Templar, would be a part of their collective investigation. Nothing would escape their study of the Mysteries through various media.

The Museum of Religion and Philosophy was scheduled to open in January of 1931. However, Svetoslav and Natacha's dream never manifested.

By 1931, The Roerich Society had become a global initiative under the imposing direction of Nicholas and Helena Roerich. The famous Russian couple had confronted many obstacles while promoting their international peace efforts in America and in India, including the insinuations they were operating a Bolshevik organization.

With their goal of creating an international Peace Pact and the challenges of managing their cultural institutions, there could be no hint of personal impropriety.

It is not yet known exactly what event instigated the termination of Svetoslav and Natacha's love affair and engagement. Yet, in light of the import of the work being conducted at the time and the residual Bolshevik rumor mongering, it is logical to assume the Roerich Society perceived Natacha Rambova, as being too heavily-laden with Valentino's Hollywood reputation. She could have posed a threat to the sanctity of their initiatives.

4 *New York Times*, (1923-current file), August 18, 1929, "Roerich Museum Elects: Theophile Schneider Is Made President of American Branch".

5 Brian Taves, *Talbot Mundy, Philosopher of Adventure, A Critical Biography*, p. 168.

From his estate in Kulu, Nicholas Roerich canceled his son's position at the Master Building in New York in 1931 and summoned him home to India. Forced to choose between his father's wishes and his impending marriage to Natacha, Svetoslav chose an allegiance to the Roerich legacy and left for India.

Natacha was devastated with the news of her broken engagement and the dissolution of plans for the Museum of Religion and Philosophy. She was furious and, according to her family, threatened to sue Svetoslav for breach of contract. Upon the sage advice of her friends, she instead left New York to find solace in an ocean voyage. Before leaving she told Talbot Mundy that she planned to move to Europe permanently.

Ironically, Svetoslav eventually did marry in 1945, and his bride was India's premier film star, Devika Rani, known as the "First Lady of the Indian Screen". Apparently, on this occasion the elder Roerich had no objections. What is interesting is that Devika Rani looked remarkably similar to Natacha Rambova. Just as Svetoslav once posed in costumes similar to characters in Valentino's films, so did Devika Rani with her hairstyle and exotic clothing no doubt remind Svetoslav of his former love, the icon of Hollywood glamour, Natacha Rambova.

During Svetoslav and Natacha's engagement, she gave him several pieces of her art including a sketch of the costume design she drew years prior which she titled, "The Egyptian Woman". In return Natacha posed for several portraits and sketches Svetoslav painted of her. These works of art survive as testament to their abandoned dream of their Museum of Religion and Philosophy and as proof of their ill-fated engagement.

Perhaps the loving devotion that is apparent in photographs of Svetoslav Roerich with his wife Devika Rani lends insight into his past relationship with Natacha Rambova. He appears a serious partner, enlightened and not one frivolous in desire or emotion. With this in mind it is reasonable to conclude both Natacha and Svetoslav's lives were impacted by their abrupt separation.

With George Wehner suffering what Natacha and the Mundy's would perceive as a complete nervous collapse, there would be no further séances and their pursuit of spiritualism as an active participation in occult activity ended. Svetoslav Roerich's departure, initiated a change in course, literally and spiritually for Natacha.

As Svetoslav sailed for India, Natacha boarded an ocean liner bound for Europe to then travel on to the Mediterranean Sea. On this crossing there were no séances held in Natacha's cabin and she no longer felt the urge to commune with the dead. Years later her secretary and companion Mark Hasselriis would comment:

"Natacha never once engaged in a séance during the years I knew her....I am of the opinion she passed that 'phase' and put virtually all of that spiritualism behind her." [6]

6 Letter from Mark Hasselriis to Michael Morris, November 7, 1989.

Fig. 107

Fig. 108

Svetoslav Roerich, Naggar, India, 1934, background painting by Svetoslav Roerich titled, *Karma Dorje*, 1934

Svetoslav Roerich, India, 1935 – 1945

"The circle of his scientific interests is striking: ornithology, botany, mineralogy, Tibetan pharmacopoeia, chemistry and its alchemical sources, astrology, comparative religious studies and philosophy, art studies, cultural studies." [7]

---

7 http://en.agnivesti.ru/the-roerichs/svetoslav-roerich/

Fig. 109

Svetoslav and Nicholas Roerich
To the right, painting titled "The Messenger", 1924, dedicated to H.P. Blavatsky

"The cross-fertilization of the arts that Roerich promoted was evidence of his inclination to harmonize, bring together, and find correspondences between apparent conflicts or opposites in all areas of life. This was a hallmark of his thinking, and one sees it demonstrated in all the disciplines he explored." [8]

8 Roerich.org

Fig. 110

Helena Roerich

"Since the mid-1920's, the Russian painter, Nicholas Roerich, Nikolai Konstantinovitch Rerikh, (1874–1947), and his wife Elena Ivanonva, neé Shaposhnikova (1879-1955), created a spiritual system called 'Agni Yoga' or 'teaching of Living Ethics' incorporating Theosophical doctrines as its basis." [9]

9 *From Synarchy to Shambhala,* by Markus Osterrieder, p. 101.

Fig. 111

Svetoslav Roerich

Fig. 112
Svetoslav Roerich, Naggar, India, 1934

"I was very interested in ornithology, zoology," Svetoslav Roerich recollected. "Helena Roerich collected for me all the necessary books – whichever ones she could find. She bought us stuffed birds, raised collections of insects, bugs. Besides, I was attracted to beautiful stones, mineralogy. She also collected for me all kinds of stones of the Urals and other types. Thus, our little world was at that time saturated with wonderful impressions" [10]

10 From S. Roerich, *Striving for the Beautiful*, p. 54, The Roerich Small Library

Fig. 114

Svetoslav Roerich, Darjeeling, India, 1924

Fig. 113

Svetoslav Roerich, @ 1920 -1923

Fig. 115

Svetoslav Roerich, India, 1930's

"Dostoevsky said: 'Beauty will save the world', or, I'd rather say that carrying the beauty into our lives should be our foundation. There is no other way. Only the understanding of Beauty, only the Good, only the desire to do every day something better than yesterday will be nurturing people's lives. Bright ideas and actual deeds are needed. Only by uniting high-minded co-workers can we pave the path to the future."[11]

---

11 Agnivesti, *We Can Not Linger*, by Svetoslav Roerich, Bangalore, July 3, 1989 and Sovetskaya Kultura, July 29, 1989.

Fig. 116

Svetoslav Roerich, Naggar, India, August 1933

Fig. 117

Portrait of Nicholas Roerich by Svetoslav Roerich

"Roerich's ambition was no less than to prepare for the coming of a New Age of peace and beauty which would be ushered in by the earthly manifestation of Maitreya, the Buddha of the Future." [12]

---

12 *From Synarchy to Shambhala,* by Markus Osterrieder, p. 101.

Fig. 118

Svetoslav Roerich, circa 1928

Fig.119

Fig .120

Svetoslav Roerich, Naggar, India, 1934, painting in background, *Karma Dorje*

"Svetoslav Roerich was convinced that Beauty could not be created without a higher ideal. Destruction of this ideal – spiritual or aesthetic – would result in the disfigurement of life and in the loss of its evolutionary pivot." [13]

13 http://en.agnivesti.ru/the-roerichs/svetoslav-roerich

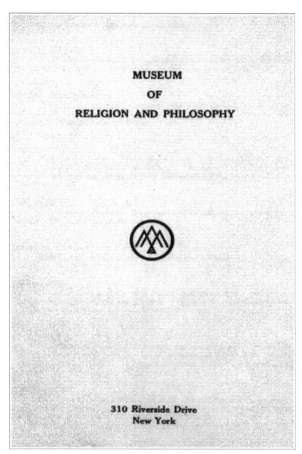

Fig. 121

Fig. 122

The Master Building
310 Riverside Drive

MUSEUM OF RELIGION AND PHILOSOPHY

OFFICERS

S. ROERICH, President
LESLIE GRANT SCOTT, Vice-President
MAJOR R. T. M. SCOTT, Vice-President
NATACHA RAMBOVA, Secretary-Treasurer

ADVISORY COMMITTEE

Alice A. Bailey
Helen T. Bigelow
Frances R. Grant
Nettie Horch
Louis L. Horch
Leila Jones
Spencer Kellogg, Jr.
Shri Vishwanath Keskar
Sina Lichtmann
Maurice M. Lichtmann
Roy Mitchell
Talbot Mundy
Rev. Dr. Robert Norwood
Professor Nicholas Roerich
Major Phelps Stokes

4

MUSEUM OF RELIGION AND PHILOSOPHY

BASIC IDEA

Visual and graphic representation of all the different phases of human endeavor embracing Philosophy or the Science of Life and the manifestation of the God-Principle.

To show the underlying unity in all religions and philosophies founded by the great Teachers and Their Followers.

The proofs of this unity to be shown or demonstrated through:

1. A collection of symbols embodied in different objects, emblems, instruments, etc., used in the various rites, mysteries and religious services.

2. Data bearing directly upon the underlying principles of unity, as it found its expression in arts, crafts, literature and music.

PROGRAM

The program will consist in acquiring collections of paintings, art objects, books and manuscripts, for a permanent museum bearing out the fundamental idea, and in arranging various publications, classes and lectures, as well as the portrayal of the fundamental ideas illustrated in dramatic form as they were revealed in various rites, Passion Plays, Morality Plays, Dramas and Mysteries. The idea will find expression through all modern facilities such as the stage, motion pictures, radio, television, etc.

PRACTICAL REALIZATION OF THE PROJECT THROUGH:

The cooperation of the various churches, philosophical societies and mystic orders in contributing to and up-building their respective representative sections, to present the true fundamental basis of their religion, creed or philosophy in its purity, and freed of accumulated misrepresentations;

The cooperation of individuals by personal efforts and donations;

Publications such as: serialized postcards depicting the lives of different Teachers; series demonstrating identical symbols, their various applications, etc.; short stories and articles in magazines; books and special periodicals demonstrating the fundamental idea of unity;

Fig. 123-124

Museum of Religion and Philosophy Pamphlet

Radio talks and motion pictures;

Dramatic performances, concerts or recitals of musical programs showing similarity of religious themes;

Permanent exhibitions of religious paintings, statues, votive figures, art objects, etc.;

A library of philosophic, religious and mystical symbols, books and manuscripts;

Exhibitions of representative ancient and modern illustrative religious paintings and sculptures.

OBJECTIVE

To ultimately erect a permanent building for the housing of these collections, exhibitions, publications, with library, theatre, concert and lecture halls for all activities.

SECTIONS

Ancient and Pre-Christian Religions

The Egyptian Religion
The Religion of the Hittites
The Religion of Babylonia and Assyria
Ancient Judaism
Zoroastrianism
Hinduism
The Parsi Religion
Mohammedanism
Mithraism
Sikhism
Sufism
Buddhism
Taoism
Confucianism
Shintoism
Shamanism
Bhon-Po
The Religion of Ancient Greece
The Religion of Ancient Rome
Druidism
The Nordic and Teutonic Cults
Slavonic Religion
Mayan, Aztec and Toltec Religions
Primitive Religions

6

Christian and Philosophic Religions

The Roman Catholic Church
The Russian Church
The Greek Church
The Armenian Church

Protestant Denominations including:
    Baptist
    Congregational
    Episcopalian
    Lutheran
    Methodist
    Presbyterian
    Unitarian

Quakerism
Theosophy
Mormonism
Modern Hebrewism
Spiritualism
Christian Science
Metaphysical and New Thought Philosophies

Followers of:
    Boehme
    Swedenborg
    Spinoza

Secret Societies

Rosicrucians
Free Masons
Knights of Malta
Knight Templars

Scientific Psychic Research

Astrology and Numerology

7

Fig. 125-126

(cont.)

MUSEUM OF RELIGION AND PHILOSOPHY

MEMBERSHIP

Patron	$1,000.00
Life Member	250.00
Sustaining Member	25.00
Sectional Membership only	10.00
Sectional Group Membership (minimum of 20) per member	5.00
Special (for information apply to Secretary)	No dues

PRIVILEGES OF MEMBERSHIP

Reference Library, Reading Room and Museum.
Services of a Museum Instructor.
Theosophical classes given under the auspices of the Museum.
50 cents admission will be charged to Section and Group Members for all Lectures.
Privilege of Lecture room twice a month for Sectional Groups or Lodges.

*Two tickets to Lectures.
*Fifteen percent discount on all books, cards, emblems, etc.
*Twenty-five percent discount on all tickets to Concerts, Plays, and Motion Pictures.

*For Sustaining or Higher Memberships only.

Lecture room available to members at nominal fee.

A book department will be maintained for the convenience of Members where books and recent publications on all subjects pertaining to the Museum may be purchased.

The Museum and Library will be opened for members after January 1, 1931.

SCIENTIFIC PSYCHIC RESEARCH SECTION

Chairman:
Major R. T. M. Scott

SUBJECTS OF STUDY

Clairvoyance—Trance—Automatic Writing—Communications between intelligences in different vibrations. Study to discriminate between communications and mind reading or telepathy and sub-conscious memory.

Psychical Phenomena—Materialization, Trumpet Mediumship, Levitation.

The Independent Voice.

Telepathy—its technique.

The Materialization of Objects.

Photography.

Thought Forms and Auras.

Dreams and Visions.

Diagnosis and Healing.

Physical effects or reactions on people of psychic phenomena. Best conditions for maximum physical results.

Influence of the human aura on plants.

Mesmeric Fluid—magnetising objects at will.

The Law of Correspondence—the correspondence between sounds, colors, plants, metals, etc., and their relation to man.

Private and Group Seances with tested professional Mediums and Psychics arranged at nominal fees.

Experimental non-professional groups and development sittings.

Lectures on the various subjects of study will be given during the season.

Fig. 127-128

(cont.)

ASTROLOGICAL SECTION

Chairman: Svetoslav Roerich

Lecturers:

Vanna Johnson   Elizabeth Aldrich
              Maud Bentley

Reading Room and Reference Library.
Classes arranged at nominal fees.

———

THEOSOPHICAL SECTION

Blavatsky Student Association

Chairman: Leslie Grant Scott

Reading Room and Reference Library.
Classes and Lectures.

———

MASONIC SECTION

ANCIENT UNIVERSAL MASONRY

Chairman: Leslie Grant Scott

Address Chairman for any information regarding the
Principles and Symbolism of Masonry.
Masonic Reading Room and Museum.

———

The above Sections have now been formed; the others are in
the process of formation.

10

DEPARTMENTS OF THE MUSEUM

ANCIENT ART

Director: Svetoslav Roerich

———

MODERN ART

Director: Howard Giles

———

LITERATURE

Director: Talbot Mundy

———

DRAMA

Director: Natacha Rambova

———

MUSIC

Director: Maurice M. Lichtmann

11

Fig. 129

275

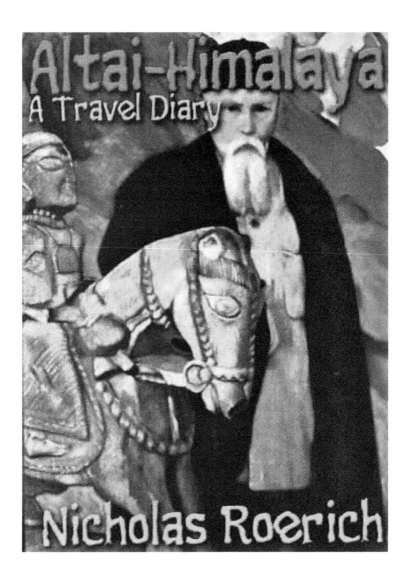

Fig. 130

"The new era of enlightenment is awaited. Each reaches in his own way. One nearer, one further; one beautifully, one distortedly; but all are concerned with the same predestined. It is especially striking to see such consciousness at a time when not the printed page, but sound itself—the human word—directs the lofty expectation. It is so precious to hear and to repeat. The Motherland of Gessar Khan, Ladak, knows that the time of the regeneration has come. Khotan remembers the Signs of Maitreya over the ancient Stupa." [14]

14 Roerich.org *Altai-Himalaya*, Part XII, Tibet (1927-1928).

Fig. 131

Svetoslav Roerich's attention is focused on the articulation of the specific textures of Natacha's garment. A parallel is drawn between the elegance and grace of the Indian figures in the background and Natacha as she crosses her hand over her lap. Her glance, slightly off to the left is evocative of her self-constructed image as aloof and cool. The manner in which her left hand is positioned and her right hand exerts little pressure further emphasizes her gracefulness and ease. Likewise, Natacha's dress in luxurious fabric in solid gold signals her affluence.

Roerich's starkly realistic portrayal of Natacha contrasts markedly with the bright pink background which conjures a sense of surreal fantasy. The pink also serves a compositional purpose in that Roerich rendered Natacha in high realism, moving her forward, away from the flaty-depicted figures behind her.

The background figures are Mughal influenced, a culture surely well-known to Roerich, who poses Natacha similarly to them, thus situating her within this art historical frame. He represents her as the embodiment of wealth and knowledge of art, history and culture. He appears to be saying in his composition, that her graceful composure is not unlike that of the Indian noble Mughal lords behind her. *(See Notes & Sources, also List of Plates)*

Fig. 132-133

Devika Rani and Svetoslav Roerich

Fig. 134

Devika Rani Roerich

"Rani's greatest achievement was that she sold cinema as an art form to the essentially puritanical upper-crust Indians. Before she became an actress, girls from Bombay's red light areas filled in as actresses because girls from decent homes didn't wear lipstick, let alone prance before a movie camera. So when Devika Rani, Rabindranath Tagore's great-niece and daughter of India's first surgeon-general, chose to make a career in films, it brought a certain respectability to the medium." [15]

15 Obituary: Devika Rani, *Independent*, March 26, 1994.

Fig. 135

Nicholas Roerich, Devika Rani Roerich and Svetoslav Roerich, Naggar, India, 1945

"Nikolai Roerich...developed an esoteric system called Agni Yoga. Their ultimate objective was to establish a vast "new country" in Central Asia, as the earthly expression of the invisible kingdom of Shambhala (the "holy place" where the earthly world is linked to the highest states of consciousness), thereby preparing humanity for a New Age of peace and beauty.." [16]

16   *The New Age of Russia, Occult and Esoteric Dimensions,* edited by Birgit Menzel, Kubon and Sagner, 2012, p. 25

Fig. 136-137 Indian Prime Minister Jawaharlal Nehru attending Svetoslav Roerich's exhibition

Prime Minister Nehru greeting Svetoslav Roerich and Devika Rani Roerich

Fig.138

The Nicholas Roerich Museum today, 319 West 107th Street, New York

"The Museum sustains an ongoing effort to spread public awareness of the intermingled roles of peace and culture, and the ways in which each sustains the other." [17]

---

17 Roerich.org.

MICHAEL MORRIS:
I WAS FASCINATED BY MY RAMBOVA

DR. VLADIMIR ROSOV INTERVIEWS FATHER MORRIS, THE AUTHOR OF *"MADAM VALENTINO, THE MANY LIVES OF NATACHA RAMBOVA"*

Dr. Rosov asks, "What prompted a Catholic priest to write a book about the dancer Natacha Rambova?"

Michael Morris:

It's a long interesting story, but I'll try to tell it briefly. I received a doctorate in art history from the University of California at Berkeley. Prior to my work on my doctoral dissertation, I completed my master's thesis, with the focus and theme of this thesis being Aubrey Beardsley's illustrations for the play "*Salomè*".

In the course of my studies, I discovered that a film was produced based on this play in which Beardsley's drawings were utilized in the design of the costumes and sets. These designs were the creation of a woman who was the wife of Rudolph Valentino. I was most interested in this production, because Salomè was the instrument that led to the death of John the Baptist. I had also been interested in the cinema for a long time, ever since my under-graduate studies at the University of Southern California in Los Angeles. My particular interest in cinema was based upon two elements; religion and art. Therefore, soon after I discovered the Beardsley connection in this production, I was off to see the silent film, "*Salomè*" in a presentation in San Francisco.

As I watched the film, I was amazed by how the scenery and costumes still held such fascination for me, despite the fact that the production was out-of-date being made in the 1920's with Alla Nazimova. I then realized I needed to learn much more about this woman, Natacha Rambova who was the artist creating such wonderful sets and costumes.

Initially, I read only negative commentary about her. Soon my interest in Rambova turned into a sort of hobby and then an obsession. By the time I was working on my doctoral thesis which was devoted to Victorian paintings of monastic motifs, I kept my focus on Rambova and it helped me to keep my peace of mind. In New York City, I was able to find a copy of Natacha Rambova's will which identified several of her heirs. With the list as reference, I began to knock on doors, to call and write many letters. Many people found the time to share information about Rambova with me.

The more I learned about this woman, the more she sparked my imagination and the more I was drawn to her. At some point in my research, I decided that I should turn my interest in her into writing a book about her. This is how the book was born. It was odd as people treated me as if I was a writer, although this was my first book. I always believed my first book would be some thesis on monks in Victorian art, but few people seemed interested in such a publication. There was interest in a book about Natacha Rambova!

"Were there conflicts presented for you as a priest as far as studying the life of a dancer?"

No, I actually think people found it intriguing that a priest could be involved in something beyond the main stream of religious art. Besides, I discovered that Natacha Rambova demonstrated a great passion for the spiritual throughout her life, from her interest as a child in mythology to her Egyptian endeavors with the Bollingen Foundation, a prestigious organization on the East Coast.

"What would you say about the relationship between Natacha Rambova's artistic work and her religious beliefs?"

Officially, she was baptized in the Catholic church. Her father was an Irish officer in the American Civil War, then a federal inspector in Utah. His first wife died and it was then he married a second time and this woman became Natacha Rambova's mother. On Rambova's maternal side there were Mormons but her paternal side was all Catholic and for this she was baptized as Catholic. In reality, she was never raised in the Catholic faith, as her parents were divorced by the time she was three years old. Her mother then took young "Winifred", her real name is Winifred Shaughnessy, to San Francisco to raise her in a secular atmosphere until she was eight years old. The young girl was then sent to England to be educated.

I believe Natacha Rambova had a natural interest in religion and mythology since her childhood although she received no specific training. Whatever she learned on the subjects, she learned on her own. When she married Valentino many years later, they did not have a marriage solemnized before any clergyman. Her second marriage, to Alvaro, did take place in a church. When this marriage dissolved, she turned to the church authorities in New York City to request that the marriage to Alvaro be annulled. This request was granted.

Although formally connected to Catholicism, she was never a dedicated Catholic. She was, however, informally connected through her theosophical research and the study of the teachings of Madam Blavatsky.

"But how did these views held by Natacha Rambova affect her work?"

She always had a religious imagination. Rambova's personal art collection contained such artifacts as a Gothic Madonna with child, and she was photographed next to this image. I think any external religiosity, in fact, had no influence over her spiritual path, which was always more deeply rooted in theosophy. She was profoundly interested in revealing how all religions, past and present, were connected and shared a same foundation.

"Could Natacha Rambova be referred to as a theosophist or not?"

Well, I think she can be, although she probably would not want to be identified with any formal philosophy or religion. I believe she was, in fact, involved in all of them.

"But she did have connections with this movement, she had connections with theosophists. As far as I understand this determines her involvement."

Natacha communicated with people who were members of the theosophical movement, but she did not attend meetings. She was seriously interested in the subject but it would be implausible to identify her personal views as being of any religion. Her mother was Mormon, then a Roman Catholic, a member of an Episcopal church and then a spiritualist and theosophist. It was Natacha's mother who formally joined all of these groups, but Natacha never formally joined any of them. She did go through Catholic training in order to marry Alvaro in the church, because this was required for the marriage. However, while she lived in New York and even in subsequent years, she never attended any church services or theosophical meetings.

In your book you write that Natacha Rambova participated in 'automatic writing.' Did this influence her work?

I posed this very question to her close relatives, whom I managed to interview at the end of their lives. Although Natacha did engage in automatic writing, I think they believed she found it slightly frightening. Natacha never delved too deeply into these type of things and by her middle age she was no longer involved in automatic writing at all. It appears to be something she utilized at a time when she experienced great stress over the unjustified guilt over Rudolph Valentino's death. The automatic writing was of no lasting importance to her although at that time she felt she needed the messages revealed to her through automatic writing.

"This is interesting, after all, in that she seems to have attached great importance to automatic writing. Because nightly, she was writing and then every morning she placed these writing as instructions for a film's executive director. Consequently, her life and her creativity was based upon these writings."

This is one of those stories, I feel defames Rambova and came about during the filming of *The Cobra*. As she was heavily involved in Valentino's Hollywood career and critical decisions were to be made, some who resented her alleged she retreated to her home to talk to the spirit world seeking her next line in a script; this is absurd. She was not eager to be involved in the production of *The Cobra*. At the time she was working on another important film, *The Hooded Falcon*, which she hoped, would be Valentino's next movie. She delegated work to others on this film and they let her down. It is a myth that she went into a trance and retreated to her home to seek improvements in this film through automatic writing. The picture was terrible. It is now available on video but is truly a boring movie. It would not have been improved if she had conjured the whole of the spirit world.

"Still, they say it played an important role in her life."

Automatic writing was not something I would refer to as her entertainment. It was an integral element of her sessions with her psychic, George Wehner, Talbot Mundy and his wife. This was a period in the late 1920's when she held faith in Wehner's abilities and when he was introducing her to certain activities of the psychic world.

When Rambova published a book about Valentino, she included her communicating with the spirits of the deceased. Almost half of the book consists of messages from the deceased, which she received either through Wehner or the group's process of automatic writing. I believe she did so in the hopes that the spirit of the deceased Valentino would reconcile with her and in this way mitigate her feelings of guilt over his untimely death. Among other things, he died as a result of her leaving him.

"Was Natacha Rambova working on 'The Cobra' at this time?

She was concerned that *The Cobra* would not benefit Valentino's career and concerned over whether they would return to produce *The Hooded Falcon*. When she was informed she would work on *The Cobra*, she surrendered her executive power to George Ullman, who I feel betrayed her. Of course, Natacha Rambova was unpopular in Hollywood, because the studios realized that it was she who managed Valentino's career on many levels. Additionally, she was not sociable and had few friends. The rumors that Rambova fell into trances and used automatic writing to dictate the production of *The Cobra* were generated by Colleen Moore, an actress who disliked Rambova intensely.

"But what about the scene in the movie, where Natacha wears the costume of the cobra?"

That is not her. It is just her costume. She had many costume designs and some were used in the films. Natacha Rambova was an artist whose costumes were made from her drawings; although I have never seen the original drawing of the Cobra costume. It has been destroyed or belongs to some private collector. She owned a great collection of her own artwork, which she painted for her own enjoyment. Sometimes she turned to her old drawings for inspiration, as she did in *Salomè*. She was always drawing upon her previous artistic ideas.

"But I did not see these drawings in your book."

There were some drawings but very few have survived. I saw several costume design sketches in private collections, but the finest of these remain the property of the DeMille family. Although I do not think these drawings have received great care, I have seen many in exhibitions that are attributed to the DeMille family. There are several original drawings with her own family. I tried to purchase them but could not. Some of her fashion sketches are kept in museums, but in general her artwork is scattered. Many of them, she destroyed herself.

"I've found her collection in the Museum of Salt Lake City, on the internet."

Yes, and it is a fascinating place to visit. I spent one week alone going through her correspondence there. Many of her personal belongings were donated to the gallery in Utah. I went there specifically to research her Egyptian collection. I found they have many other items including furniture, portraits, jewelry and letters. Her personal collections are housed in Utah and at the Brooklyn Museum in New York. She donated many of her Egyptian rarities to Utah and also to a Museum in Philadelphia; a museum of fine arts houses her Asian art. They maintain a closed gallery with such things as her Tibetan tangkas which require a special admission to view.

"What can be said about Rambova's personal relationship with Svetoslav Roerich?"

I would have liked to write about this, all that I learned, primarily from Daniel Entin, the Director of the Nicholas Roerich Museum in New York.

"But you didn't write anything."

I had to comply with an agreement with the trustees of the Roerich Museum agreeing that I would not publish anything concerning the love story of Natacha Rambova and Svetoslav Roerich in my book. If I had received permission to cover this, I think I would have said they were friends and not delved too deeply, despite their being evidence as proof. Daniel Entin clearly stated to me that there are letters in the Roerich archive standing as evidence of the fact that Natacha Rambova planned to marry Svetoslav.

Apparently, the Roerich family resisted such an idea; a marriage to this woman from Hollywood bearing a great reputation. They hoped Svetoslav would marry someone else and consequently, his father Nicholas Roerich summoned Svetoslav to India. Natacha Rambova initially planned to sue him for breaking his promise to her; there was such a law in the 1920's. When an engagement had already apparently taken place and it was broken, a lawsuit could be filed for breech of promise to marry.

Today such a definition does not exist in legal parlance, but then she did threaten to sue him for breech of promise, as she was planning on marrying him. Have you seen Svetoslav's photo? He is the very type of man who attracted Rambova. At first she fell in love with Kosloff, a Russian dancer. By the way, the origin of her pseudonym is attributed to Kosloff. He was originally from Oranienbaum, a small town on the Gulf of Finland near St. Petersburg. Local residents called their city, "Rambov".

Then she fell in love with Valentino, a Hollywood actor. Then Svetoslav as her third love story as he was always elegantly dressed with delicate features and very handsome. Additionally, you can recognize again her fascination with the Spanish Count, Alvaro. All of these men were foreigners and in a way, romantic figures.

"But how did they meet?"

They met in the Master Building. Svetoslav had an apartment and studio on the top floor. Natacha had her own apartments on the 20th and 21st floors. Talbot Mundy and his wife lived on the 18th floor. They met as they lived in the same building. Svetoslav painted several portraits of Rambova; I've seen only one...the one Mr. Entin showed me. It is exquisite and exciting and the only one I saw in the Roerich Museum. However, there is evidence he painted more than one.

"Is the fact that Natacha Rambova lived in the building of the Roerich Museum accidental?"

I think she wanted to live there with Talbot Mundy. She was on friendly terms with him and his wife. He was a writer. If you want to know more about the relationship with Roerich, then there a man in Washington who you could interview. He is the biographer of Talbot Mundy. It was he who helped me connect with the Roerich Museum, because he researched what was going on in the Master Building when he wrote his biography. There were in residence artists, writers and intellectuals all interested in Roerich's ideas about culture, peace and religion. They felt comfortable there and deliberately settled in this building, a place populated by people of similar ideas.

"One more question, Was Egypt an important aspect of Rambova's destiny?"

I would say that the art and religion of Egypt fascinated Rambova. She firmly believed that Egyptian mythology had its basis in reality. She did not practice Egyptian rituals and never tried to actually revive the ancient religion. She was attracted by religious ideals both in the East and the West. She was interested in Egypt as a civilization. Rambova did not engage in spiritual practices, as some artists, occultists or magicians did. Natacha was not so much interested in this, although she did own a ring which was considered alchemical.

It once belonged to John Dee, a great magician and wizard at the court of the Queen of England, Elizabeth I. He owned the ring and an alchemical vessel. These sacred objects somehow were passed down to the ancestors of the Spanish Count, Alvaro, whom Natacha married. He gave them to her on the occasion of their wedding. Rambova bequeathed the ring and the alchemical vessel, a most valuable property, to the Salt Lake City Museum. They were transferred there, but disappeared mysteriously. The alchemical vessel was an alabaster bowl, used in some sort of magical ritual.

"Is is known what this ring looked like?"

Yes, I saw a photograph of the ring and a drawing made of the vessel by her secretary. He is still alive, his name is Mark Hasselriis and he lives in New York. He is a true believer in the Egyptian religion. I learned a great deal from him about Natacha Rambova's Egyptological interests. Mark Hasselriis was in Egypt with her. He executed many sketches of her belongings, her archaeological discoveries as well as the ring and the alchemical vessel.

"Was it an Egyptian ring?"

I don't know. It was set with some precious stone but I can not give you a good description. I have never seen the ring; only a photo. It seemed to me to be oval and set with onyx.

"Was the ring somehow used in the mysteries?"

It seems to have once been used in rituals. Natacha only knew that there was a magical connection between the ring and the vessel. Mark Hasselriis said that he had once witnessed this vessel in her room and it phosphoresced in the dark, shining like a huge emerald....

Berkeley, April 21, 1999

CHAPTER SIX

Fig. 139

View of Bellver Castle, from Gènova, Mallorca, Balearic Islands, Spain

BETWEEN THE THUNDER AND THE LIGHTNING

In an effort to cope with the sudden loss of her fiancé Svetoslav and her plans for the Museum of Religion and Philosophy, Natacha embarked on an extended Mediterranean cruise. She was no longer a stranger to heartbreak and confronted the turn of events by heading for calmer seas.

While Rudolph Valentino's manager, George Ullman once likened Natacha to Cleopatra,[1] it would seem her charms were still able to exercise a fascination over men. As she sailed to the Balearic Island of Mallorca, the captain of the vessel, Count Alvaro de Urzaiz, courted the rebounding Natacha. Charming her with his good looks and aristocratic demeanor, the Spaniard soon became her fourth great love and second husband.

Natacha and Alvaro married, first in a civil ceremony in Paris and then, in deference to his family, in a second ceremony in the Church of San Francisco in Palma, Mallorca. Upon the church's recognition of their marriage, Natacha assumed the surname of "de Urzaiz". Natacha Rambova de Urzaiz and her husband Alvaro settled first in Gènova at the villa San Ferreret but soon relocated to Peguera. There they designed and built a villa by the sea in nearby Cala Fornells which they called Ca Na Tacha; "Ca" meaning "house" in the Catalan language.

Natacha and Alvaro's lives on Mallorca were initially idyllic; even pastoral with panoramic visages of sea, sky and rocky coastline. The Mediterranean acted as balm for Natacha and unlike her serious Hollywood portraits, she is seen smiling and relaxed in photographs taken at San Ferreret and Ca Na Tacha. She and Alvaro gained the admiration of the local citizenry when they launched a business of restoring villas and intervened in a local cave system by ingeniously installing lighting and pathways. Natacha opened the caves, "Ses Coves" to tourists, exploiting them commercially for the first time. She also opened a café beside the entrance to the caves, which still exists today.

Several elders in Gènova recall how Natacha also opened a garment workshop in the village; employing five or six women. During the Spanish Civil War, the women sewed military uniforms, with their salaries paid by Natacha. She is remembered fondly for her exceptional appearance and residents often came out of their homes just to see the beautiful American woman pass by.

The many guests visiting Natacha and Alvaro's Mallorcan homes included his relatives from Madrid and her Hollywood and New York acquaintances: Talbot Mundy, Dawn Allen, artist Mai Mai Sze, Catalan portrait painter Federico Beltran-Masses and movie stars Mary Pickford and Pola Negri. Their famous guests were provided with quaint accommodation and a literary and artistic salon ambiance.

Despite the political rumblings on mainland Spain in January of 1936, Natacha and Alvaro traveled with his brother Mariano and Natacha's mother Muzzie, to the Middle East to visit Greece, Turkey and Egypt. In Luxor, Egypt, Natacha met with Howard Carter, famed English archaeologist and Egyptologist who discovered the tomb of King Tut-Ankh-Amon fourteen years prior. In 1924, Carter visited America and the notoriety of his presence sparked "American Egyptomania." Howard

---

1 "Cleopatra is her greatest prototype in history." *The George Ullman Memoir*, p. 183.

Carter consequently achieved celebrity status.

Although he was besieged by countless requests for interviews and refused many, he did not deny Natacha Rambova's request to meet him when she visited Egypt in 1936. In fact Carter granted her his full attention.[2] Her lengthy conversations and time spent with Howard Carter served to intensify her own interest in ancient Egyptian culture.

Of her first trip to Egypt in 1936, she wrote,

"I felt as if I had at last returned home. The first few days I was there I couldn't stop the tears streaming from my eyes. It was not sadness, but some emotional impact from the past—a returning to a place once loved after too long a time." [3]

The euphoria Natacha experienced in Egypt would be short-lived. She and Alvaro returned to Mallorca and their Ca Na Tacha home amid mounting political turmoil and social unrest. Battle lines were being drawn during the initial days of the Spanish Civil War and both sides arming, each determined to exact their victory.

Despite the remote location of Ca Na Tacha, life for Natacha and Alvaro became one of unavoidable political and military strife as the proliferation of the conflict soon brought the civil war to their door step.[4] There were no longer casual terrace gatherings of friends nor visitors trekking from America to enjoy the serenity of the de Ursaiz hospitality.

As Spain grew dangerously divided and engaged on several battlefronts, Natacha was not one to remain silent in regards to her political opinions. Naively underestimating the violent intolerance of both sides of the civil war, she soon placed her life in danger.

Her outspoken public defense of Mallorcan intellectual, writer and Civil Governor of the Balearic Islands, Antonio Espina would force her frantic escape from Mallorca. By confronting a priest during a service in the Cathedral about his inability to prevent the abuse of Espina, she exposed herself and put her life in imminent danger.[5] Within hours she was secreted, with her dog Bimbo, out of her home and aboard a coal freighter bound for France and the Hudnut Chateau at Juan les Pins. Natacha left so suddenly, she did not pause to pack her belongings; leaving all behind with Alvaro in Ca Na Tacha.

Muzzie would recall her shock, seeing a coal-blackened Natacha walking up the driveway to the chateau with her puppy Bimbo in her arms.

Her experiences with the mounting social and political tensions in Spain, her stressful exodus and the uncomfortable journey aboard the coal freighter, levied an immediate toll on Natacha. Within a short while after her arrival at the chateau, she suffered a major heart attack. Her exile then became one of slow recuperation as she focused on the teachings of mystic philosopher, George Gurdjeiff and the advancement of her theosophical studies.

While the Spanish Civil War brought misery to the people of Spain and as Alvaro became more militarily involved, Natacha pursued her Egyptian fascination by traveling to London to study with Egyptologist, S.R.K. Glanville at University College. It is not known when she left England, however she did not return to New York, but to the Chateau Juan les Pins.

Alvaro visited Natacha only a few times at the Chateau, where they posed for photographs and appeared to maintain a cordial exchange. This despite her inability to return to Spain and Alvaro's lack of interest in leaving Spain. On one visit he told Natacha that he had fallen in love with another woman. Their marriage was

---

2   Mark Hasselriis tells Michael Morris, "Howard Carter refused a lot of people who came in droves. How could he refuse Natacha Rambova?"

3   Letter from Natacha Rambova to Ann Wollen, March 1, 1965.

4   Battle for Mallorca, August 16 – September 12, 1936.

5   Account of Natacha Rambova's support of Antonio Espina by William James.

over and Natacha made plans to return to America.

In the fall of 1936, perhaps during the initial days of her hiatus at the Chateau Juan les Pins, Natacha wrote an account of her civil war experience on Mallorca which she titled, "Arriba España", or "Up Spain"; "Arriba España" being the battle cry of Generalissimo Franco's Nationalist Fascist forces. Her essay, published here for the first time, is accompanied by an introductory historical analysis by renowned visual artist, documentarian and Mallorcan Rambova authority, William James.

In his introduction, he defines the various elements of the Spanish Civil War critical in understanding Natacha's essay. The war was not a conflict with a specific date of engagement but one that escalated over time through a sequence of events brought about by a complex political situation. William James has contextualized Natacha's political opinions of the war, which later changed direction and made her a refugee fleeing from her home on the cliff in Cala Fornells.

William James' Introduction and the first publication of "Arriba España", are presented along with a collection of photographs, also published for the first time of Natacha's life with Alvaro on Mallorca.

These remarkable photographs are shared by courtesy of Mallorcan resident, Maria Salomé Juaneda Pujol, Natacha and Alvaro's goddaughter. Maria's father, Juan Juaneda Palmer was Alvaro and Natacha's chauffeur and mechanic and her mother, Lorenza Pujol Roca, their maid. Maria Salomé's mother and father first met Natacha and Alvaro while they were living at San Ferreret in Gènova and the two couples moved together to Peguera and the villa Ca Na Tacha.

After Natacha left Mallorca, Juan and Lorenza lived at Ca Na Tacha for many years, acting as caretakers until Alvaro sold the house in the late 1950's. Many of Natacha's possessions, furniture and works of art were shipped to America after the war, when it became clear she would never return. Natacha asked that whatever possessions remained; clothing, jewelry, photographs, her record player, a red leather and silver dressing case, be given to her goddaughter. Maria Salomé has safeguarded and treasured Natacha's belongings since that time and some years ago she organized an exhibition of her collection in Gènova. The exhibition inspired much interest among local residents, particularly those old enough to remember Natacha. Maria Salomé also backed an initiative to have a street in Gènova named in honor of Natacha Rambova.

Most recently, the Es Baluard Museum of Modern and Contemporary Art in Palma, Mallorca organized an oral history education project for primary school children in Gènova. The children were asked to interview elderly residents about the history of their neighborhood. A group of children spoke with Maria Salomé who announced she was Natacha Rambova's goddaughter, explaining Natacha's history, who she was, her marriages and how she came to live in Gènova.

Intrigued by her story, the Museum's education officer, Sebastià Mascaró, asked to meet Maria Salomé and was introduced to her by Catalina Ruiz, the school teacher supervising the program. Sebastià Mascaró felt that the story of Natacha Rambova's life in Mallorca and the memories of Maria Salomé and her parents deserved to be recorded for posterity.

It was then he invited visual artist William James to design a relevant art project for the Museum and a meeting was convened between William James, Maria Salomé, her daughter Rosa, Catalina Ruiz, Sebastià Mascaró and Tonina Matamalas, a member of the Es Baluard Museum staff allotted to assist the project. So began the two-year process of research and documentation, eventually leading to an audio-visual documentary installation shown at the Es Baluard Museum in October – November, 2016.

During that first meeting, Maria Salomé opened her old albums of photographs, spread out the collection of Rambova's jewelry, shawls, turbans, even a passport and a tube of "Natacha Rambova" branded lipstick. To the amazement of those present on that auspicious day, the accouterments of Natacha Rambova's life lay before them as a rarefied glimpse of her five years in Mallorca before she was forced to run for her life, never to return.

William James later contacted Michael Morris in search of a copy of Arriba España, hoping to include this in his Es Baluard Museum tribute. He did not hesitate to share news of the discovery of Maria Salomé's collection. The connection was made, the guardianship of the artifacts rewarded as Ms. Maria Salomé Juaneda Pujol agreed to grant Michael Morris permission to publish her photographs and announce news of her guardianship of Rambova's treasures in this publication.

It is interesting to review the newly-discovered evidence of Natacha's life on Mallorca, before the outbreak of the civil war and note her transition from Hollywood glamour to a more natural and less staged presence. She is seen wearing loose trousers, sandals yet still an occasional turban. She lolls on the beach with her friends and dogs and appears to be thriving physically in the sun and ocean proximity.

These were Natacha's halcyon days just prior to a war that would not only result in a change of her appearance but a change in the course of her intellectual pursuits as well. Her idyll would be short lived and end abruptly. Yet within the pages of Maria Salomé's photo albums, Natacha Rambova is seen reveling in the sunny Mediterranean climes with her Spaniard love Alvaro, her dogs, Toni and Bimbo, friends and new in-laws.

Fig. 140-141

The De Uzaiz Residence at Son Ferreret, Gènova, Mallorca

Fig. 142

On the Terrace at Son Ferreret, Artist Mai Mai Sze, on left

Fig. 143

Terrace Gathering, from left, Pola Negri, Alvaro, Mai Mai Sze

Fig. 144

Son Ferreret, Mai Mai Sze, second from left, Natacha Rambova, center standing

Fig. 145

Alvaro, center, Natacha, right

"...a gathering of Alvaro and Natacha with Alvaro's aristocratic family...Alvaro's family was not too delighted that a woman from Hollywood decorated the family tree for a while. You can even decipher that in the photo where Natacha made a peripheral pose. As I remember, she takes her revenge on those relatives by the way she describes then in *Arriba España*." [6]

6   M. Morris writes to William James.

Fig. 146

Son Ferreret, De Urzaiz visiting relatives, Alvaro second

Fig. 147
Talbot Mundy, reclined, Natacha and Alvaro, far right

Fig. 148

Alvaro, seated right

Fig. 149

Gènova guests

Fig. 150

From left, Talbot Mundy, Natacha Rambova and Alvaro - 1932

"Natacha Rambova wrote that she had moved to the town of Gènova, just outside the capital city of Palma, on the island of Mallorca. There she was renovating villas and renting them to tourists, and promised Dawn and Talbot she had just the place for them...When they arrived at Palma de Mallorca, Natacha, now aged 35, surprised them by introducing her new husband." [7]

7   Taves, Brian, *Talbot Mundy*, p. 199-200.

Fig. 151-152
Ca Na Tacha, Peguera

"The villa was noted for its simple planes, sharp-edged modernity and gleaming white wash." [8]

---

8   Note written on reverse side of photograph by Ann Wollen.

Fig. 153-154

Terraces & architectural detail, Ca Na Tacha

Fig. 155-156
Interiors, Ca Na Tacha [9]

9 …"the heads on the columns here are also found in photos of the Whitley Heights living room.." M. Morris Notes.

Fig. 157-158

Interiors at Ca Na Tacha

Fig. 159

Seating Area, Ca Na Tacha

"Nearly ten years after Valentino had expressed his dream of one day buying the deserted fortress on the island of St. Lerins, Natacha had her castle by the sea." [10]

10 M. Morris, *Madam Valentino*, p. 204.

Fig. 160
Natacha and Federico Beltran-Masses, on right, Ca Na Tacha

"...the photo of Natacha with Beltran-Masses on the steps in the living is a real wonder. Little did Natacha know that is was Beltran-Masses who convinced Rudolph Valentino to hire the Pinkerton Detectives who followed her into her nightly soirées which led to her divorce. Here, she is entertaining him in her home!" [11]

---

11   M. Morris Notes.

Fig. 161

Natacha, on right

"...She was not one for smiling in front of the camera. According to Maria Salomé, Natacha never appeared in swimming costumes but adopted a standard summer wardrobe of wide, high-waisted trousers, skimpy top and espadrilles, usually topped with the eternal turban. She swam, but did so mysteriously and invisibly." [12]

---

12   William James commentary.

Fig. 162
Natacha, Toni, a guard dog and Bimbo at Cala Fornells

Fig. 163
Natacha, seated left on sea wall

Fig. 164-165
Alvaro at Cala Fornells

Fig. 166-167

The De Urzaiz Yacht, "Yzarra" at Cala Fornells

Fig. 168
The gentleman in the black cap is Maria Salomé's father, Juan Juaneda Palmer.

Fig. 169
Turtle Fishing Aboard the Yzarra, Natacha on left

Fig. 170

Tony and Bimbo, asea

"One could swim in the numerous rocky coves, or "calas", as the Mallorcans called them. And explore the diverse scenery of the island, from its sandy beaches to its craggy mountaintops." [13]

---

13 *Madam Valentino*, p. 202.

Fig. 172

Alvaro in Egypt, 1936

Fig. 171

Alvaro

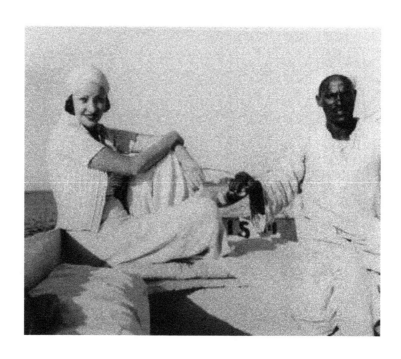

Fig. 173

Natacha on the Nile, 1936

"Natacha was particularly excited to visit what she called 'the fountainhead of the world's greatest cultures'.." [14]

---

14   *Madam Valentino*, p. 207.

Fig. 174

Howard Carter

Fig. 175

Natacha Rambova in Egypt, 1936

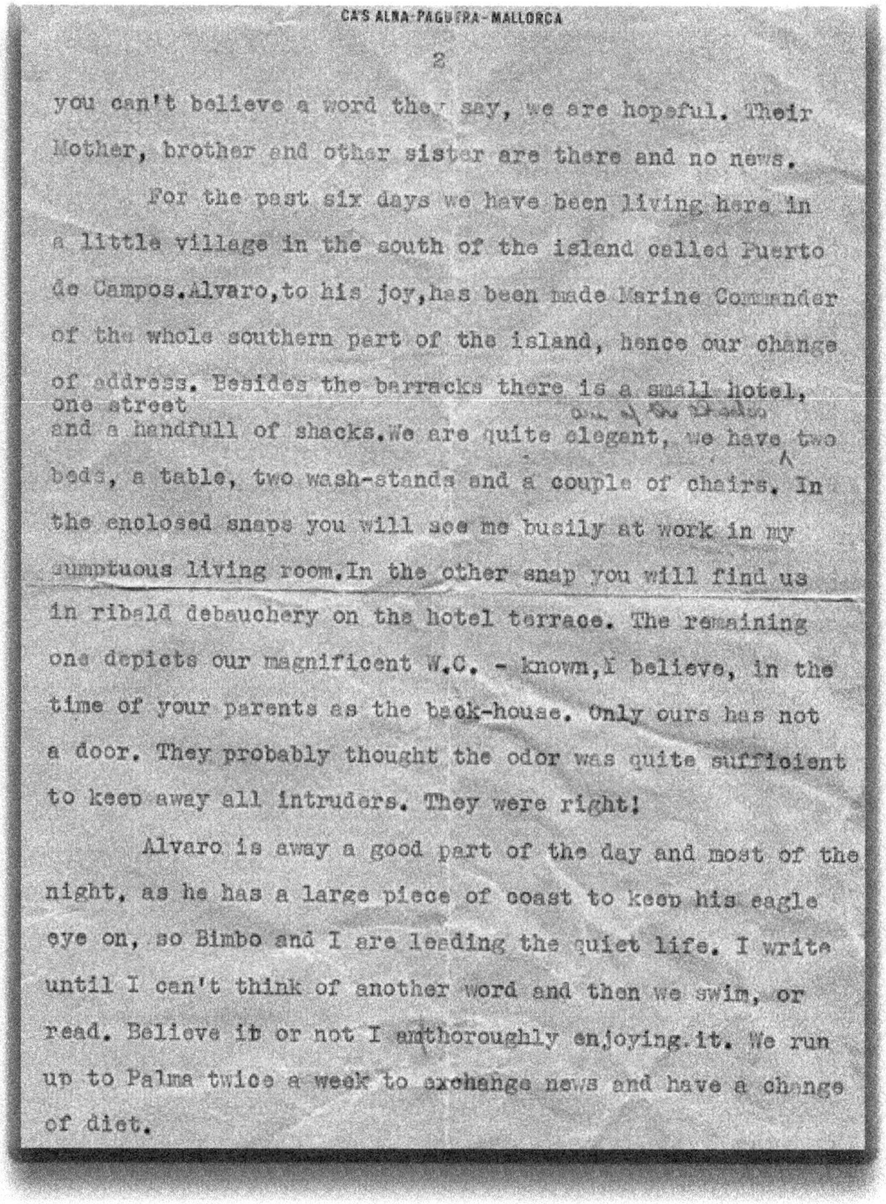

you can't believe a word they say, we are hopeful. Their

Mother, brother and other sister are there and no news.

For the past six days we have been living here in

a little village in the south of the island called Puerto

de Campos.Alvaro,to his joy,has been made Marine Commander

of the whole southern part of the island, hence our change

of address. Besides the barracks there is a small hotel,
one street
and a handfull of shacks.We are quite elegant, we have two

beds, a table, two wash-stands and a couple of chairs. In

the enclosed snaps you will see me busily at work in my

sumptuous living room.In the other snap you will find us

in ribald debauchery on the hotel terrace. The remaining

one depicts our magnificent W.C. - known,I believe, in the

time of your parents as the back-house. Only ours has not

a door. They probably thought the odor was quite sufficient

to keep away all intruders. They were right!

Alvaro is away a good part of the day and most of the

night, as he has a large piece of coast to keep his eagle

eye on, so Bimbo and I are leading the quiet life. I write

until I can't think of another word and then we swim, or

read. Believe it or not I amthoroughly enjoying it. We run

up to Palma twice a week to exchange news and have a change

of diet.

Fig. 176

Letter Home from Natacha

Fig. 177

Siesta at Ca Na Tacha

Fig. 178

Drawings by Natacha Rambova of De Urzaiz family heirlooms she received as wedding gifts

"...The alchemical jar of Dr. Dee which was in the possession of the De Ursaiz family and presumably came from the Emperor Maximilian. The jar is about 3" or a bit more in height. It is made of a type of alabaster or marble and has a warm tint. The relief on the surface shows an alchemical phoenix rising from a pool of flames. To each side of it are three vortical images of flame in the center of which are symbols of the planets, thus forming a 7-fold motif. The jar's symbolism represents the transmutation of the elements and planetary powers so that the phoenix becomes the glorified body of the spirit. Inside the jar is stained with cinnabar, the red mercury salt known as vermilion and this "trace" no doubt alludes to the process of alchemy which the jar symbolizes: the transmutation of "baser metal" into the "gold" of the phoenix. "

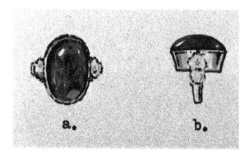

Fig. 179

"...The Imperial sapphire ring presented by the Holy Roman Emperor Maximilian to the De Ursaiz family. It is reputed to have been formed of pure "alchemical" gold made by the famous Doctor Dee (alchemist and astrologer to Queen Elizabeth I and Lord Cecil Burleigh). The dark sapphire weighs about 10-15 carats. The upper surface is somewhat scratched or worn. " [15]

---

15 Both Descriptions by Mark Hasselriis as included in his correspondence with Michael Morris.

Fig. 180

Studio portrait of Natacha Rambova taken in Palma de Mallorca

Fig. 181

Natacha at the Chateau Juan les Pins

Fig. 182
Alvaro Visits the Chateau

Fig. 183

Natacha Rambova, passport photo, @ 1940

"Now I realize that Natacha was at times 'controversial' and I will not gainsay it, she could be. Posterity has to view a life and evaluate it by its own standards and according to the information available to it. However, the young Natacha was, as far as I can determine, quite different in certain respects from the mature Natacha..." [16]

---

16 Letter from Mark Hasselriis to M. Morris, dated September 16, 1989.

Fig. 184

Alvaro and his second wife, Esperanza Maldonado y Chavarri on their wedding day

THE CAVES OF GÈNOVA
"SES COVES"

Fig. 185

The bar and restaurant, Ses Coves" first established by Natacha Rambova

"To help lure tourists to Gènova, Natacha negotiated a lease on the caves there, one of the natural wonders of the island. She installed electrical illumination throughout the rock forest of stalactites and stalagmites, and constructed diverse paths along which visitors could wander through a geographical fantasy land." [17]

---

17 *Madam Valentino*, p. 202

Fig. 186

Fig. 187

Stairs and passageways in the caves of Gènova

Fig. 188

Fig. 189

Fig. 190

Fig. 191

The cistern in the caves of Gènova

328

Natacha Rambova's Mallorca Today

Fig. 192

Ca Na Tacha today, from the sea

Fig. 193

Ca Na Tacha

Fig. 194

View of Gènova neighborhood today

Fig. 195-196
The street in Gènova named in honor of Natacha Rambova

A long view to the sea

A Tribute to The Guardian

Fig. 197

Ms. Maria Salomé Juaneda Pujol

Fig. 198

Maria Salomé Juaneda Pujol sharing her Rambova collection

Left to right: Catalina Ruiz, primary school teacher and supervisor of the oral history project, Tonina Matamalas, assistant to William James assigned to the project by the Es Baluard Museum, Maria Salomé, her daughter Rosa and William James.

Fig. 199

Natacha Rambova Brand Lipstick – Shade "Raspberry"

"It is possible that Rambova designed this jewelry herself, as she had previously designed the bracelet for Rudolph Valentino. Proof of a cosmetics line is less evident. She may have been encouraged by her stepfather Richard Hudnut to pursue a line of cosmetics in Europe, as was suggested by Dawn Allen in her biography of Talbot Mundy, but no additional evidence exists."[18]

Maria Salomé's guardianship of these artifacts has provided proof of the existence of Rambova's cosmetics line. The lipstick is photographed displayed on one her turbans.

---

18 Vaughan, Heather A., *"Natacha Rambova, Dress Designer (1928 – 1931), Dress, The Annual Journal of the Costume Society of America*, Volume 33, 2006, p. 34.

Fig. 200-201
Natacha Rambova's Lipstick

Fig. 202 Maria Salomé's cache of photographs

Fig. 203

Fig. 204 Childhood photograph of Natacha Rambova

Fig. 205

Fig. 206 Natacha Rambova's jewelry, fan, china and passport

Fig. 207

Fig. 208

INTRODUCTION & HISTORICAL ANALYSIS

OF NATACHA RAMBOVA'S "ARRIBA ESPAÑA"

by

William James

Natacha Rambova wrote this 23-page essay shortly after the outbreak of the Spanish Civil War. She argued the cause of the rebel uprising led by army generals against the elected government of the day, and hoped to sway the opinion of the international community in their favor. She sided with the traditionalist and conservative right. Her title – *Up Spain* – is a translation of the falangist salute *¡Arriba España!,* one of the most memorable elements of the symbolic apparatus adopted by the movement's leader José Antonio Primo de Rivera in imitation of Italian and German fascism.

Natacha Rambova's reactionary views will jar contemporary sensibilities. But we read *Up Spain* with the hindsight of history – the evolution of the Spanish Civil War, its escalating cycle of violence, the subsequent events of the Second World War, Nazi horrors, and the 40-year dictatorship that was to follow in Spain. *Up Spain* must be read in the context of Natacha's inevitably piece-meal view of the events, her obvious political naivety, and the circumstances of her marriage.

It is clear that two main factors influenced her views. First and foremost, there is the figure of her husband, Álvaro de Urzaíz y Silva, and the feelings of disenfranchisement felt by himself and his circle during the years of the Spanish Second Republic leading up to the war (1931-36). Secondly, an understandable fear of communism (the fate of property owners in the Russian revolution was still a relatively recent memory) and, closely related to the former, a distaste for class hatred. It is one of the recurring catastrophes of history that the privileged remain unaware of their privileges and rarely comprehend the feelings of the under-privileged; this is clear in much of Natacha's writing.

Up Spain has remained unpublished until now for unknown reasons. Nor is it clear whether Natacha ever made any attempt to publish her article. As the Spanish Civil War progressed and General Franco emerged as a dictator, we do not know how her views may have changed. According to her secretary of many years (1949-66), she never spoke of her five-year sojourn in Spain, her marriage to Álvaro de Urzáiz (she displayed no photos of Álvaro at home), or expressed any opinions about the tragedy that befell Spain, to which she had been a witness.

It would appear she drew a line through that period of her life and turned her attentions to new interests. The reasons for this are a matter for speculation. But after the bombing of Guernica by the German Condor Legion (in April 1937), international attitudes to the Spanish Civil War shifted dramatically. At its outbreak, the war was seen as an internal conflict – the U.S. government banned the export of arms to either side – but with Guernica, Germany's involvement on the rebel side (until then denied by the Nazi regime) became a proven fact, and the horrifying images of the suffering of the civilian population consolidated public opinion in favor of the legitimate Republican government. After that moment, it would have been difficult to publish *Up Spain* in America. But perhaps Natacha no longer wished to.

She accused the ruling class of complacency: *"Wealth centered in the hands of indolence and indifference does not tend towards national strength or progress."* Natacha had many opportunities to observe the wealthy and privileged in Spain at close hand as her husband belonged to just this class. Álvaro's relatives and immediate social circle enjoyed full membership of the ancient oligarchy that had traditionally enjoyed power and privilege in Spain – Catholic, conservative, and traditionalist. Álvaro's relatives considered his marriage to a Hollywood celebrity unsuitable. It would appear that Natacha did not think much of them either – they bored her. The opening pages of *Up Spain* provided her with an opportunity for revenge on her in-laws and their social milieu: *"Everyone knew everyone else, knew what everyone else was doing. The latter required little ingenuity as no one did anything that was not done by everyone else. No one dared brave ridicule or criticism by an original thought or action"*

Spain in the early twentieth century was a backward agricultural country bitterly divided by inequalities of every kind, and held in the iron grip of an ancient social, economic, and religious order. Ruled by an oligarchy of mainly landowners with a smattering of industrialists, the Catholic Church also had immense political power and was involved in many areas of social provision, particularly education (and illiteracy remained at over 50%). An antiquated rural economy depended on a vast workforce laboring all the hours of daylight for a pittance. Some 10% of agricultural workers – *jornaleros* or *braceros* – were landless day laborers, hired and fired at the convenience of the farmer. Often, the only employment was during harvests and despite starvation wages, *jornaleros* would have to make meager pay stretch over indefinite periods of unemployment. If a harvest failed or drought set in, there was no work and the *jornaleros* would go hungry.

Meanwhile, the Spanish nobility – Álvaro was a count, his mother had been lady in waiting to the princesses – was one of the least dynamic aristocracies in Europe, mainly living on income from agricultural estates, *latifundios*, in which as absentee landlords they took a minimal interest. Few made any effort to foster more modern and efficient forms of economic activity by investing in new industries, or even to optimize the productivity of their land. At the same time, they enjoyed wealth, power, influence, and prestige. During the reign of King Alfonso XIII, nobles occupied many key government posts. The nobility also dominated the army and navy.

A long tradition of army intervention in national affairs made the officer corps a major player in the evolution of history. Overmanned, top-heavy, and ill equipped for military action, the armed forces seemed to lack any real professional function but instead constituted an autonomous socio-political force. The only active area of operations was in the small Spanish protectorate of Morocco. Officers aiming at promotion sought to serve there and were regarded as an elite – the *africanistas*. It was in this context that General Franco first rose to prominence. When political and institutional instability weakened the state (which it frequently did), the military elite would intervene as the arbiter of national affairs. In a country made up of territories with very different characteristics, and indeed different cultures, many aspects of Spanish history have been characterized by tensions between the central state and opposing forces of regionalism. In this context, major sections of the Spanish officer corps regarded themselves as the guardians of stability, always favoring the nationalist, Castilian culture of a centralized state.

Spain remained neutral in the first world war, exports boomed, the economy underwent a sudden spurt of growth, but inflation and inadequate wage rises made working people's living conditions worse, which further declined in the post-war slump. Grass roots social agitation drove a strengthening workers' movement spurred on by the Bolshevik triumph in Russia and awareness of the widespread political mobilization underway across post-war Europe. But oligarchic liberalism prevailed, accompanied by mounting problems of unemployment, poverty, and labor unrest.

With strikes, uprisings and strife mainly in Andalucia and Catalonia, the three-year period 1918-1920 became known as 'three years of bolshevism,' when employers in Barcelona resorted to hiring hit-men – *pistoleros* – to gun down union leaders (soon after the authorities would adopt identical methods to restore law and order!). In this context, the CNT (*Confederación Nacional del Trabajo*, National Worker's Union, an anarcho-syndicalist trade union) grew and radicalized; the more moderate UGT (*Unión General de Trabajadores*, General Workers' Union) also increased its membership. A tiny Spanish communist party (PCE – *Partido Comunista Española*) was founded in 1921. These three groups would thereafter compete to become the representatives of the working class.

Anarchists – mainly represented by the CNT – were an important element of the political landscape in Spain, perhaps a response to the fierce regionalism felt by many Spaniards and their resentment towards the idea of a remote centralized state (particularly in Catalonia). In a country in which the largest sector of the working class resided in the country, the idea of self-organization and a grass roots politics emerging in local communities had widespread appeal.

In 1921, the Spanish army suffered a devastating defeat at the Battle of Annual in Morocco against combatants of the Rif region. The massacre discredited military policy and competence and in 1923 parliament called for an investigation into the interference of King Alfonso XIII in the debacle and into ubiquitous rumors of army corruption. The army responded by mounting a *coup d'état* in September led by Miguel Primo de Rivera, which gained the backing of the king, who appointed him Prime Minister.

The new dictator rejected the constitution in the belief that parliamentary failure had thrown Spain into turmoil and that by governing without politicians he could restore the nation. Initially he saw this as a short-term project but the monarchist dictatorship endured until the end of the decade and soured many Spaniards against the monarchy, while others welcomed the cessation of political instability. Primo de Rivera set out to modernize the economy by investing in new infrastructure. Although a series of ambitious public projects did much to reduce unemployment and stimulate the economy, inadequate funding caused sharp inflation to the detriment of ordinary people's living conditions. But the dictatorship could only govern by the permission of reactionary forces – the Army, the Church, the monarchy – and failed to tackle Spain's most urgent social and economic problems, which would inevitably call for a shift in the status quo.

As the king had backed the dictatorship, and as economic conditions worsened particularly in the wake of the Wall Street Crash (1929), the monarchy became a symbol of oppression to ordinary people, and a Republican movement gained ground. The dictatorship was overthrown in January 1930 and Republicans rallied to fight for their cause in municipal elections held in April 1931. Ostensibly to elect town councils, the elections were understood by the population as a contest between monarchy and republicanism. The Republicans won a landslide victory, the king went quietly into exile, and April 14th saw the birth of the Spanish Second Republic.

The monarchist dictatorship of the twenties was the background to Álvaro's adolescence and early youth, when his family continued to occupy a secure position of prestige as members of the ruling class. They participated in court life from their ancient mansion in the center of Madrid not far from the royal palace. *"They remembered their duties at Court, the Court functions and balls... They mused and laughed, contented and happy in the memories of the past. The Past, in which they continued their lives in the dignity of tranquil comfort..."* The advent of the Republic would have been a traumatic moment in their lives, and Natacha gives some evidence of their resentment *"Some blamed these annoying times on other nobles who had not been loyal. If they had all stuck by El Rey, things would not have come to such a pass!"* Álvaro was educated in England for a career in the Spanish Navy and entered the navy as a lieutenant at some point in the late twenties.

One of the first reforms launched by the new Republican government in 1931 aimed to rationalize and modernize the top-heavy armed forces and by doing so reduce a potential threat to the Republic. Firstly, the government obliged all officers to pledge loyalty to the Republic (refusal to do so constituted resignation). Then, new legislation offered officers the opportunity to retire from the services on full pay, placing them on the reserve list. It was just those officers who were unhappy with the turn of events who chose retirement (leaving them with time on their hands to plot the Republic's downfall), and this is certainly how Álvaro came to withdraw from the navy at such a young age. Other members of Álvaro's family and circle did the same: *"we had two cousins and a friend staying with us at the time... all officers retired since the revolution of '31."* It is significant that here Natacha refers to the declaration of the Republic – the outcome of a democratic vote – as a revolution; this gives us a sense of the terms in which those events had been described to her, and the feelings of those around her regarding the overthrow of the monarchy.

Following the declaration of the Republic, general elections returned a coalition of socialists (the PSOE, *Partido Socialista Obrera Española*, Spanish Socialist Workers' Party) and the Republican Left Party whose first task was to draw up a new constitution (passed by parliament in December). An important feature of the constitution were articles designed to make Spain a lay state, separating church and state by denying the church any role in public life, particularly education. This also involved a declaration of religious freedom (making religion a matter of personal choice rather than public obligation), the nationalization of some church property, the cessation of all financial subsidies to the church (previously priests had received state stipends), and a more liberal attitude to divorce.

An explosion of popular rejoicing in towns and cities across Spain welcomed the proclamation of the Republic. This was accompanied by a wave of anti-clerical feeling manifested as the burning of churches and convents mainly in Madrid, Seville, Granada, and Malaga. Anti-clericalism was nothing new in Spain. For the previous hundred years, Spaniards had been divided by vehement differences of attitude toward the Church and its role in society. The church was seen as integral to the ancient ruling order that was preventing Spain from modernizing, as a branch of government, the psychological branch of authority, its 'thought police.'

Spaniards' opinion of the church often marked their position as left, center, or right on the political spectrum. The term anti-clerical applied to all those who wished to see a reduction or elimination of the Church's influence on national life, to make religion a personal matter with no place in social or political affairs, in the belief that the authoritarian structuring of religion as it had been in Spain was tyrannical. This view was shared among socialists and anarchists alike, the urban and rural working classes, among middle class liberals, Republicans, and even many believing Catholics.

Natacha Rambova was naturally horrified by anti-clerical violence and *Up Spain* gives many examples of the shocking violence of attacks on priests, nuns and church property in the period before and after the outbreak of the civil war. In addition to extreme cruelty to the victims, she understood the violence as an attack on art, culture and history, *"the destruction of priceless treasures of history and art"* the very things that fascinated and inspired her throughout her life. But, although she was appalled by manifestations of anti-clericalism, she does not acknowledge the political implications of the church's historical involvement in government. These acts of violence were acts of political symbolism, perpetrated in spontaneous outbursts of a fury so overpowering that its protagonists no longer recognized the humanity of their victims. We must ask ourselves what conditions had driven people into this state of blind rage.

For decades, moments of social unrest had been accompanied by violent outbursts of anti-clericalism, resulting in all sorts of atrocities. The wanton violence of these attacks contained an odd mixture of political protest and fury for past injustices, endowed with an eerie symbolism that was perhaps a response to the fervent mysticism and superstition of the church itself (for example, the disinterment of the embalmed cadavers of nuns as a response to the zealous custom of kissing the bones of dead saints). Centuries of moral dictates and repression enforced by the Spanish Inquisition were entrenched in the national imaginary. Mental illness in Spain frequently took the form of religious delusion. But events in Mallorca, *"our Island of Calm,"* were always a pale shadow of those taking place on mainland Spain; Natacha describes a church burning at the Majorcan village of Esporles, with this peculiarly Spanish blend of political conscience and superstition: *"The statue of their Madonna had been known to work miracles! She would be angry. No one now wished to lay despoiling hands on her sacred replica. They conferred. At last they reached a decision. Reverently they removed their caps and entered the church. With care they lifted down the sacred statue, the altarpieces and paintings, with care they carried them to the house of the padre. The Virgin would surely not wreak vengeance on them now! They were safe to proceed. With enthusiasm they burnt the church."*

Faced with the anti-clerical outburst in the spring of 1931, the new administration was slow to put a stop to the attacks on church property. Their reluctance to intervene immediately, and a passing remark allegedly made by Republican Left minister Manuel Azaña that he would prefer all the churches in Spain to burn than a single Republican be harmed, was taken by the right as evidence that the Second Republic was actively anti-religion and anti-church. Although many Republicans were anti-catholic on an individual level, the legislative agenda was simply intent on separating religion from government. But after centuries of close involvement between church and state, this was not likely to go smoothly. The church and its supporters fought back.

The newly elected socialist coalition optimistically embarked on a program of reforms aimed at modernizing the nation and alleviating the atrocious day-to-day conditions under which many working people lived (the *bienio reformista* – reformist biennium, 1931-33). This meant reforming one of the most backward nations in Europe and leading it into the modern era, a process that had taken decades to evolve, if not centuries, in other European countries. After the jubilant show of support for the proclamation of the Republic, the government felt that this placed a seal of approval on their program.

Agriculture was the main source of national income and employment and its organization and management determined the insuperable inequalities suffered by half the population. Agrarian reform, designed to ease poverty among the landless *jornaleros,* was the *bienio reformista's* most ambitious project. Legislation was introduced to expropriate farmland without compensation from the larger estates (*latifundios*), which would be turned over to the landless and make them self-supporting. Some half million hectares were expropriated from sixty of the richest landowners and this evidently affected the Urzáiz family (and others in their circle, no doubt): *"They would now undoubtedly be indemnified for their confiscated fincas* (farms), *or the fincas might even be returned."* Industrial workers had already had the working day reduced to eight hours and the same rule was applied to agricultural workers. Letting the land lie fallow as a means of boycotting the legislation was prohibited under threat of confiscation.

A new education program – one of the Republic's success stories – saw the creation of some 10,000 new schools and 7,000 new teachers; education was to be free, compulsory, and non-religious. New labor laws were drawn up by the socialist Minister of Labor, Largo Caballero, which introduced arbitration structures with equal representation by employers and employees, a forty-hour week, and an inspectorate to ensure that legislation was applied.

The reforms themselves were moderate, cautious but inevitably required some redistribution of power and wealth. In reality they were insufficient to reverse the economic and social divides inherited from previous eras. Moreover, they were delivered in a relatively short time-span for a country accustomed to the stagnation of an established order: *"Everything will take care of itself, nothing ever happens in Spain."* And the *bienio reformista* came at a particularly unfortunate moment coinciding with the Great Depression. Public funds were insufficient to see reforms through. A generalized fall in profits made it difficult for landowners and industrialists to offset the economic cost of reform against business income. They closed ranks against the Republic. It might be expected that a program of reform designed to meet the needs and aspirations of the mass of working people within a democratic state would be ensured of a successful outcome, but the government did not realize how easily reactionary forces, backed by propaganda and well-funded campaigns, could mobilize opposition to change.

Despite criticism of the upper classes as represented by Natacha's in-laws and their like, *Up*

347

Spain continues in support of the right's intransigent opposition to reform and to the Republic itself. She evidently accepted the arguments of her husband and others around him and viewed the Republican left with mistrust and trepidation. Social and economic divisions on the island of Mallorca were always milder in comparison with mainland Spain. Natacha failed to recognize the justice and urgency of the reforming ambitions of the *bienio reformista*. Had she been witness to the extremes of poverty and the cold-hearted indifference with which workers were treated in some parts of Spain, perhaps her views would have been different.

In a climate in which the social divide between servants and their employers were almost insuperable, María Salome' Juaneda Pujol's parents, maid and chauffeur to Natacha and Álvaro, reported that while Álvaro could be rude and overbearing (and short-changed them over household expenses), Natacha treated her staff with consideration, warmth and sympathy and always did her best to soften social differences.

As the legislature proceeded, the *bienio reformista* was faced with growing criticism from both supporters (impatient for change, disappointed with the modest nature of the reforms) and opponents. The government found it increasingly difficult to push their program of reforms forward and elections were called in November 1933. The main opposition to the government came from a newly-formed alliance of right-wing parties, the CEDA (*Confederación Española de Derechas Autónomas* – Spanish Confederation of Right Groups) under the leadership of Gil Robles, a strident and vocal opponent of the *bienio reformista*, who declared himself the defender of "order and religion," pledging to reverse the agrarian and other reforms underway and to restore power and privileges to the church. These were "the rights" as Natacha calls them, who fought against the Republican Left-socialist coalition in the November election, evidently supported by herself and the Urzaiz family.

This was the first time women had voted in Spain (another feature of the new constitution). Many sought the guidance of the parish priest and were advised to vote CEDA. Moreover, increasing ideological divisions split the vote on the left. The anarchist CNT – opposed to parliamentary system on principle – urged their members not to vote at all. The CEDA won but with an insufficient majority to govern, which led them to form a coalition with the center Radical Party.

This marked the beginning of the *bienio negro* (black biennium 1933-35), when the newly elected legislature set out to undo the reforms initiated during the *bienio reformista*, provoking the fury of the left both within parties and among the grass roots proletariat. The confiscation of land belonging to the grandees was halted and the labor law providing agricultural workers with the same protection as industrial workers was annulled. It is said that impoverished laborers looking for work were told by landowners "let the Republic feed you." Employers, encouraged by CEDA policy, refused employment to unionized workers. When disputes got out of hand the Civil Guard moved in to keep order, backing the interests of the reactionaries. This was a politics of retaliation in which the CEDA's ambition was to return to the pre-1931 status quo by canceling the reforming ambitions of the socialists. At a time of high unemployment resulting from the depression (12% of the workforce in the winter of 1933-34) and with no welfare arrangements to support those out of work, hardship was widespread and extreme.

Socialist disappointment drove the PSOE, now under the leadership of Largo Caballero, to radicalize dramatically in resistance to the influence of the CEDA, and draw up a new program of reforms with a distinctly revolutionary flavor:
  - Nationalization of the land
  - Dissolution of all religious orders, with seizure of their property
  - Dissolution of the army, to be replaced by a democratic militia

A revolutionary committee was formed and threatened to organize an uprising but ill prepared for such action, this was in reality an empty threat intended to force the CEDA to proceed with caution. A series of strikes in the early months of 1934 all failed, but fired the flames of revolutionary zeal. Militancy swept through an infuriated working class.

The situation reached a head when the CEDA achieved increased representation in parliament, and anarchists and socialists called a revolutionary general strike in the autumn of 1934. The strike immediately exposed rifts between the Spanish Socialist Worker's Party (PSOE), its affiliated trade union the UGT, the main organizers, and the anarco-syndicalist CNT, who doubted the political efficacy of strike action. While a stoppage in Madrid struggled on, strikes collapsed in other parts of Spain, with the exception of Asturias. Here miners seized a number of Civil Guard barracks and took control of several towns where they set up revolutionary committees to govern the areas they controlled. The government interpreted this as all-out revolution and sent in the army led by generals Franco and Goded to suppress the rebellion.

The Asturian miners, armed with weapons seized from the civil guard and mining explosives (deployed with professional know-how) managed to resist for two weeks. But when troop deployments arrived by sea and took the anarchist controlled ports of Gijon and Avilés they met little resistance, and this defeat spelled the end of the strike. The suppression of the strike was as harsh as it could be with looting, rape, on-the-spot executions, and torture; as many as 3,000 miners lost their lives, another 30,000-40,000 were imprisoned. Many individuals on the left were imprisoned in other parts of Spain too, including Mallorca.

Franco believed that the uprising had been carefully prepared under supervision and guidance from Moscow, declaring "this war is a frontier war and its fronts are socialism, communism and whatever attacks civilization in order to replace it with barbarism." [1] The right-wing press came up with the notion that the uprising had been the product of a foreign Jewish-Bolshevik conspiracy. Here lie the origins of much of Natacha's rhetoric in *Up Spain* that the subsequent actions of the right were a crucial, glorious and timely move to save Spain from a Bolshevik revolution instigated from abroad. Over and over again, *Up Spain* views the Republic as a puppet state with Russia pulling the strings. There is little respect for the Republican causes of democracy, universal suffrage and a lawful constitution. Instead, Natacha sees the Republic as an affront, an opinion surely originating with her husband.

During 1935, the CEDA continued efforts to build a corporate legalist right wing state within the constitutional framework of the Republic. In response, the Republican Left leader Manuel Azaña encouraged parties on the left to unite to oppose the CEDA by coming together to fight in the next election. He persuaded the socialist politician Indalecio Prieto to resume relations with the Republican Left party (as during the *bienio reformista* coalition). This involved a split within the socialist party between the revolutionary ambitions of Largo Caballero (and many grass roots members) and a politics conducted within the Republic's constitutional framework. Repeatedly Manuel Azaña pledged his support for a constitution based on universal suffrage and aimed at social reform. Later, the increasing power of the CEDA within government drove Caballero to accept a new coalition of groups on the left to fight in the next election, named the *Frente Popular* (Popular Front).

In the autumn of 1935, various corruption scandals involving key politicians in the Radical Party led to the resignation of Radical party ministers and elections were called. The elections took place in February 1936. They would be the last elections held in Spain for the next forty years. The *Frente Popular* promised to resume the reforms begun during the *bienio reformista*, guaranteed

---

1 Ed. Carlos Jerez-Farrán, Samuel Amago, *Unearthing Franco's Legacy: Mass Graves and the Recovery of Historical Memory in Spain*, 2010, Notre Dame University Press, p. 62.

amnesty to all those detained as a result of the 'October Revolution' of 1934, and to implement a process of increased regional autonomy. The CEDA and other right parties declared their campaigns to be 'counter-revolutionary,' in opposition to the supposed threat of a worker's revolution. They also argued against the potential rise of regionalism if the *Frente Popular* came into power. This time CNT members, with anarchist representation in the coalition, were encouraged to vote. The *Frente Popular* won the day, but by then it was perhaps already too late to save the Republic and democracy.

After the suppression of the miner's strike in 1934, the government had found it increasingly difficult to contain social and political conflict. The reversal of the reforms begun during the *bienio reformista* and the repeated and heavy-handed thwarting of opposition by the CEDA generated a climate of bitterness and hatred that was bound to explode sooner or later *"Anxiety, fear and class hatred hung like a pestilence in the air. The proletariat glowered and waited."* A mounting breakdown in law and order characterized the period leading up to July 1936, with self-organized militia forming among many different political groups. Some historians date the real start of the civil war as the autumn of 1934.

This period saw the rise of the *Falange* founded by José Antonio Primero de Rivera, son of the former dictator, in imitation of Italian fascism. Natacha reports that by 1936 the younger members of the Urzaíz family had joined the *Falange*. *"He, of course, was a Falangista. So were all the young members of the family although they refrained from discussing it before their parents."* And they were armed: *"Yes, they all had their guns–well hidden. They only asked to be allowed to use them."*

Unbeknown to Natacha, who gives several accounts of outbreaks of lawlessness during those months that she consistently blames on the left, the *Falange* made deliberate contributions to the breakdown in law and order. Such actions were not isolated incidents but followed a preplanned strategy intended to provoke conflict and lawlessness that could later be used to justify a *coup d'etat. Up Spain* makes it clear that by the spring of 1936 the young falangista's were impatient for the uprising that was to come. The left-wing press warned of the imminence of a nationalist rebellion too.

In the months before the rebel uprising in July 1936, and for years afterwards, the nationalists disseminated propaganda and a series of documents they claimed were evidence that a Bolshevik revolution had been planned for August, and years into the regime it continued to justify the rebellion as necessary to save Spain from communism and Soviet domination (dubbing themselves the *Movimiento Salvador* – the Movement to Save Spain). This argument involved coloring anyone opposed to the uprising as 'red.' Nationalists applied the term communist to all the elements that made up the left, and Natacha does the same in her account of events, repeatedly referring to all on the Republican side as communists: *"In our own village of Peguera we knew there were many communists."*

It is true that the municipality of Calvià, which includes Peguera, was one of the few in Mallorca where the *Frente Popular* won a majority in the 1936 elections but by supporting the *Frente Popular*, voters were opting for a non-revolutionary coalition representing may different factions, some more moderate than others. According to the French writer Georges Bernanos – like Natacha, an eyewitness of events before and after the outbreak of war in Mallorca – the number of communists on the island barely reached a hundred.

It is true that the left did include sectors bent on "the rule of the proletariat" to quote Karl Marx, many of whom were grouped around Largo Caballero: *"Caballero and Prieto ... huge crouching monsters of destruction on the horizon."* But the political landscape in Spain was bafflingly complex, and very fragmented on the left, encompassing all sorts of political groupings with wide-ranging, often conflicting, ideologies and objectives that could cross classes, regions, allegiances, and interests. It was relatively easy to unite the right as the interests of different groups and parties were fairly compatible, a matter of blocking change and maintaining an old and familiar order.

In fact, the formation of the *Frente Popular* coincided with Russian communism's realization that it must focus its efforts on defeating fascism in Europe. The truth is that the Comintern urged the Spanish communist party and the Spanish proletariat to unite with non-revolutionary parties on the left to achieve a socialist state by democratic means in order to isolate and abbreviate fascism. Communism was to be achieved by long-term gradual evolution driven by the will of the people. The threat of communist revolution was a fabrication, an instrument of propaganda used by the right to justify the overthrow of the Republic in the pursuit of its own interests.

In different areas of Spain, support for or resistance to the rebellion in July 1936 tended to follow the election results in February; areas that had voted to the right supported the nationalist side and areas that had voted *Frente Popular* remained Republican. Majorcans had voted mainly to the right, and in Palma the rebel uprising on July 19th had immediate success. Cases of resistance in other parts of the island capitulated almost as soon as the nationalist forces arrived. This did not make much sense – any opponents to the new regime would soon be shot. Detachments of soldiers moved around the island and, supported by local *falangistas*, set about establishing the new order by detaining any elements regarded as a threat.

Lists had already been drawn up: Republican mayors and councilors, state school teachers, union members, party members, anyone who had taken part in a strike or a demonstration, people who never went to church, in other words, anyone who could be suspected – even remotely – of Marxist, anarchist, or anti-clerical ideas were registered on those lists under the common denomination of 'reds.' As many as two thousand individuals were detained during the first few days, many of whom would be executed without trial.

Countless atrocities were committed on both sides during the Spanish Civil War. But the victor in any civil war is bound to kill more because of the imperative to eradicate the cycle of fury and hatred from which the war arises. This was certainly the case in Spain. In Mallorca, the individual victim would be taken at night, whether from prison cell or from his bed at home, to be shot and abandoned, typically in the ditch at the side of a road. The suspect would be shot in the face to make it more difficult to identify the cadaver. When the body was discovered the next day, a doctor was summoned to issue a death certificate; too frightened to speak out, he would write down the cause of death as 'cerebral hemorrhage.'

It was in the context of these reprisals that Natacha's feelings changed direction. Her friend's husband, Antonio Espina, former Civil Governor of the Balearic Islands had been detained, and his wife was afraid he would share the cruel fate of so many other Republicans. She asked the Bishop of Palma to intervene with the authorities to save him but was refused. [II] In an act of great personal courage, an outraged Natacha made her way to the cathedral and interrupted the service shouting at the bishop "When will you stop the slaughter?" This immediately raised doubt about her allegiances, and it became clear that she must leave the island at once or be detained herself.

Evidently, she had not understood the ruthless nature of the regime that she herself supported. At that time, many Republicans were attempting to escape Mallorca without much success. As a foreign celebrity, Natacha Rambova almost certainly had covert assistance from the *Falangista* authorities. It was the end of her marriage. She would never set foot in Spain again.

What became of Álvaro? He had signed up in support of the nationalist rebels on the first day

---

II Espina's wife was not the only person to seek assistance of this sort from the Bishop. Their pleas fell on deaf ears. In a letter to The Vatican's Secretariat of State in 1938, Bishop Miralles denied all knowledge of executions in Mallorca, thereby refusing to acknowlege what everyone else on the island knew.

of the insurrection, *"The following week my husband was made Naval Commander of the Southern coast of the island and we left for the port of Campos."* The importance of this role suggests that perhaps he had been chosen for the position in advance, perhaps as part of a prior arrangement to which he was party (although, if this was the case, Natacha probably knew nothing about it). Effectively, Franco's dictatorship restored the ancient social order that the Republic had sought to dismantle. With alacrity Álvaro resumed his career and the entitlements he had been brought up to expect.

He thrived under the new regime both during the war and the dictatorship that followed. He occupied high-ranking posts in the navy and in 1942 led an expedition bearing his name (*La Comisión Urzaíz*) to Nazi Germany to study the *Kriegsmarine* with a view to modernizing the Spanish navy. He spoke fluent English and acted as interpreter in the negotiations between the U.S. and Spanish governments that led to the Pact of Madrid in 1953, one of the key events in the history of the dictatorship. This role placed him at the heart of the regime. Álvaro and Natacha were to meet again on several occasions and while relations between them were cordial, their marriage was over. Natacha could not return to Spain. Álvaro now had too much at stake to go after her.

Up Spain is a significant historical document published here for the first time. It gives us a vivid eyewitness account of the first months of the Spanish Civil War in Mallorca. It is also a portrayal of the narrow political outlook of the conservative, monarchist right, characterized by reaction to the advent of the Second Republic. Although Natacha Rambova sided with the Republic's opponents, *Up Spain* does not give us much idea of any positive political ideal that she might have envisioned for Spain beyond these few words: *"In the hands of General Franco, who is a disciplinarian with energetic modern ideas, Spain may have a great future; she may rise again to reclaim her position of past grandeur. These hopes of the future are voiced in his words, 'All citizens of the new Spain must work, there will be no place for the idle or for those who have lost their pride of race in the pursuits of foreign amusements.' "* The form that Spain's "great future" might take is extremely vague. When she put pen to paper in the autumn of 1936, Natacha did not foresee, nor could have done, that Franco's Spain would be the only dictatorship allied to fascist Italy and Germany to survive beyond 1945. [III]

III Other sources: Interviews with Majorcan historian David Ginard i Féron; Interviews with Natacha Rambova's goddaughter, María Salomé Juaneda Pujol; Anthony Beevor, *The Battle for Spain*, Phoenix, London, 2007; Georges Bernanos, *A Diary of my Times*, Borriswood, London, 1938; David Ginard i Féron, *El moviment obrer de Mallorca i la Guerra Civil (1936-1939)* (The Majorcan Worker's Movement and the Civil War [1936-39]), Publicacions de l'Abadia de Montserrat, Barcelona, 1999; Paul Preston, *The Coming of the Spanish Civil War. Reform, reaction and revolution in the Second Republic*, Routledge, London, 1994; Jean Schalekamp, *De una isla no se puede escapar* (From an Island there is No Escape), self-published, Palma de Mallorca, 1987.

Fig. 209

The Falange insignia as propaganda poster

Arriba España!

by

Natacha Rambova de Urzaiz

To quote Mr. Winston Churchill, "It is without doubt that the enormous influence exercised in Spain towards a state of revolution had Russia for origin....Without the communist intrigue carried on in Spain for six months prior to the movement, we would never have had to witness the present horrors." - A country so naturally rich, in such a state of decay, was bound to attract alien acquisitiveness.

Wealth centered in the hands of indolence and indifference does not tend towards national strength or progress. That has been the tragedy of Spain. With wealth goes responsibility; those who have refused to take their responsibilities have had to pay bitterly for their short-sighted idleness. As always, the exceptions have had to suffer for the generalities. In the last five years that Spain has been my home I have watched with growing apprehension the gathering clouds of this storm.

Yet those who should have been the most interested were content to rest placidly voicing their favorite expression, "Everything will take care of itself, nothing ever happens in Spain." It is unfortunately a characteristic of the Spanish people that they utterly refuse to look ahead; preparation bores them. They have a genius for emergencies. Although there is no one who so loves his peace, yet there is no braver, fiercer fighter once aroused.

In the hands of General Franco,[1] who is a disciplinarian with energetic modern ideas, Spain may have a great future; she may rise again to reclaim her position of past grandeur. These hopes of the future are voiced in his words, "All citizens of the new Spain must work, there will be no place for the idle or for those who have lost their pride of race in the pursuits of foreign amusements." Let us hope the slaughtered, tortured thousands will not have met martyrdom in vain. There is no country with greater latent possibilities; my one wish is that she may realize them.

Arriba España, A Vencer!

When we had been in Madrid the year before, things had been different. The Rights were then in power. Hopes were focused on Gil Robles. All would now be well.

The streets were filled with bright, expensive cars; I had never seen so many stream-lined Chryslers and LaSalles. The side-walks were crowded with women smart in Paris clothes. Confidence was being restored. Wealth was cautiously emerging from its seclusion – not yet entirely convinced of the safety of conspicuous daylight. Sallying forth gradually with more boldness, it kept one eye ever on its refuge; for a hasty retreat at any loud rumbles of the Lefts.

The cinemas and bars, the two principle places of amusement of the elite were crowded. "The Bengal Lancers" had been playing to weeks of enthusiastic acclaim. At all smart hours it was impossible to be served at the Bakanik or Chicote's. Even the large and more democratic Aquarium was packed. One lunched or dined at the Bar Club; frightfully expensive, but excellent food!

We had come to Madrid to attend a wedding of a close member of my husband's family.[2] In consequence, we viewed wedding presents and trousseau, attended formal family luncheons or less formal cocktail parties. Life, like a barely moving, sluggish stream, flowed slowly through extraordinary hours and rutty routines.

We rose about noon, dressed leisurely and sauntered to some bar, sooner or later to be joined by the same friends of the day before. Madrid, I discovered, was in reality but a very small Main Street. Everyone knew everyone else, knew what everyone else was doing. This later required little ingenuity as no one did anything that was not done by everyone else. No one dared brave ridicule or criticism by an original thought or action. One lunched about two-thirty. After lunch one siesta-ed until six; the hour when the first move cinema-ward was made. A few of the very energetic played golf. Some of the older generation went for a drive through the Pardo before tea.

Still belonging to the younger generation, we went to the ciné. Afterward the men went off together to Chicote's. We, the women, went home to our own apartments. The next hour and a half was again spent in our dressing rooms; although, since the Republic, no one dressed for dinner unless for a very special occasion. At ten, we gathered in the salon to gossip lazily until the arrival of male friends and members of the family. Dinner was scheduled for ten; we rarely sat down until eleven.

Dinner was usually a tedious affair ending about one in the morning. Some of the men had been to the Country Club and discussed club gossip. At times, politics entered the conversation. This latter topic rarely reached any pitch of heated argument. The Rights, gracias a Dios, were again in power. They would now undoubtedly be indemnified for their confiscated fincas, or the fincas might even be returned. They could safely leave matters in the hands of Gil Robles. Why discuss or worry!

Some blamed these annoying times on other nobles who had not been loyal. If they had all stuck by El Rey, things would not have come to such a pass! Others disagreed and said in reality it was all the King's fault; he had been too democratic. How could he expect to keep his position if he drove himself around in a Ford and sat amongst the audience at the cinema. He was altogether too intelligent, too broadminded for a King. Today, the English royal family were the only ones who understood and held their position. They knew the value of tradition; were never seen except surrounded by fitting ceremony.

Look at University City. That again was the King's idea; it had been, in fact, his hobby. He wished education for his people. A great mistake! If everyone became educated who was going to do the manual labor; impossible in Spain for Spain was an agricultural country. They had all agreed on this so many times it had become boring. The conversation returned to more amusing subjects. They debated the merit of Greta Garbo in "Queen Christina". Some found it too theatrical.

At tea I listened to the older generation. Over their tea cups, in high-ceilinged rooms hung with family Goyas, Sneyders and Velasquez, they discussed the goings and coming of their respective families. They shook their heads over the strangeness of the times, over the wild life of the younger generation. In their day there had been no bars! They would sigh and allow their minds to wander along more pleasant channels. They remembered their duties at Court, the Court functions and balls; they recalled anecdotes. They laughed and whispered about that time when the Duchess of So-and-So had so well put the pushing Countess of So-and-So in her place. Dear Sophia was really a character as she never lacked the exact word at the right moment! They mused and laughed, contented and happy in the memories of the past. The Past, in which they continued their lives in the dignity of tranquil comfort. Yes, the older generation still remained contentedly in the past, the younger generation blindly and indolently in the present. It seemed it was left to the people to live in the future.

This year on our visit to Madrid we found things very changed. It was appalling that so much could alter in a year. The Lefts were now in power! [3]

The Rights, as usual, had done nothing with their opportunity. Gil Robles had gone down a failure. A good man who had tried to temporize, to sit on both stools at once; inevitably he had fallen between the two, both parties now looked upon him with suspicion. So the Lefts were again in power, more Left than ever. Largo Caballero and Prieto had loomed like huge crouching monsters of destruction on the horizon. Azalia, who after all did stand for order, was now paradoxically the one hope of the Rights. A short year before he had been looked upon with antagonism and hatred! Ca! He was a Left Republican!

Gil Robles

The streets were no longer filled with bright stream-lined limousines; small Fords and second-hand cars had taken their place. Anxiety, fear and class hatred hung like a pestilence in the air. The proletariat glowered and waited. Confidence had gone. Money had beat a hasty retreat to its underground refuge. The side-walks were no longer crowded: there were now no women in the smart Paris clothes. Everyone this year was economizing – whether one needed to or not.

No one was very interested in the cinemas or bars. It was no longer smart to go to the Bakanik, to dine at the Bar Club. If one dined out it was at some small bistro or restaurant tipique, where one had the very excellent but modest plat du jour, at an even more modest sum. If one went out in the evenings it was to the "boite", a very chummy, democratic affair where no one dressed. The music was supplied by an American boy on the piano. The one subject of conversation, even here, was – politics.

Being country cousins from Mallorca, we still enjoyed the cinemas. "The Tale of Two Cities" was playing at the Capitol and had created some indignant interest. It was so unwise to show such a picture at such a time! Such obvious revolutionary propaganda! Those awful Spanish titles, just written to incite the people to more fury!

After the ciné one evening before going home, we thought of stopping at the Aquarium for a drink. When we arrived we found the Civil Guard at the door. No, we could not go in; a bomb had been thrown there about fifteen minutes before. A bomb! Anything serious? No, nothing much. It appeared in Madrid there were two waiters' unions. The two unions did not agree. The waiters employed here were all from one union, the others had thrown the bomb in protest! No one paid much attention, these occurrences were common. The bar would doubtless reopen in a day or two.

Another evening we wandered to another place. This was also shut. Two men had just had a gun battle; they had disagreed on politics. We passed in front of the Club Militar. The day before women had thrown corn through the open windows. "Corn", they said, "for old hens!" The Militar did nothing but cackle when the time had come for action.

There were no social activities this year. Many of our friends of the year before were in more amusing Paris or Biarritz; so with the family we usually dined quietly at home. During dinner, conversation was often interrupted by the now familiar sound of distant booms. Boom! Boom! Sometimes not so distant but quite frighteningly near. The house would vibrate. Quiet settled over the dining room table as the booms were counted. Three! Four! Five! When they ceased we would speculate as to where the booms had been thrown. The evening before the striking workers had blown up the sewer pipes. Any buildings in the process of construction were certain to be bombed. One really never knew what would happen next or who next would disappear. On all sides the Falanges were being arrested and thrown into prison. The butler, who had friends everywhere it seemed, would have the news for our morning coffee. Nothing was ever to be found in the papers; everything of interest was strictly censored.

Politics, our one topic of vital interest, would be resumed. Had we heard? The son of the doorman had been arrested! He, of course, was a Falangista. So were all the young members of the family although they refrained from discussing it before their parents. This last news made them feel their honour had suffered a serious affront; how belittling that one of their servants should be the first in the household to go to prison for their cause! Most of the older members, through personal loyalty to Gil Robles, still persisted outwardly in belonging to his Action Popular although their hopes and interest were obviously with young Primo de Rivera, the leader of the Falanges.

After dinner in the drawing room the conversation would be resumed. The women discussed with horror the burning of the Churches and the hideous atrocities inflicted on the nuns. What would become of the poor children cared for by Grandmama's charity? - the government was going to close the home. Would they be turned into the streets? Many of them had been brought into the world by the nuns, had been cared for by them while their mothers worked; many had known no other mothers. These same nuns who nursed the poor without reward, who cared for their children, were the ones who had just been attacked, beaten; one had had her face and teeth crushed in by the book of an infuriated communist mother. And the government allowed such things, apparently encouraged them. To what, they asked, was this going to lead? The men in groups conversed in lower tones.

José Primo de Rivera

Such a state of affairs could not go on. Why must one wait? They were impatient to get going. (was it possible these were the same bored, indifferent men of the year before! Were they at last awakening to vital realities?) Were they to wait until they were all murdered in their beds, they asked? That very day stones had been thrown into one of the windows on the second floor. The windows in the womens' apartments of the floor below had to be kept closed to shut out the brutal threats of the U.H.P. -Unios Hermanos Proletarios! -United Proletarian Brothers! Who paraded with linked arms in red shirts singing the International and shouting Viva Russia!

This waiting was insupportable, people must think they were cowards. Looking at their parents and the women, they lowered their voices still more. Yes, they all had their guns – well hidden. They only asked to be allowed to use them. But orders were orders, they must wait; it would be folly to start the fire rashly before they were ready. Hundreds were joining their party daily, many even of the Lefts, disgusted and disillusioned by the atrocities. The government, by its persecutions of the Falange party, by unconstitutionally declaring it illegal, had proven unwittingly their greatest aid; their patron of propaganda. There is nothing a Spaniard loves like a martyred cause.

The men strangely disappeared at all hours of the day and night. There were mysterious whisperings and meetings. The youngsters were difficult to repress and keep in order. The organization of the party, to everyone's surprise, was going ahead with efficient strides. It was whispered the long awaited moment was scheduled for September. They would then be ready! There was an even more exhilarating whisper; the Militar were joining them! Calvo Sotelo, on whose shoulders rested their greatest hopes and expectations, was to lead the new movement of joined forces. Viva España! Arriba España! The enthusiasm was contagious!

☙❧

We returned to Mallorca. Life settled again into its lazy, peaceful routine. The fresh, sweet smelling ozone of our Island of Calm,[4] soon banished from our nostrils the nauseating odor of pestilential class hatred which permeated the streets of distant Madrid. Those alarming incidents of our visit now seemed scenes from an improbable nightmare.

In consequence, we were shocked when one of our servants, returning from her monthly week-end to her village, brought tales of the burning of Churches in several parts of the island. In her village the padre had received a threatening note demanding his immediate retirement. The same night he had closed his church and left. The peasants shook their fists and were pleased with themselves. Their village was noted for its Left tendencies. Russia would no doubt hear of their valor and reward them!

The following day several of the women began to wonder what would happen if someone died! There would be no one to administer the last sacraments; they would be certain to go to Hell! Their children could not be baptized, their young people could not be married! In terror they fled after the padre and begged him to return.

In Esporlas, another Left village, they also decided they would burn their church. They marched importantly to the entrance door. They hesitated. No one, it seemed, wished the honor of being the first to desecrate the abode of their Saints. The statue of their Madonna had been known to work miracles! She would be angry. No one now wished to lay despoiling hands on her sacred replica. They conferred. At last they reached a decision. Reverently they removed their caps and entered the church. With care they lifted down the sacred statue, the altar pieces and paintings, with care they carried them to the house of the padre. The Virgin would surely not wreak vengeance on them now! They were safe to proceed. With enthusiasm they burnt the church. Viva Russia!

In our own village of Peguera we knew there were many communists; we refused to take seriously their rather childish illiterate enthusiasm. The little cafe and adjoining tienda, where we bought our vegetables, was their meeting place and club. One evening when we passed for a walk they were shouting, "We demand the release of Comrade Prestes. We demand the release of Comrade Prestes." We stopped and asked who Comrade Prestes was? They looked from one to another, each hoping someone else would answer; it became obvious they did not know. We smiled. It had never occurred to them to ask who Comrade Prestes was? Or why they should be demanding the release of a Brazilian communist in far off South America. It was just one of their most effective slogans like their other favorite, "Our children are starving, we demand bread and a living wage!" The fact that our leading communist, the little fat cafe owner, was not only a rich man with farming properties but also the father of a large and, from appearances, rather overfed family, did not seem to them at all amusing.

They glared at us in silence. Their importance as brave communists was being doubted. We smiled. Their looks said, well, wait and see! They muttered and looked sullen. One more valiant than the rest again repeated feebly, "We demand the release of Comrade Prestes." He received no encouragement and subsided into an embarrassed silence. We moved on.

⊰৯⊱

On the afternoon of July fifteenth, my husband and I went as usual to the village for the mail., When the daily paper was unfolded we were startled into horrified silence by the headlines, CALVO SOTELO ASSASSINATED![5] Calvo Sotelo the leader of the Renovacion Española! The man who was to lead the new movement of the Militar and Falanges to a glorious victory! The man who was to save Spain for the Spaniards, who was to lead a new Spain forward to resurrection and life! Stabbed and shot by the new Sovietic government assassins! It was incredible! We couldn't adjust our thoughts.......Again poor Dolfuss! Calvo Sotelo, the Spanish Dolfuss! What would happen now? We were not ready! For weeks, months, young Primo had had difficulty in restraining his impatient young patriots; would he be able to hold them back? Had the time for action come at last?

Calvo Sotelo

We jumped into the car and rushed for Palma. Everywhere we saw quiet, anxious groups. Everyone was asking the same question, "What would happen now?"

Saturday morning we went again to Palma to attend the Requiem Mass for Calvo Sotelo, to be held in the lovely old Church of San Francisco. At the funeral services in Madrid there had been a demonstration; many had been killed. Would there be a demonstration here? It was obvious, from the expressions on the faces of the men, that tensely their hopes favored that probability. They were longing for a chance, an excuse to unleash their rage, their indignation; to retaliate for this last insupportable, cowardly atrocity.

The Church was crowded. In a clearing in front of the altar we could see the draped catafalque lit by many candles. The benches in the fore-ground, as I expected, were mostly filled with the bowed heads of women in their black mantillas. To my surprise they were insignificant in comparison. I had not expected to see the masses of men, young men, Falangistas and Carlists, that were crushed, standing on each others toes, into every available corner; the overflow extending through the carved Gothic portals and out into the square.

At a given moment in the service the entire congregation lit the long slender candles that, I now noticed for the first time, were held in every hand. My husband whispered this ritual was unknown on the peninsula, it was a custom individual to Mallorca. The musical chants, the incense, the muttered prayers, vibrant with emotion in the soft glow of thousands of small flickering lights, contrasted strangely, I though, with the almost suffocating atmosphere of strained explosive tension and watchful glances that darted from side to side.

When the services were over, the women were told to keep back while the men pushed through into the rapidly filling Plaza. On all sides they whispered, the electric awareness increased, hands stole cautiously to suspiciously bulging pockets. There might be a demonstration, a bomb thrown, but they were ready. They might be caught, but not unprepared!

361

Slowly the tension relaxed, the expressions of fierce determination faded, the women came out into the sunlight, little groups formed; apparently casual conversations were resumed. The low buzz of mid-day human flies settled comfortingly over the warm still square. With many, "Adios, adios, hasta luego," the groups disbursed. Our island, seemingly was again calm. For the moment nothing had happened. It brought, however, the realization; we had not known there were so many Falanges in Mallorca.

✵

The strained feeling of prolonged, restless anticipation made it impossible to remain at home and continue our now futile routine of life. The following morning found us again in Palma. The city was sparkling with news. Things had begun to happen. News, rumors – unknown but fully explained with individually enlarged details – were on every tongue. Papers were being grabbed from the hands of running newsboys. One paper said, "Soon there will be a conflict such as Spain as never seen before...." a culmination, in nothing less than CIVIL WAR, the hunt for man, crime and barbary converted into political instruments! The Culpables? The Responsibles? Lefts? Rights? Hatred, vengeance, despair! The causes are old. It is not now the hour to think of causes, but of solutions. There is no time to philosophize...it is a question of hours and minutes, it will be worse for those who still refuse to see, to act, who persist in their comfortable attitude of "Todo se arreglara" - all will arrange itself.

The troops in Morocco had rebelled against the government! The Army was in revolt! General Franco had left the Canary Islands and had taken charge of the troops and the Legion in Spanish Morocco. Everywhere the Falanges were rising to join and offer their strength to the rebels! The Civil Governor of the Balearics was confined! The Military Governor, General Goded, had taken over authority! The detained Falange leaders were being released from prison. The conflict had apparently begun.

General Goded

A State of War was declared in the Balearies. The Military Commander gave notice that "in defense of la Patria" he had assumed absolute control; he was resolved inflexibly to maintain order and authority. Anyone, for whatever cause, by act or word, showing the slightest resistance to the salvation movement ODF Spain, would be detained. "With the same exemplitude we will punish any signs of intent to instigate strikes of sabotage of any kind. Anyone in possession of arms must immediately turn them over to the barracks."

The newly appointed Civil Governor asked the citizens of Palma to resume their normal life, to open all shops, cafes, bars and cinemas. In the afternoon the Municipal Band gave a concert under the trees on the Borne – the main thoroughfare.

After issuing his orders, General Goded left in a hydroplane for Barcelona to take over the military command of the forces of Cataluna.

All telephone and telegraph communications with the mainland were cut. The familiar streets of Palma presented over night a new and strange aspect; groups of soldiers with machine guns were posted in front of all principle buildings, on all strategic corners throughout the city. The streets were patrolled by armed Falanges in blue shirts, bands of black and red bearing the Falange insignia of crossed arrows around their arms. Trucks and cars bristling with soldiers and Falanges with protruding guns, circulated the streets and roads.

Across the street from the Formentor Bar – where all Palma seemed to congregate to discuss the latest rumors, we watched the tired soldiers with their growing beards. For six days they did not leave their posts. We watched the laden trucks delivering their meals, women arriving with cigarettes, huge ensaimadas and other specially cooked dainties. The men sent them cool drinks from the bar. When at last they could be relieved, none wished to relinquish such favored posts. As one of them remarked, "If this is war, may we never have peace!" Troops marched everywhere to the accompaniment of clapping hands and enthusiastic shouts of "Viva España, Arriba España."

The next few days, filled as they were with anxiety, still held their absurd surprises and moments of humor. People we had never suspected of any political interest, suddenly blossomed forth in full Falange regalia – or as characters of suspicion. One acquaintance, a mouse-like little sculptor, turned miraculously into an efficient Falange leader strapped in a belt of businesslike guns.

Another, developed into a dastardly Communist; to the sad discomfort of a friend whose unfortunate wife, with tragic lack of discrimination, chose one of our most hectic days to deliver herself of their joyously awaited heir. Her husband had just rushed her to the clinic when to his horror soldiers arrived to remove the doctor; a communist agitator of important dimensions, so it was said. In vain did he plead that the doctor be allowed to remain until the anxious moment was over. They regretted, they could not assume the responsibility without permission from Headquarters. Frantic, he dashed for headquarters......when he returned the blessed event had taken place; the new arrival having shown her independence and disdain of a communist doctor. Obviously a full fledged Falange baby, declared the proud father - Another incident to confirm my belief that doctors and priests should refrain from politics.

⋙⋘

Then the bombing began![6] This was prefaced by the advent of a plane over Palma which sprinkled the city in leaflets of communist propaganda. The city smiled contemptuously. The following day it returned, this time its propaganda was in the form of hand grenades. Contempt turned to fury! How dare they bomb a civilian population – even with hand grenades. A few of the less brave decided the air of Palma was a trifle warm; they would spend a few weeks in the cooler atmosphere of their country houses.

That night over the radio we listened to Radio-Barcelona proclaim to the waiting world that they had that day bombed Palma of Mallorca; the rebel city now lay in smoking ruins. Palma laughed scornfully; except those who had members of their family abroad who realized the agonizing heartaches such lies would cause.

Possibly our scorn reached Barcelona for the following day the bombing began in earnest. My husband and I were buying cigarettes for the soldiers when we first noticed the hum of the planes. Before our packages could be paid for there was a deafening boom and a crash. A moment later another. I fumbled with my purse while my husband dashed out into the street. The shop owner and her two children had disappeared below the counter. As I tried to count out the money, I was surprised to find that my hands were shaking. I was not conscious, however, of fear but of a suffocating excitement, intense exhilaration. That same dreaded quivering excitement – near to nausea – one experienced at a bull-fight!

As we fell into our car a man dashed out, "Señor, go quick, quick, there are two of them. One big bomb has just fallen across the way. Go. Go." He disappeared and so did we; as fast as the car would take us. The roar of the planes sounded very near, I craned my neck and looked up from the side of the car; a huge flying monster seemed perversely to be following over us. After the first fifty yards we regained our composure and slowed down. Trying to out distance a plane going over a hundred an hour was obviously absurd.

In their excitement soldiers were rushing into the street, firing their rifles, they popped from all sides; an erratic modern melody to the accompaniment of the low, steady, pup-pup-pup-pup-pup-pup of the machine guns. Pup-pup-pup-pup-pup they went again.

We stopped at the first post of soldiers and delivered our packages to the slightly astonished Sargent. His face clearly expressed his views of people who chose such a time to deliver cigarettes; his words extended gracious thanks. All a prelude to the vital interest of the moment. "Yes, the swine are using real bombs today. That last has done plenty of damage." He shook his head, " If only we had some anti-air!" With heads tilted back we watched the giant birds circling and white in the sunlight overhead. Boom! Then another – Boom! At any other time we would have been filled with admiration for their beauty. Now their grace meant death! And was repaid with resentful hatred. A little below them, against the blue of the sky, I could see puffs of whitish smoke

At the Battlefront at San Servera

from the bursting of shells of our answering guns. If only we could reach them! But they were flying high.

We moved on to the next post which was by the railway station. As we drew up a car with a red cross flag and soldiers on the running boards passed at full speed in the direction of the hospital; it held the first victims of the bombs. Later we heard there had been four killed and seven wounded.

ॐ॰ॐ

The bombings became a daily occurrence; twice daily occurrence would be more accurate as from now on we received regular morning visits at eleven thirty and again at five thirty in the afternoons. Some days one plane, some two, three, even seven. During the day, in consequence, the city became deserted except for soldiers and Falanges. To buy supplies all marketing must be done before eight in the morning. After that the shops were closed, the streets dark with people laden with food baskets going for safety to the hills; until the following morning at five when they would return for more provisions. The terror of the people was pathetic; it was their first experience of war tactics and chaos on their Island of Calm. After the first bombing, the roads leading out of the city were crowded with people lugging mattresses, bird cages, baskets of food, followed by straggling children and dogs. Every cart and car that the city possessed was heaped with white faced trembling human bundles. In one cave, in the hills back of Palma, seventy people remained in horror without food for three days and nights. Senseless panic ruled the stricken city.

We soon found that panic was contagious; the foreigners caught it also – English, German, French and Americans – they clustered in terrified groups of indecision. Many had their homes and businesses here and were torn between their possessions and their fear of death.

Warships were now crowding the harbor as well as the usual steamers of call. The radio, newspapers and posted notices now warned all foreigners to leave. The steamers and warships would take all refugees to Gibraltar or Marseilles. The American Consul arrived to take charge of the Americans. An English officer with the usual British efficiency toured the island to notify all foreign and British subjects that after the following morning they would not be responsible for anyone deciding to remain. But here were few who remained. I watched the heavily laden tenders going back and forth, back and forth from the landing to the ships. When the last one left, carrying all my foreign friends and acquaintances I watched it go with uncertain feelings. For the first time it occurred to me that possibly an island was not the most comfortable spot from which to watch a revolution. Once the last boat left there was no escape. The horrible atrocities committed by the communists came oftener to mind and with them the threats of the communist in our own village of Peguera.

These threats had come as a distant shock. If we had thought of it at all it was to flatter ourselves that we were liked by our surrounding peasantry. What reason had we to think otherwise when at one time or another most of them had worked for us and our relations had been most friendly. Their men had built our house, had terraced our garden, one farm supplied us with milk, another with eggs and chickens. We had always attended their local fiestas, contributed to their various causes and collections.

These cherished illusions of mutual sympathy were destined to be exploded by the first bombs thrown from the attacking communist planes. Our unpleasant awakening came about in the following way.

The first day of the revolt, the men of our household had rushed with enthusiasm to inscribe themselves as volunteers – we had two cousins and a friend staying with us at the time – as they were all officers retired since the revolution of '31.

With the commencement of the bombing they were often sent off on different commissions which left the women of the household without the usual comfort of male protection. My maid[7] and the cook soon became hysterical; they wished to return immediately to the safety of their own village. I tried to calm them with the assurance that they were perfectly safe, what could possible happen? "If the Reds should come the men of the village will protect us until our soldiers arrive!"

"No, no, señora, you do not understand, you must not trust them. They are only waiting for the support of their comrades to come here and cut all our throats and burn the house down! They have told us so many times. Now that the red planes have arrived they say their friends will come soon, soon!"

Although this was a shock, it was hardly news that could be taken seriously. It was really too absurd! However.....it seemed as well to saunter to the village for a casual talk with the little cafe owner. We had been having a strike of farm hands on the neighboring fincas; this might serve as an introductory subject of conversation.

In spite of the fact that the price of almonds had dropped to half their value in the past three years the men were now demanding double wages, shorter hours and better housing conditions. The owners, many of the peasants themselves, had replied that the crops would have to be left to rot, with no market for their produce they could no longer afford the old wages to say nothing of the new demands.

But it was not the problem of the wages which seemed most to upset the men, it was the idea that they had to sleep on the floor – what more perfect example of abuse for their propaganda! "You do not know, Señora, how we are treated. We are made to sleep on a bit of straw on the floor, crowded together like animals. Such conditions cannot go on. We will not go back to work until we are given beds and treated like men!"

"You are right, Juan! It is time you learned to sleep on beds but I hardly see that you can blame this on the proprietors. You know, as well as I, that in most of the farm houses on the island the peasants, both owners and men, sleep on the floor under just these same conditions, whether from habit of preference I can't say!" [8]

I knew of one progressive owners who had sent his son to England to study the more modern methods of farming. When his son returned he had attempted many reforms; one of them in the housing conditions of his men. He had installed beds and mattresses; in less than a week the beds had been stacked outside or converted for other uses. The men had insisted they were more comfortable as they were; they wanted nothing to do with his foreign innovations.

But this incident made no impression on my companion. He obviously disbelieved me. I, with all of my kind were against them. His expression settled into stubborn animosity, "Si, si, Señora, I know what you think but we have a right to live like men, to earn a living wage, to have food for our children and soon now we will have it!"

"But that is absurd, everyone wants you to live like men and have food for your children. Here on our island your children have never gone hungry. But you must see that you cannot ask for double wages when the farmers have no market for their crops. Most of last years almonds are still unsold. These problems can only be solved slowly, by the government changing their custom restrictions, making new commercial treaties, creating new markets and helping the farmer as well as the laborer until changes in present conditions can be made. Taxes must be raised, horded money put into circulation for the benefit of the country...." I realized suddenly that my listener understood not one word of what I was saying. As I paused he continued, "No, no, Señora, you will see, soon we will take the fincas and we shall have everything."

"Yes, but that will not solve your problem. Look what happened in Madrid when the men took over the tramlines. They immediately doubled all salaries and shortened the hours of work. All very well until funds came to an end, then the worker's committee had to beg the government to take them over."

"No, no. We understand. We have been told you would tell us just such things. But is is not true. Soon you will see."

"And what are we going to see? You are surely not thinking of doing the same dreadful things that the communists have done on the peninsula?"

He hesitated, then nodded slowly. "Come now, Juan, we have always been friends, you cannot tell me that you would actually come to our house to kill us! You can't think such things seriously?"

"Well, Señora, maybe I wouldn't but there are many who would."

I could only marvel at the power that could, with such devilish efficiency, transform kindly lovable peasants into instruments of death and destruction!

The following week my husband was made Naval Commander of the Southern coast of the island and we left for the port of Campos.

Our house was a rather primitive, one story affair built on the beach facing the small island of Cabrera: lately taken by the Reds. The vivid description of the conquest of this island as told over Radio-Barcelona had cheered us for days. If all of the red "conquests" were like this one we felt we had little to worry about. According to their reports, after forcing the submission of the garrison they had marched in triumph from village to village where they were acclaimed with feverish enthusiasm by the inhabitants, flags flying, bands playing. Apart from the lighthouse keeper there were held a dozen carabineros with their wives and children who lived in the few houses on the tiny port. Such was the garrison they had so valiantly conquered. The only other inhabitants consisted of a number of wild goats and a fair amount of rabbits. There were no villages on the island. As it was without provisions of any kind its only possible use was as a temporary base in the event they contemplated an invasion of Mallorca.

It was for the preparation against just this invasion that all our efforts were now being centered. My husband was away most of the day and night preparing and supervising the vigilance of the coast. Trucks laden with soldiers passed to and fro. At night I could hear the heavy guns rumble by as they were taken to their hidden positions. The nights were filled with activity.

The days were sleepy and quiet; our only diversion was to watch the planes as they passed overhead on their way to the bombing of Palma, plus an occasional glimpse of an aggravating submarine that hovered about Cabrera. But our peace was not for long; it soon ended after the arrival in our midst of a young Mallorquin by the name of Crespi, the proud owner of an old avionetta, whose sole ambition it appeared was to bomb and sink the red submarine. On the second day his impatiently awaited opportunity arrived. At once he was off, with the entire village rushing to the beach to watch the fun.

The submarine was passing slowly between two islands when it first sighted the small plane. It quickened its speed and started to zigg-zagg crazily. Crespi circled, straightened, then swooped. We held our breath as we watched his first bomb drop slightly ahead into the sea and heard the pup-pup-pup of the protesting defense guns. He mounted and circled again. Another bomb, then another. One fell very near the mark.

Crespi – The Mallorcan Aviator

We shrieked our enthusiasm as we saw him returning; his small supply of ammunition, we thought, having come to an end. We watched our hero proudly as he circled the sandy stretch which served as a landing field. His maneuvers were repeated several times before we realized something was wrong. Suddenly the motor stopped and to our horror we saw the plane dive, crash on its nose and turn slowly on its back.

Before anyone could reach him he had crawled out from under, intact and still holding in his hand a live bomb. Why the bomb had not exploded, our hero been blown to atoms was a mystery that remained unsolved. Providence works in strange ways! The following morning we were again quietly contemplating the red planes pass when to our surprise they turned and started to circle. We were going to be bombed! A retaliation, obviously, for our attack on their submarine the day before!

The plane was now overhead as we watched it in fascination. The first bomb fell with a deafening report not twenty metres away on the beach. The astonished and terrified villagers scuttled indoors, hysterical with fright. I made for the thickest wall I could find, collecting a sobbing old woman and a young girl on the way. We flattened ourselves against the wall and waited. Crash! Another fell on the other side of the house. We could hear shrapnel hit the walls, one bit splintered the shutters on the window. For more than half an hour bombs rained around us.

When at last the planes departed, a demented rush to evacuate began. Women and children ran creaming through the streets. Laden carts, wagons and old cars piled with bundles of hastily accumulated belongings dashed past, driven madly by shouting men. In less than an hour not a soul remained; except for an occasional soldier, a few stray chickens and dogs forgotten in the panic, the streets were empty.

There had been but two casualties. Providence had again taken a hand. One bomb had fallen close to a house, blowing in the door and seriously wounding two of the inhabitants huddled within. Strangely both were reds from a neighboring village. Before they could be lifted into the cart that was to take them to the nearest hospital, Civil Guards arrived with the warrant for their arrest. They were suspected of attempting to spy out the positions of our hidden game.

When discussing this coincidence I was told of another, even more strange. When the red planes had bombed the village of Inca there had been but one casualty, also a communist. When he had seen the red planes overhead he had dashed into the street waving his clenched fists in their comrade's salute and crying, "Viva Russia!" Before the shouted acclaim had died on his lips, he was blown to atoms by a falling bomb. "Truly a sign of God's vengeance" was the awed opinion whispered by the devout villagers.

Undoubtedly we owed the attack to Crespi's little plane which still lay a gleaming target on the sandy stretch in back of the scattered houses of our one main street. As it had been righted the enemy was ignorant of the fact that is was not a useless wreck, their attack but a waster of ammunition. That night our soldiers moved it to an isolated field where it was left, only slightly hidden, as a bait to detract any future planes from the houses and barracks.

The bait worked. At six the next morning we were favored with another visit at which at least twenty bombs were sacrificed on our tempting wreck. Their submarine was obviously undesirous of another bombing; they were taking no chances. Every night the poor remains were carefully removed – an apparent attempt made to hide them – every day the red planes returned intent on their work of destruction. Our men were in high glee over the success of their strategy. In the end it cost the enemy well over a hundred bombs, a pilot and a good plane.

We were also deluged with propaganda leaflets calling on all workers to rebel against the Military Fascists and join the liberating forces that in a short time will come to save you! Soldiers, rebel and kill your leaders. You do not have to obey their orders! Join the loyal forces! These inflammatory epistles of the "legal" government were signed by representatives of the the General Union of Workers, the Socialist Party and the United Youths.

During the first attack our men were ordered not to fire, to give no sign of life. Without opposition the red pilot became more and more bold

Plane Brought Down on Punt Amer Beach

descending within a few hundred feet to drop his bombs. Suddenly we retaliated with fire from two hidden machine guns. Our strategy was again successful; he departed hurriedly leaving a trail of smoke behind. Watching, we saw him make for Cabrera. Our bullets must have hit a vital spot as he was forced into the sea between two islands. Later the crippled plane was towed into port by the submarine.

The following day we were shelled in retaliation; the shells falling on an isolated stretch of beach. No damage was done. An order was now issued notifying the villagers to return, life must continue normally; all shops and cafes must reopen. Anyone not complying within three days would have their property confiscated. Slowly and fearfully they returned. A semblance of calm was restored; for the first time in many days we had fresh bread and milk, vegetables and meat were again to be had. During the interval we had lived on a diet of deserted chickens, supplemented by the contents of old tins.

When a plane was now heard the men rushed for refuge to the small caves and crevices that honey combed the beach, the women and children were herded into an ancient underground oven. Although between times life continued almost normally, I made the unpleasant personal discovery that eight days of continuous bomb dodging had had their effect on my nerves.

But our renewed calm was not for long; news of the red conquest of our sister island of Ibiza, with grim details of more atrocities, again threw the villagers into a state of panic and despair. Remembering the lying descriptions given over the radio of the bombing of Palma, the exaggerations of their occupation of Cabrera, we refused to believe these latest reports without reliable confirmation. Unfortunately we were to receive tragic confirmation from four eye-witnesses who had escaped on a small fishing boat; four horrible days spent in the blazing sun without food or water. Amongst the survivors was the mayor of an Ibithian village. One of the refugees died from the results of exposure shortly after reaching our port of Andraitx. We now knew the invasion of our own island was imminent.

As there was but a narrow stretch of water between us and their base at Cabrera it was thought possible that we might be favored with the brunt of the disembarkment. In the event of a night landing the houses on the beach would be between two fires, our own guns in back, the landing reds in front. In consequence the village was again evacuated. I was ordered back to Palma.

To my surprise I found Palma very changed in the short time I had been away. On the surface everything was normal; the city went with calm determination about its daily business. Only when sirens screamed their warning of the approach of enemy planes was there a rush for doorways marked REFUGIO. In a few moments the streets were emptied. Only with the second safety siren did the people emerge again from the cellars to go quietly on, seemingly oblivious to the interruption.

Along one street I noticed a long patiently waiting queue, three or four abreast. When I inquired for what they were waiting for, I was told the Military Commander of the Island had issued an appeal for gold. Completely cut off from the mainland our supplies must be bought from foreign nations. With the present devaluated currency we should have to pay in gold. I was witnessing the response to his appeal. My throat tightened with emotion as I noticed the quantity of peasants, the tranquil resignation on their weather-worn faces; for the salvation of their country they had come to offer their few gold pieces, the gold buttons from the sleeves of their regional costumes, the trinkets that had been treasured and handed down for generations, the gold that represented the dowries of

Gold & Valuables Donated to the War Effort

their daughters. Looking at the preponderance of the peasantry in the waiting line I wondered if the wealthier classes would respond with equal sacrifice.

But calm was only on the surface. Underneath I found the emotions of the people keyed to the snapping point. Unspent passion would flare up on unexpected faces. Every tongue carried tales of horrors they were powerless to avenge. Every foreign warship that entered the harbour brought new evidence of atrocities being perpetuated by the reds. Newspapers were scanned for new causes of indignation and rage. Resentment was being stirred to dangerous hatred against certain foreign powers that still stupidly prattled of the necessity of upholding the "legal" government of Spain – A "legal" government of Spain that was Russian – a government whose apparent idea of law and order was to allow and encourage senseless slaughter, the burning alive of priests and helpless nuns, the violation of women, the mutilation of innocent children and the destruction of priceless treasures of history and art. Nations, many of whose representative papers still persisted in describing as "rebels" and "insurgents" the men who were giving their lives to save not only their own country but the civilization from the contagion of class hatred, turned to madness; from an epidemic of such insidiously aroused brutality and cruelty that is made the most hideous episodes of the French and Russian revolutions pale in comparison.

Daily we listened to harrowing descriptions of eye-witnesses of such viciousness as the murder of the Naval officers in Cartegena; bound and thrown into the sea with weights tied to their feet, of the murder of the hostages of the prison ships in Barcelona who to save ammunition had been drowned in the same inexcusable way.

From an officer on a British warship I heard the following details of their rescue of sixty nuns. The necessary permission to evacuate had been applied for to the committee – the representatives of the anarchist F.A.I., the C.N.T., the U.G.T., the P.O.U.M., etc. - but had been refused.

Casualty of the War

Permission was only grudgingly given for the three or four English nuns numbered amongst the sixty; who stubbornly refused to leave without their sisters. Persistently hoping to be able to wangle more favorable replies, the officers of the ship invited the different representatives on board one evening for drinks. After several hours of flattering attentions and freely circulating cocktails, the mess room rang with loud protestations of friendship, the atmosphere became matey. In a rash burst of geniality one of the committee asked what they in turn could do to show their appreciation of such hospitality. The hoped for moment had arrived – he was asked for the lives of the sixty nuns. There was an awkward silence broken at last by a welcome "Caramba!" Yes, why not, after all what were sixty miserable nuns in return for such hospitality, nothing must be allowed to stand in the way of their friendship! Without delay the nuns were fetched and put on board before the committee with more sober daylight could repent of their generosity.

In spite of the incomprehensible attitude of the British government – under the influence of their Soviet-minded Mr. Eden – too much praise cannot be awarded to the British Navy for their ceaseless humanitarian efforts which have resulted in the rescue, from worse than death, of thousands of innocent victims. I asked one officer how, after having seen with his own eyes the horrors committed by the Communists in Spain, he could account for the seeming blindness of the British opinion, as voiced by articles in the *London Times* to the effect that no illusions must be made, the British public prefers Communism to Fascism. He could only answer that being a sailor he did not pretend to fathom the intricacies of politics, he only regretted that more influential men could not have witnessed personally a few of the horrors he had had the misfortune of seeing.

❦

The disembarkment took place on the southern coast of the island at Porto Cristo and the beach of Punt Amer early on the Sunday morning of August 16th. The tension and dreaded anticipation under which we had been living was such that the news came, I think, as a relief; the worst at last had happened! There was now something to fight, something on which to vent pent up emotions.

Our troops and Falange militia were rushed to the front. The protection of the capital was left to the "segunda fila", old men, civilians who clasped their guns with pride and fierce determination.

We hung on the radio for news! Crowds waited in anxious silence for the proclamations of the Military and Civil Governors. "Be calm, Mallorquines, the Reds shall not pass! Our valiant soldiers and our beloved Falange are hourly advancing, the enemy shall be forced back into the sea. Soon you shall hear that not a red remains on our island. Go to your homes in peace, rest in the knowledge that your protection is in good hands."

And daily we waited for the news that not a red remained. Days passed. Anxiety increased. The realization grew that victory would not be easy; our troops were outnumbered, our advance checked by the continuous, murderous rain of bombs and machine gun fire from the red planes. It began to be obvious that victory was not so assured. Our one cry now was for planes. Why were we not sent planes? Daily we were told that General Franco was sending them, the planes were on their way, they would arrive the end of the week, the beginning of the week, tomorrow, day after tomorrow. But no planes arrived. Our troops in the interim retired to "better" positions and again to "better" positions!

The Destruction of Buildings in Porto Cristo

It was not until the fourth day after the landing that I knew my husband was safe. I had heard he had been amongst the first arrivals at Porto Cristo; after that nothing. Then he and another Captain of their battery arrived for a hasty conference with the Commandante Militar; after which - a rush for fresh clothes. Like all of the volunteer officers they had been dressed in monos – overalls, of which now only muddy shreds remained to tell of days spent throwing themselves on the ground to avoid the bursting shells.

Avidly, I listened to their snatches of first hand news. Yes, everything was alright. They were now in better positions, they were holding their lines. Their men were wonderful, poor devils, they were getting used now to the bombs. God, if we only had some planes. Knowing we have no defense against them the "canallas" swoop right down on top of us to pepper us with their machine gun fire. But we did get one of them; he fell out at sea. A bit more news from the prisoners; they say they haven't had food for three days. There is a lot of discontent amongst them; they were told they had only to land and walk into Palma, the villagers were waiting to hail them as their deliverers, they were promised rich loot. Some of them have refused to fight. Don't worry we'll pull through. With that they were off.

New men were being called daily. In front of the barracks you could see them lined up in the weirdest assortment of clothes; the uniforms were giving out. Here and there groups were being put through the paces by exhausted officers. Girls dressed in the blue shirts of the womens' Falange were handing out cigarettes from big baskets. Camions laden with new rifles drew up. Other camions crowded with men off for the front were waiting for last minute orders. Shouts of Viva España! Arriba España! Snatches of the stirring Falange hymn,

Cara al sol, con la camisa nueva	Face to the sun, in the new
que tu bordaste en rojo ayer....	shirt that you embroidered
la muerte si me lleva y no te vuelve	yesterday in red....if death
a ver.....	should take me and I don't return
Volveran banderas victoriosas.....	Our flags shall return victorious.
Arriba escuadras, a vencer!	Up squadrons, to win!
Que en España empieza a amanacer!	Spain in beginning to rise!

More days passed. War was making itself felt; everywhere women were frantically sewing on shirts, trousers, underwear for the soldiers. Material was giving out; as cloth, buttons and thread grew scarce they became more fanciful in color. Donations of supplies, food kitchens had been started for the poorer families who men were at the front. You could no longer buy sugar, coffee or rice. The supply of foreign tinned goods had come to an end. Olive oil and potatoes were being rationed. Gasoline permits were becoming more and more difficult to obtain. There were new appeals for gold. Women with baskets made the rounds of houses and shops; collections were being made of everything, everywhere.

Travel on the roads was becoming more difficult and dangerous. Old men and young boys with itching fingers and precariously pointing guns stopped you at every bridge or turning, every village entrance and exit. It was usually wise to have a Falange escort.

Going back and forth to Nanacor – headquarters for the front – with contributions of cigarettes, anis, herez, biscuits for the soldiers of my husband's battery or clothes for the officers, I heard many stories. One boy had been with the first group of Falanges to attack on the morning of the landing. They had been ordered to advance down a hill and take up positions behind a clump of bushes at the bottom. Half way down they saw what they took to be another group of Falanges advancing to meet him. When they were almost up to them, they were suddenly fired upon. To their bewilderment they realized too late the others were communists camouflaged in blue Falange shirts. His younger brother had been shot before his eyes. He still looked bewildered and unbelieving.

Another had had his brother taken prisoner. They had been in the thick of it for six days with little time for food or sleep and no relief. Exhausted, the night before they had settled down to snatch a few hours of rest, leaving some to guard while the others slept. They awoke to find themselves surrounded; a few fought through and escaped in the dark. His brother was missing. He wondered whether he was still alive – how was he to tell his mother. Silence – in which we passed kilometres of strangely still farms, here and there cattle grazing with wise unconcern, occasional children with arms outstretched in the Falange salute shouting lustily, "Arriba España!" "Yes," he continued his thoughts, "I suppose by now he is dead. I hope so, for him it would be better."

Some came back with trophies, red arm bands marked U.G.T., a stained red shirt, an ugly looking knife with horrid smears, "Blood", said its new young owner with pride. One showed me an impressive silver cigarette case, "Oh, yes, these communists, they do themselves well!"

When things looked at their worst – the reds had just landed a large number of reinforcements from their "hospital" ship, the "Marquis de Gomilla", their planes had dropped announcements giving us twenty-four hours to surrender, several of our smaller ports had been shelled – albeit feebly, it did not improve our optimism – we were notified there was to be a bombardment of Palma by air and sea. Their dreaded "Jaime I" and "Libertad" were known to have left Malaga in our direction. The attack was scheduled for midday. At eleven we watched with mixed feelings the departure from the harbour of all foreign warships. The exodus was led by the British, the Americans close behind followed by two Germans and the Italians.

At a quarter to twelve, we – which included the American Counsul – were near the lookout of a fort, in the hills high above Palma; preferred seats for the spectacle which was to take place in fifteen minutes, a spectacle which might mean anything between the destruction of our city and the sinking of the red fleet by our fortress guns.

We stood expectant in the hushed glare of the noon sun, eyes straining the sky and horizon for the first sight of the enemy. The minutes dragged by; twelve came and went, twelve o'five, ten, fifteen, twenty. A faint whirr was heard in the distance; the planes were coming. Several white specks were now discernible. We hardly breathed as they grew in size. At last they were over us; huge white hydros. They began to descend lower and lower, circling the helpless,city. Nerves taut, we waited for the first shattering boom! None came. Why weren't they bombing! A shout went up. We saw the men at the fort running out waving their arms in the air, patting each other on the back, shaking hands. Stumbling over rocks and bushes we ran to join them. "Nuestras aviones! Nuestras aviones!" Our planes! Our planes! They could hardly have chosen a more dramatic moment for their arrival.

By one o'clock we decided the bombardment was off; now that we had planes to defend us, had the reds changed their minds? We returned to Palma to find the city in a state of delirium of joy. Vivas and arribas rang out on all sides from the grinning, excited faces. Our long awaited pilots were accompanied to their hotel by a mob hysterical with relief. A few days later more planes arrived from General Franco; this time some fast chasers to protect our bombers. The day of their arrival they took the enemy by surprise, bringing down and destroying five planes and killing the commander of the red air squadron.

Our planes now took the offensive, in turn the enemy lines were bombed without respite. From that day on not one red plane reappeared. We intercepted frantic radios from Captain Bayo – the commander of the red forces – demanding help from Barcelona and the return of their planes to protect their lines. His S.O.S. went unanswered. Their ships were bombed by our pilots and withdrew to a healthier distance. Their men were becoming demoralized; at night from our lines they could be heard fighting amongst themselves.

Radio-Barcelona was heard calling for volunteers for Mallorca. They would be paid ten pesetas a day. A new, bigger and better expedition was being equipped! Let them come, we are now prepared! We had planes and more than twelve thousand men under arms. Orders were given for our concentrated offensive; the attack that was to free us once and for all from our unwelcome intruders. The night before it was to begin, I drove my husband to the front lines. He had been on a hurried commission to Palma returning too late for the last camions leaving for the front. In consequence, I was commanded into service.

From Manacor, the road to Porto Cristo slopes gently to the sea. Once beyond the village we drove without lights; our route lay in full view of the red lines and within range of their guns. We crept through the stillness; tree stumps and boundary posts emerging from the dim light to make my heart thump; each one an imagined Red. Some I know had filtered through our lines.

We arrived at our destination, were stopped and gave the whispered password. The position of the battery was on a small hill dominating the port. The sea was glimmering silver in the moonlight. There was not a sound to be hear; surely this was not war! We climbed to a lookout and I was shown the enemy lines below us. They were very near; by crawling quietly forward our men had been able to listen to them conversing. I asked why there was no firing going on. I was told that both sides were having supper; supper over, someone would fire in the air and the war would recommence. I was introduced to the battery mascot, a pup from an abandoned farmhouse that had attached itself to the men. One soldier told me proudly that is was very clever; when it heard the planes overhead it flattened itself on the ground beside them, not moving until the danger was past.

Our advance pushed forward rapidly. Under the incessant shelling of our guns, the bombing of our planes, the red lines were in hasty retreat. Dawn on the final day of the battle saw the arrival of the red reinforcements. They never landed; what was first taken to be a disembarkment was soon discovered to be the reimbarkment of the surviving red forces.

The disordered haste of their departure was such that quantities of guns, rifles, munitions, cars, an armored truck, valuable medical supplies had been abandoned. Even their loot in gold, jewelry and church ornaments, mostly stolen from the rich peasantry of Ibizia, had been left behind.

Amongst the prisoners were French and Russian communists and an Austrian anti-Fascisti officer. Put off by our rapid advance, we captured five of their best machine gunners, they were women; the sans-culottes of our Spanish revolution - in spite of the red cross bands tied around their arms. When ordered to surrender they had all raised their clenched fists in the communist salute and shouted, "Viva Russia!" They were not cowards like many of the men who had given themselves up with cries of "Arriba España!"

A day or two following our victory my husband took me on a tour of the battlefields. In Porto Cristo the Sanitary force was still at work; the air reeked with the fumes of burning bodies heaped here and there on smoldering piles. The red losses had been heavy; they left well over a thousand dead. The streets were littered with debris, the decaying carcasses of mules and

Destruction Inside a Porto Cristo Church

horses, corners and crossings were barricaded with stacked furniture and mattresses. The houses that had escaped shell fire were perforated with holes, knocked through for gun positions; the filth inside indescribable. In one house there were twenty-seven dead. It was curious how callous one soon became to death.

I also visited the remains of the village church; the altar lay in blackened ruins, the sacred statues heaped in corners; the majority had had their heads hacked off.

Isolated reds were still being found; while there we saw two taken prisoners. They had been hiding on the outskirts of the village. They were probably young. It was difficult to tell by their haggard, unkempt, bearded faces.

Our victory at last complete it was celebrated by a triumphant march into Palma of our returning men. The days program began with an impressive Mass of thanksgiving held in the open air. Although it rained from early morning no one minded; the streets were impassable, nothing could dampen the spirits of the enthusiastic, shouting people. We witnessed a proud display. The man-force of the island was now under arms, for hours we watched them pass; infantry, machine gunners, Carlists with bright red berets, blue-shirted Falange, the valiant "death battalion" with shaved heads and many beards, the captured enemy cannon, several of the damaged red planes, dozens of Communist and Catalan flags dragged in dishonour through the mud. Many of the men had their mascots; pet roosters, rabbits, goats, dogs, one carried three small kittens in his cape.

A well deserved peace was restored to our Island of Calm.

Cut off as we were nearly four months had passed without news of family or friends on the peninsula. Many we knew were in Madrid at the outbreak of hostilities; the harrowing details of life in the capital were such that we avoided dwelling on the subject.

Due to the shortage of Naval officers, my husband was now ordered to the mainland; via Rome and Gibraltar. In Rome to our joy we met several members of the family from whom we heard the following varied accounts.

My husband's brother, with his wife and infant daughter, was visiting his in-laws in San Sebastian when the revolution commenced. As well-known members of the aristocracy, they were under immediate surveillance; any attempt at flight over the frontier was in consequence impossible.

Through the help of devoted servants they were able to disappear into hiding on the morning their arrest was to have taken place. Daily it became more obvious that their escape from San Sebastian was imperative. A house to house search for them was being made. Separately, as members of their cook's family, they were smuggled to a neighboring Spanish port. Although personally loyal, the cook was a communist and as such able to obtain the necessary passes.

Hardly had they arrived when the wife's mother and father were discovered, arrested and put in prison. The daughters who fought to accompany their parents were brutally beaten back. My sister-in-law was separated also from her husband; with a friend, he was in hiding in another part of the town. It would have been fatal to attempt to see him. Their situation was desperate. Every day brought the news of the deaths of relatives and acquaintances.

Through mutual foreign friends their plight was brought to the attention of an Englishman whom it was hoped would help them. The rescue work of this heroic old man, who alone, with total disregard of personal danger, accomplished the escape of several hundred innocent victims, would fill a fascinating volume. He became in truth the Scarlet Pimpernel of the Spanish revolution.

For several years he had spent his summers in this northern seaport; occupying a small house in the poorer quarters of the town to be close to the people in whose local problems he took a sympathetic interest. He encouraged their supportive efforts by awarding prizes, helped them obtain reforms and privileges and so gained their trust and affection. Due to their friendship and his influence with many young radicals he was able to save the lives of countless unfortunates.

Here, as in all ports, British ships were evacuating their nationals. Amongst these many nurses accompanied by their small charges whom they refused to leave; the parents in many cases being dead or in prison. In contrast to the loyalty of these splendid English women, there was one despicable exception; a secretary to one of the Consulate officials. Part of this creature's duty was to check off the departing British subjects.

When the nurses arrived with their charges she refused, on the excuse that they were Spanish subjects, to allow the children – some infants in arms – to be taken on board. Not one nurse, however, departed, all preferring possible death to the desertion of their children. This incredible situation was eventually brought to the attention of those in authority, the inhuman interference of this creature brought to an end. Our small niece, in the arms of my sister-in-law's youngest sister, was sent out in this way with other rescued children through the help of the "Pimpernel". Soon after he was able to smuggle out the two remaining sisters; their escape was not easy.

In a small dinghy he had rowed them to the side of the waiting ship, as they were about to board they were discovered. The communist guard on shore hastened alongside prepared if necessary to remove them by force. Against their wishes and the advice of the Captain he had taken full responsibility; returning with the communists as hostage. When last seen he was surrounded by an angry mob. With the influence of his radical friends, he was later released.

Through other means, which I am unable to disclose, he also effected the escape of the mother and father from prison; both parents and daughters meeting unexpectedly in Biarritz. They had arrived through different routes, within a few days of each other. Their tireless rescuer was unable however to manage the escape of my brother-in-law and friend before the departure of the last British boat; on which he left himself hoping to arrange for another to return.

One stormy night the two men, accompanied by my brother-in-law's dog whom he refused to leave, made a last desperate attempt at escape in a stolen rowboat. Before they had gone far it capsized. He saved the dog, but passports and identification papers were lost. With their last hope gone they returned dripping and chilled to their hiding place.

My mother-in-law, waiting over the frontier in despair, was introduced to the "Pimpernel". He had finally been able to arrange for the call of another boat, was returning himself by train that night to continue the rescue work of those still remaining in the hands of the reds. He assured her he would again cross the frontier with her son; he was now an old man, life was no longer very dear, the little time left him he would give gladly to help those to whom he had become so sincerely attached in these last terrible weeks.

As the Nationalists were closing in, the situation was becoming more desperate. The trapped reds venting their rage on innocent prisoners, the massacres mounted daily in total and in horror.

Unable now, under the increased vigilance, to smuggle out any further victims he was forced to think of another plan. As many of the red leaders were now equally interested in contriving the escape of their families he was able to make terms: for the lives of sixty of his friends he would agree to arrange the escape of sixty of theirs. They immediately wanted to know the names of the sixty he proposed to take. Knowing he would never obtain permission if the names were known he replied, that realizing the danger to them if the names of their people become known he agreed to take their sixty with no questions asked; his sixty likewise to remain unknown.

When the anxiously awaited boat arrived, all was prepared. The embarkation took place cautiously at night; in equal numbers the enemy refugees were taken on board. The last to leave was the "pimpernel" himself accompanied by my brother-in-law and his friend; they had lived five appalling weeks in a small damp cellar.

When the boat arrived in the French port strategy had again to be used; the quai was crowded with reds ready and waiting to attack any landing white refugees. Our people were hidden discretely below. Not until hours after the communists had landed, the quai again cleared, were they taken off.

In other parts of the peninsula family and friends had not fared so well.

In Madrid, the Conde de Torre-Arias had been brutally murdered. His crime being that he paid taxes amounting to several thousand pesetas a year. Walking along the street with his wife he had been accosted by a group of communists who demanded his identification papers. All he had with him was a tax receipt; enough to send him to his death. In spite of the pleas of his wife he was dragged away. The following day his mutilated body was found amongst others at the cemetery where many of the murders took place; it saved the executioners the bother of cartage. The beheaded body of another relative was found here; he had taken precaution of tying his visiting card around his ankle for identification.

A cousin had been betrayed while trying, with a friend, to escape in disguise. Dressed as a peasant woman she had been about to step into a third class carriage of a train when she was arrested. The guard was accompanied by her maid who pointed her out saying, "That is no peasant woman; she is my mistress the Countess-------." Since this incident nothing further has been heard of her.

Another friend owed his escape to a cigar. He had been in prison for several weeks under the strain of momentarily expecting his final visit to the cemetery. One morning he was called. He accompanied his red guard in silence out of the prison, down several streets, around several corners. His guard stopped suddenly, "Señor Marques, it will be quite safe for you to go alone from here." He looked at the man in unbelieving astonishment; he was asked if he recognized his face. "No, my friend, I do not think I do." The guard proceeded to describe a dinner he had given at a smart hotel just prior to the revolution. He concluded by saying, "I was a waiter at your dinner. When it was over you thanked each of us in turn, giving us each a cigar. I appreciated that. Good luck, Señor Marques!" In another moment he was alone and free. His life for a cigar!

A gentle, charming woman of our acquaintance is now in France, hopelessly insane. She and her husband, bound and gagged, were force to watch the violation of their sixteen-year-old daughter. Their amusement over, the Marxists then proceeded to murder the husband and daughter before her eyes. She was unconscious and rescued.

From the small village of Posadas, in the province of Cordoba, which borders the estate of a friend we were given the following enlightening details of the rule of the communist government of Spain.

The first victims of the "liberating" red militia – who took possession of the village on the eighteenth of July – were two young girls, sisters who were considered the beauties of the countryside. They were ruthlessly violated by one after the other of the comrades; their agony enduring for hours. Their bodies, with that of their mother, were found horribly mutilated at the bottom of a well. House after house was explored for further objects of pleasure; their fancy mostly being appeased by little girls between the ages of eight and ten. The massacre of the parents was carried out methodically. Each day a new street was checked off their list, entire families were wiped out. This butchery continued for nearly six weeks – until the arrival of our troops. Before their retreat they slaughtered the few that remained; leaving not one living creature to greet our men. Of the population of an entire village only two boys, who had escaped into the hills, were left.

At our entry into another village women and children were found hanging by their pierced jaws on butcher hooks along the wall. In another an old man, with his two small grandchildren on his knees, had been nailed to his chair; they had then been covered with gasoline and burned alive. These are but a few of the atrocities described to me by reliable eye-witnesses. Thousands of such cases authenticated by official documents exist in the files of Señor de Sangroniz, General Franco's chief of public services.

I regret if the description of these horrors has shocked the sensibilities of some of my readers; it could not be avoided. It is obvious from opinions expressed in many English and American newspapers and periodicals that there still exists in certain circles of these countries the most appalling ignorance as to facts. Articles that declare at all costs the "legal" government must be upheld and helped against the "rebels". Articles that profess the most profound sympathy for the loyal men fighting so bravely for their liberty and democracy!

"Liberty" that judges it a crime for a man to wear a tie – for this reason alone many have been shot on sight in Barcelona -"liberty" that condemns to death even those of the same party whose views may be slightly more humane or temperate. A "democracy" that ignores the political rights of its citizens in over sixty-five percent of this territory! A "democracy" patterned on anarchy and imposed by torture, murder, destruction! Such is the Liberty and Democracy of the legal government of Spain as directed and supervised by Soviet "Ambassador" Rosenberg in Madrid and supported by poor deceived fools made mad by provoked class hatred. Fools carried away by ignorance into believing the ephemeral vision held before their eyes of a workman's paradise where none need to work! So they cry, "Viva Russia!"

A few days ago I read the account of a meeting held in Madison Square Garden, New York City, at which American citizens subscribed fifty thousand dollars to help the legal government of Spain in its heroic fight for liberty and democracy! Hell is indeed paved with these two misused words as well as good intentions! As an American I think those of my countrymen who do not know, should know, on what they are wasting their sympathies and ever-ready generosity.

A point of "extreme regret" and criticism of the Nationalists seems to have been the fact that General Franco has brought to his aid the Moorish troops from Africa. Is this criticism a case of ignorance, loss of memory or merely more Komintern propaganda? I seem to remember during the World War that France brought her native troops from Africa, England, and many regiments of her native troops from India – amongst whom were some of her fiercest fighters of Afghan border fame – and America contributed with her African-Americans. Have our sensibilities become so tender since nineteen eighteen? Or has reason been so undermined that what was then permissible and right to use against the German people is now a crime to use against the enemy of Spain, an enemy that has exceeded in genius for brutality and insane ferocity all records of any war or revolution in modern times or past! The Spanish Nationalists are fighting not only for their lives but for their liberty and the right to remain Spanish. They have no desire to be a vassal soviet state of Russia. In their fight, which is also a fight for civilization, as on the outcome depends the security of many nations, they need and will use every decent weapon at their command. Thank God! It is no longer necessary to say, "May they win!" They have! - doubt no long exists as to the outcome.

1 In February 1933, General Franco was appointed Military Commander of the Balearic Islands by the then Minister of War, Manuel Azaña. Azaña's intent was to remove a potential conspirator opposed to the Republican Left from mainland Spain. Natacha and Álvaro made his acquaintance in Mallorca and he evidently impressed them. A relationship with the Franco family continued and later Álvaro let one of their properties at Gènova, *Los Escalones*, to Franco's brother Ramón when he was (controversially) appointed commander of the hydroplane base at Puerto de Pollensa in the north of the island. María Salomé recalls being given his daughter's old dresses to wear.

2 Probably June 1935, occasion of the marriage of Álvaro's brother Mariano de Urzáiz y Silva to María del Pilar Azlor de Aragón y Guillamas, Duchess of Villahermosa.

3 Spring 1936, following general elections won by the left coalition, *Frente Popular*.

4 "Island of Calm", A reference to the book *La isla de la calma* (1912) by Catalonian artist and writer Santiago Rosiñol. At the turn of the century numbers of painters from Catalonia, Europe and South America settled and worked in Mallorca, seeing the island as an earthly paradise, and their decision to travel there as symbolizing a rejection of modern industrialization and commerce.
It is true that in Mallorca, during the years and months leading up to the outbreak of the Civil War, political and social unrest did not reach the extremes of mainland Spain but the apparent calm contained increasing political frustration among the worker's movement, the constitution of new socialist groups in the towns and villages (many of whose members were imprisoned following the strikes held in the autumn of 1934), the burning of several churches, and the bombing of the *Casa del Pueblo* in Palma (House of the People – social center that housed various workers' social and political groups) by *Falangistas* in the spring of 1936 (luckily no life was lost but easily might have been).

5 Calvo Sotelo, leader of the monarchist party *Renovación Española*. A vehement critic of the Frente Popular's failure to maintain law and order in the Spring of 1936, he was assassinated on July 13th in an apparently unplanned and spontaneous attack by a group that included member of the security forces, apparently as a reprisal against the shooting of socialist militant José Castillo the day before, probably by *falangistas*. The news of the murder of Calvo Sotelo had an enormous impact on supporters of the right (as Natacha makes clear) and would appear to have precipitated the nationalist uprising a few days later.

6 Mallorca was important strategically and Palma was bombed from the Republican aerodrome at Reus in Catalonia, during July and August 1936, the first raid taking place on July 23rd. As no planes were stationed on the island during the early days of the war, the only defense was from anti-aircraft guns but the planes flew too high (a prize of 5,000 pesetas was offered to anyone who achieved a hit but was never claimed). There were casualties although few (nine lost their lives, 39 were injured). Later, large numbers of planes belonging to the Italian Aviation Legion (fascist Italy and Germany actively supported the Nationalist uprising) were stationed at the Mallorcan air base at Son Sant Joan, making Mallorca an impregnable stronghold. From Son Sant Joan, countless air raids set out to bomb Republican-held cities in the East of mainland Spain. Some five thousand citizens lost their lives in attacks on Barcelona, Tarragona, Valencia and Alicante.

7 María Salomé's mother, Lorenza Pujol Roca.
8 During the 1950s, Álvaro acquired (or perhaps inherited) a sizeable estate in Segovia on mainland Spain. On one occasion in 1957, María Salomé's father, Juan Juaneda Palmer, was required to drive there to deliver Alvaro's car – a Cadillac – which had been left at Cala Fornells. Juan reported that the half dozen or so families who worked the land (including women and children) slept on Álvaro's kitchen floor!

CHAPTER SEVEN

Fig. 210

"In Egypt, the local people of Luxor called Natacha the 'Sitt Mudir', which is roughly translated as the 'Boss Lady' although a 'Mudir' in Egypt is a Governor." [1]

---

1 Mark Hasselriis letter to to Michael Morris, Nov, 7, 1986 p. 7.

"My assessment, at the early age of 23, was that Natacha knew well what she needed to do, she directed the expedition with patience and the necessary skills required to get the job done. You can imagine the amazement and wonder of our Egyptian friends. There we were in a male dominated society, being led by this extraordinary woman whose mannerisms alone caused them to stop and stare."[2]

2 L. Fred Husson, Letter to Michael Morris dated August 20, 1990.

ENVELOPED BY THE MYTH OF THE AGES

In 1939, Natacha left the Hudnut chateau on the French Riviera to return to New York City. In fragile health and suffering from allergies, she made a sojourn to the dryer climes of Arizona where she planned initially to build a home. Within a short time she returned to New York and an apartment at 140 West 55th Street.

Discarding the glamorous trappings of her Hollywood past and the casual attire of Mallorca, Natacha began to adopt a stylistic appearance associated with academia. Tweed suits replaced her turbans and silks and symbols, comparative religion, astrology and dream analysis became the primary focus of her daily life.

She delivered lectures, conducted classes in her apartment and performed an "oracular technique" she observed first in Egypt in 1936. [3] This involved the reading of the imprint of a person's hand after it had been pressed into sand. Natacha soon earned a respected reputation as an astrologer, capably calculating natal charts as well as imparting dream analyses.

Her lectures and classes[4] were attended by New York's intellectual community, many of whom she knew through her affiliation with the Roerich Society, including artist and scholar Mai-Mai Sze, Taoist scholar Chang Chung-yuan, costume designer Irene Sharaff and painter Buffie Johnson. Photographer and authority on India, Dorothy Norman, Indian art scholar, Stella Kramrisch and poet and playwright Mercedes D'Acosta were also, at various times, Natacha's students. Upon Natacha's return to New York, she also rekindled her friendship and professional affiliation with Alice Bailey, noted occult teacher, author and founder of New York's Arcane School.

Despite Natacha's popularity, the predominately spiritualist focus of her work did not endear her to the academic community she aspired to impress. Her publication of articles on physical therapy and yoga appearing in *The American Astrology* magazine from February 1942 to June 1943, no doubt contributed to her lack of acceptance by a skeptical academia.

Yet, it was with an open mind she moved beyond what she was then considering to be the passé subject of theosophy to delve further into her quest to connect all ancient civilizations through their symbols and religious traditions. As she grew increasingly serious in her research, she owed allegiance to no academic institution or particular school of thought and it is still a matter of discussion whether this was an advantage or a disadvantage for her.

It would be in one of her classes that Natacha made the acquaintance of a kindred spirit, Maud Oakes. As one of Natacha's students, Maud Van Courtland Oakes' field of research was indigenous art, language and symbolism. Just as Natacha began to turn her full attention on the subject of ancient Egypt, Maud was completing the recording of the ceremonial rituals of the Navajo in Arizona.

Natacha and Maud forged an immediate

---

3   Oracular Technique as related by Mark Hasselriis. M. Morris archival notes.

4   McQuire, William, *Bollingen, An Adventure in Collecting the Past*, pp. 89-90, " In the winter of 1943-44, she (Maud Oakes) was attending classes on symbolism, myth, astrology and Theosophical thought given by Natacha Rambova in her apartment."

professional and personal affiliation through their unorthodox research methods and similar interests and remained lifelong friends and supporters of each others work.

Maud also held no formal academic degrees or training yet unlike Natacha she was garnering the attention of academic authorities in her field. In the introduction to her book, *The Two Crosses of Todos Santos*, anthropologist Paul Radin sheds light upon this conundrum of scholars with no academic credentials such as Natacha Rambova and Maud Oakes.

"The important thing in Miss Oakes book, from the point of view in methodological implications, is the fact that the author is not a trained historian and, indeed, makes no claim of being academically trained at all. If, as most of us believe, a proper, rigorous academic training is a prerequisite for good anthropological field work, how are we to account for Miss Oakes achievement? The answer must be that no academic training can give an individual historical insight or the ability to establish rapport with other individuals. The capacity to see things as a true historian sees them – that is, historical vision – appears to be something a person is born with. Proper academic training can improve and deepen this vision and make it more effective. It can do no more. "[5]

Maud's influence was fortuitous. Natacha's scholarly pursuits would benefit as Maud's work received acceptance in great measure due to the support of Mary Mellon, President of the Old Dominion Foundation. Mary Mellon's Old Dominion Foundation, later known as the Bollingen Foundation, funded their "fellows" research of ancient cultures. It was Maud Oakes who first introduced Natacha to Mary Mellon. Natacha made an immediate impression upon Mary Mellon and as a consequence she was provided with a resource of continuous, generous grants enabling her

ensuing years of study, research and field work.

By the time Natacha met Mary Mellon, Maud Oakes was conducting field work in Guatemala, in a Quiché village in the Cuchumatan Mountains. There she was recording and studying the Mam, an indigenous people still living according to the Mayan calender and culture.

In November of 1945, Natacha requested Mary Mellon appoint her as Maud's official assistant.[6] She also asked Mary Mellon to expedite her obtaining a passport in order to travel to Guatemala. There, she planned to review Maud's notes in search of Mayan influences relevant to her study of comparative religion and symbolism.

After receiving the official appointment from Mary Mellon, Natacha flew from New York to New Orleans and then on to Guatemala. She spent a few months in the Mam village of Todos Santos with Maud before returning to New York.

"By 1946, Natacha pressed on with her symbolistic researches under Bollingen patronage, along with her classes, analytical practice, astrological counseling and public lectures."[7]

Inspired by the success of Maud Oakes' independent scholarship, Natacha applied for and received her first financial grant from the Old Dominion Foundation specified for use in her research to *"make a collection of essential cosmological symbols for a proposed archive of comparative universal symbolism."[8]*

In December of 1946, two months after the sudden death of Mary Mellon, Natacha requested a second grant from the Old Dominion Foundation, reorganized in December of 1945 as the Bollingen Foundation.

---

5 Oakes, Maud, *The Two Crosses of Todos Santos*, introduction by Paul Radin, p. 5.

6 Letter from Natacha to Donald D. Shepard, dated May 22, 1945.

7 William McQuire, *Bollingen*, p. 159.

8 Letter from Natacha to A.W. Schmidt, June 15, 1946, "I believe it will interest the Foundation to know that the research work made possible by the grant..."

Her application outlined her plans to travel to Egypt where she would conduct research on the ancient symbolism of gem and stone scarabs.

Her grant was approved and in February of 1947, she sailed for Egypt launching nearly five years of research there supported by Bollingen Foundation funding. Upon her initial arrival in Cairo, Natacha met with renowned Egyptologist Alexandre Piankoff. Piankoff was born in St. Petersburg, Russia in 1897 and by 1947, he was a French citizen, married and dividing his time between an apartment in Paris and a home in Cairo. While in Cairo, he devoted his time to translating the inscriptions on the Royal Tombs of Thebes. [9]

Alexandre Piankoff and Natacha Rambova's first meeting was held in the library of the French Institute of Archaeology. Egyptologist Dr. I.E.S. Edwards, shared details of this meeting with fellow Egyptologist Rosalind M. Janssen.[10] Dr. Edwards was in the library when Natacha first met Piankoff and recalled their lengthy, animated exchange. The professional and personal relationship between Alexandre Piankoff and Natacha Rambova first inspired in the French Institute library in Cairo would continue for the remainder of both of their lives.

As Natacha then traveled south from Cairo to Luxor, she began filing her reports to Jack Barrett, President of the Bollingen Foundation via lengthy, descriptive letters. In February 1947 she wrote,

"If Cairo was changed at least Luxor was not. The little rambling (Luxor) hotel with wide verandas set in one of the most beautiful natural gardens in the world was just as I had seen it last. The same sleepy-eyed waiter, the same house boy doing the same rooms and the same old gardener who picked forbidden flowers

and produced them from behind his back firmly expecting baksheesh.

At dawn the next morning I looked from my window to see the first faint light break through the star speckled darkness with an aura of green to rose to silhouette the giant palm trees standing like guarding sentinels of the gods." [11]

Alexandre Piankoff remained in contact with Natacha and advised her to expand the focus of her research grant from the symbols on scarabs to the study of his French translation of the *Book of Caverns,* a religious composition inscribed on the walls of the tomb of Ramesses VI.

In November of 1947, Maud Oakes joined Natacha in Egypt. Maud would utilize the opportunity to further her own research but she was uncomfortable working in the narrow passageways of the tombs. Convinced Natacha was summoning questionable energies by disrupting the tombs, Maud departed for the nineteen day return sail home to New York.

In 1948, the Bollingen Foundation awarded Alexandre Piankoff a grant to record the inscriptions on the entire tomb of Ramesses VI. Natacha was appointed acting head of the expedition. The research objective of the Piankoff and Rambova expedition also included the recording of the Pyramid Texts of the nine Fifth and Sixth dynasty pyramids at Saqqara, south of Cairo.

During the initial days organizing the expedition, Natacha interviewed a young epigrapher, (an archaelogical artist) Mark Hasselriis. He was recommended by another member of the impending expedition, Egyptologist Elizabeth Thomas. The talented, twenty-five year old Mark Hasselriis had just completed his first season as epigrapher at the University of Chicago's, Oriental Institute in Luxor. According to his resumé he served,

"...the Field Expedition of the Oriental Institute

9 *"Alexandre Piankoff (1897–1966)"* Extrait Du Bulletin De L'Institut Français D'Archèologie Orientale, T. LXV.

10 Janssen, Rosalind M., *"Rambova and Piankoff: Tying up Loose Ends",* Göttinger Miszellen, 156 (1997) p. 67.

11 Letter from Natacha to Jack Barrett dated, February 1947 from Luxor, Upper Egypt.

of the University of Chicago as an Epigraphic (archaelogical) artist during the season of 1946-1947, at Luxor, Egypt. In 1949, he joined the Expedition of the Bollingen Foundation under Dr. Alexandre Piankoff, of the French Institute of Archaeology in Cairo and Natacha Rambova, research scholar in Comparative Religions, to assist in the recording of the Tomb of Ramesses VI, and the Golden Shrines of Tutankhamon." [12]

By October of 1949 the members of the Bollingen Foundation's Egyptian expedition, Natacha Rambova, Alexandre Piankoff, Elizabeth Thomas, Mark Hasselriis and a photographer, L. Fred Husson convened at the Mena House near the pyramids.[13] Mark Hasselriis and Fred Husson were lodged at the University of Chicago's Oriental Institute with Natacha and Elizabeth Thomas in the Luxor Hotel about a half a mile south of the Oriental Institute. [14]

From October until the following March they recorded and photographed the tomb of Ramesses VI in its entirety. According to L. Fred Husson, Natacha and her expedition crossed the Nile river from Luxor on a barge each morning, with Natacha's small dog in tow,[15] where she would set up near the entrance of the tomb to do her work.

By April of 1950, the recording the tomb was complete and the move was made to Cairo for work on the golden shrines of the tomb of King Tut-Ankh-Amon. Additional field work took place in Saqqara south of the Pyramids of Gisa. As Husson wrote,

"In addition to the above mentioned assignments, we photographed parallel religious texts in several other tombs in the Valley of the Kings." [16]

The expedition was not without tension and on several occasions Natacha grew short-tempered. Piankoff would later blame Fred Husson and Elizabeth Thomas' departures from the expedition on Natacha's "Irish temper."[17] Natacha was livid when she discovered Fred Husson was exhibiting a "montage of his photographs in the Oriental Institute at tea break". She demanded he remove the photographs as they belonged to the expedition and were not for public display. [18]

Mark Hasselriis nearly left the expedition but Natacha made her amends, acknowledging his "eloquent" criticism of her behavior with a box of chocolates. Alexandre Piankoff intervened in the role of peacemaker between Natacha and her young artist and Mark agreed to remain in Egypt for the final months of work. He wrote his "letter of grievances" to Natacha and then wrote his family in March of 1951, lamenting he was *finished with this type of work*. He added, *"Egypt is a strain on the system and in time it attacks the health of its visitors."*

In addition to researching, recording and directing the logistically complex expedition, Natacha returned to New York several times to negotiate funding with the Bollingen Foundation and conduct preliminary editing of the material gathered in the field.

Late in 1951, she returned to New York to

12   Mark Hasselriis' handwritten "Resumé", Courtesy of John G. Rae III and Susan Rae. All Rights Reserved.

13   Michael Morris archival notes from interview with L. Fred Husson, also Bernard Bothmer, *Egypt 1950, My First Visit* " Husson's darkroom at Chicago House.." p. 33.

14   In Luxor, Mark would stay at the Oriental Institute where.."I had a room and a drafting room. Natacha Rambova stayed at the Luxor Hotel." Michael Morris notes from Mark Hasselriis interviews.

15   Natacha's small dog in tow, Bernard V. Bothmer, *Egypt 1950, My First Visit*, Edited by Emma Swan Hall, p. 33.

16   Husson interview with Michael Morris, April 9, 1990.

17   Mark Hasselriis writes, "I was lonely in Chicago House after Fred Husson left. She (Natacha) had a disagreement with Fred and he decided to leave. I was lonely and she was picky and testy. A blow up occurred and she sent me a box of chocolates. Piankoff said calm down. 'She's tempermental – She's Irish!' "

18   Letter from L. Fred Husson to Michael Morris dated, August 20, 1990.

begin in earnest the task of editing Alexandre Piankoff's Egyptian translations. Natacha's editing of the Bollingen publication of Piankoff's *Egyptian Religious Texts and Representations,* would consume the next decade of her life. Her devotion to the historical and cultural significance of the work remained foremost despite the sacrifice of the completion of her own life's theses.

Natacha's professional relationship with Piankoff complicated when she agreed to assume control and management of his financial affairs. Piankoff's increasing reliance upon Natacha in this regard caused their professional relationship to deteriorate. Despite the stress of their many disputes, a mutual professional respect endured.

There are contrary reports regarding Natacha's relationship with Alexandre's Italian wife, Helene. One version portrays the two women as being amiable and bonding over their love of little dogs. Another version has Madam Piankoff in fits of pique over Madam Rambova with Madam Rambova maintaining a politically cool demeanor with Madam Piankoff. The tensions were inevitable as Natacha assumed almost total control over Helene's husband's business affairs.

While Alexandre maintained addresses at 30, Rue de Juillet in Cairo [19] and an apartment in Paris with his wife, in New York City Natacha ran "Alex's" bank accounts, was granted his Power of Attorney, guarded the only copy of his *Last Will and Testament* and worked feverishly editing his life's works. [20]

In light of their involvement, the letters penned from Alexandre to Natacha appear quizzical in their contrary sentiments of professional formality and affectionate intimacy.

"Dear Miss Rambova..." Alexandre would begin a letter while closing the missives with *"Yours as Ever, Alex".* [21]

Natacha's patience with "Alex" eventually wore thin and she appealed several times to the Bollingen Foundation requesting she be relieved of her time-consuming and arduous editing responsibilities. She stated she was reaching the limits of her physical and mental capabilities regarding Piankoff's Bollingen Egyptian publications.[22] However, the lengthy tomes were slowly being completed and in great measure due to the support and technical assistance of Natacha's circle of friends and scholarly associates, most notably Mark Hasselriis.

---

19 Address of Alexandre Piankoff in Cairo, letter from Vaun Gillmor at Bollingen Foundation to Piankoff notifying him of Natacha Rambova's death, dated June 6, 1966.

20 Natacha assumes control over Piankoff's personal business affairs, letter from Vaun Gillmor to Maud Oakes, August 25, 1966.

21 Bollingen Foundation file, letters Piankoff and Rambova.

22 Natacha Rambova's letters to Bollingen Foundation... "As you know, and as I have told Piankoff many times, I do not wish to do any more editing until I have finished my own work..." letter dated, August 25, 1958.

Fig. 211

Maud Oakes in Todos Santos, 1946

"From Jung in Zurich to Jeff King in New Mexico and Zimmer in the world beyond, we are part of some huge plan or creative force. You have a very important role to play in it. Maybe that is why you have been given this heavy load of gold, maybe that is why when you are the real Mima you become like a symbol of the sun. You are already the alchemist starting to transmute your gold – both inner and outer..." [23]

Fig. 212

Mary Mellon "Mima"

"The best description I could give of Mima as she was then, before the asthma got bad, Maud recalled, "was that when she walked into a room, you'd feel that the sunlight had come in. She was radiant." [24]

23 Letter from Maud Oakes to Mima (Mary Mellon), 1943, McQuire, *Bollingen*, p. 71.

24 McQuire, *Bollingen*, p. 10, painting by Gerald L. Brockhurst, 1938.

Fig. 213

Passport Photograph – 1945

"....On my passport application my married name de Ursaiz, is also given. Although separated from my husband and having had no communication from him since 1940, it is still my legal name. I was born in this country in Salt Lake City, Utah, on Jan. 19, 1897, both parents being American. My mother, Mrs. Richard A. Hudnut is still living and resides at 30 West 56th Street, New York City. I retained my American citizenship at the time of my marriage. You will pardon my burdening you with these details, but I felt you might need them in reference to my passport application..." [25]

---

25 Letter from Natacha Rambova to Donald D. Shepard, Vice President of The Bollingen Foundation, dated May 22nd, 1945.

Fig. 214

Maud Van Cortlandt Oakes

"I have no degree to my name and no works published to my credit," she wrote (Mary Mellon, Mima at the Old Dominion Foundation), "But I have always been deeply interested in symbolism and I can honestly state that I am completely devoid of any form of racial prejudice. Having dabbled in painting since childhood, I have trained my eyes to be unusually observant."[26]

---

26 *"Dona Matilda of Todos Santos"* by Lanfranco Rasponi.

Photo courtesy of the Epigraphic Survey, Oriental Institute, University of Chicago

Fig. 215

Chicago House Staff photo, Luxor, Egypt, 1946-1947,
Mark Hasselriis, third from right, back row standing

Fig.216

Mark Hasselriis, Chicago House Staff, Luxor, Egypt, 1946

Fig. 217

Elizabeth Thomas

"Natacha did not get along with Elizabeth Thomas - a graduate from the Oriental Institute and a member of the expedition."[27]

27 M. Morris archive, M. Hasselriis inteview notes.

Fig. 218

The Luxor Hotel

"About Egypt, I do not know what to say – Donald Hansen, a student of mine now teaching ancient Near-Eastern Art and Religion at the Art Institute at NYU has just returned from a hurried trip during the Christmas holidays to see the sight of their new diggings. He reports mobs of tourists everywhere and reservations practically impossible unless made ahead...Try and find a place in Luxor as you should see the temples and tombs of the kings..."[28]

28 Letter from Natacha to Ann Wollen, January 19, 1964.

Fig. 219

The Cataract Hotel

"...I had been told the only hotel in Aswan was The Cataract, which turned out to be a great morgue of a place stifling in declining magnificence, with prices in accord with its rating as the most expensive hotel in Egypt. Arriving just in time for lunch, I was shown to the screened off corner of a huge black dining room where a handful of intimidated guests were whispering their conversations. Not a ray of light entered until I asked if we might have a blind lifted and a shade pulled so that we might at least see the famed view up the river – which we were presumably paying such tariff to see.

A young American couple – obviously honeymooners – sitting at the next table gave me a grateful glance and forgot to whisper. The food like everywhere else in the place was for show – to be seen but not eaten. Discovering a small but gay and refreshing hotel on the main street called The Grand, I went there later for tea to fill up the emptiness left by the uneatable lunch. This little hotel, run by an Egyptian married to an efficient French woman, is spotlessly clean with good, simple and well-cooked food. I sat in a charming garden and made note of it for future use as the rates, full pension, are less than half that of The Cataract."[29]

---

29 Natacha Rambova writes to Bollingen Foundation President Jack Barrett from Luxor, Egypt, February 1947.

Fig. 220

Bernard V. Bothmer, Alexandre Piankoff, Helene Piankoff and Natacha Rambova at the temple of
Edfu, (Esna) south of Luxor, January 1950

"Natacha didn't want to be photographed at that time at all, so any photos Fred (L. Fred Husson)
may have taken were taken sub-rosa."[30]

30 M. Hasselriis write to M. Morris, September 16, 1989.

Fig.221

"Last evening I drove back from Karnak at sundown along the banks of the Nile. Looking across to the foothills beyond, there was one continuously moving picture filled with opalescent light and veils of deepening mist shading from violet to indigo. Here you move in a land of silent mystery not of this world – yet there to be read by those who can – a land which has seen the far distant past in its greatest glories and will remain to see the distant future all unmoved. The only other country which has this same quality of eternity and cosmic space is Arizona. No wonder the myths of Egypt are all of cosmic gods, and their designs the sublime conceptions of minds ever dwelling in the nearness of far-off worlds. The stars at night hang in the sky like friendly and familiar lamps one can reach up, touch and become part of as they light the way." [31]

---

31 Natacha writes Jack Barrett at Bollingen Foundation, Feb. 1947.

Fig. 222

Epigrapher Mark Hasselriis of the Piankoff and Rambova Bollingen Expedition, 1950

Fig. 223

The Nile

"...After watching the evening sunset over the Nile, I very often stopped into Sayed's shop to talk if no one was there. One very hot day I had happened to ask if the heat did not effect the dogs here and if people were often bitten. He said yes that it happened quite often but that if you were in the village or here it was not serious. Seeing that he was weighing further explanation I told him that our American Indian medicine men had cures that the white doctors did not know about and told him one or two stories of their cures.

He said they also had a sure cure and that he himself had proven its efficiency two summers ago. If you were bitten he explained that you must at once remove your shoes and hit the wound seven times with the sole. Then you must get seven dates, seven pieces of bread, seven pieces of cheese and some holy water. A Coptic priest was then called and he divided these evenly between each member of the patient's family. When all the household have partaken then there is no further fear of rabies and there are no ill effects from the bite...All of this was told with such a matter of fact belief that it was not to be questioned." [32]

---

32 Natacha writes Jack Barrett at Bollingen Foundation.

Fig. 224

Saqqara - South of the Pyramids of Giza
Showing the Pyramids of Zoser (3rd Dynasty) left and Unas (5th Dynasty) right

"....The material I was able to gather here was well worth the trip up, where for four hours I choked and smothered in dust. The fine white dust defies all precautions and preparations when the wind blows. Before leaving we had a three day Sirocco which changed the weather and ushered in the real summer heat and dust..."[33]

---

33 Natacha writes Jack Barrett at Bollingen Foundation.

Fig. 225

Hypostyle Hall, Temple of Karnak, Thebes

Fig. 226

M. Hasselriis drawing of the Udja-Eye of Tut-Ankh-Amon

Fig. 227

Divinities on the Exterior Doors
of the Shrine of Tut-Ankh-Amon by M. Hasselriis

Fig. 228

Detail of Pillars, the Temple of Karnak, Thebes

Fig. 229-230

"...She was always pointing out details in my drawings which I occasionally missed in representation and others yet to be drawn I should attend to. I rarely omitted details in fact, but at times I might overemphasize them since some drawings were to serve as mere diagrams and others were best done as facsimiles. I counted every dot, if dots there were since in some cases these were number symbolism and in other cases might be such..."[34]

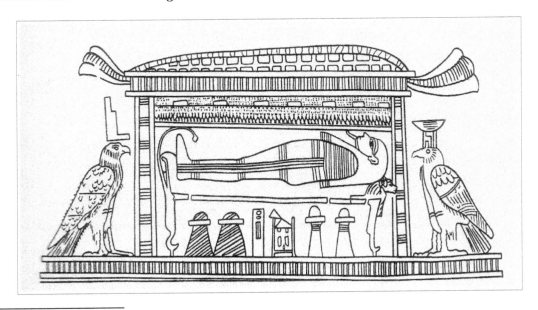

34 M. Hasselriis writes to M. Morris on October, 6, 1987.

403

Fig. 231

Detail of the face-plate from the tomb of Ramesses VI

404

Fig. 232

Hatshepsut with Amun-Re, from the Temple of Karnak, Thebes

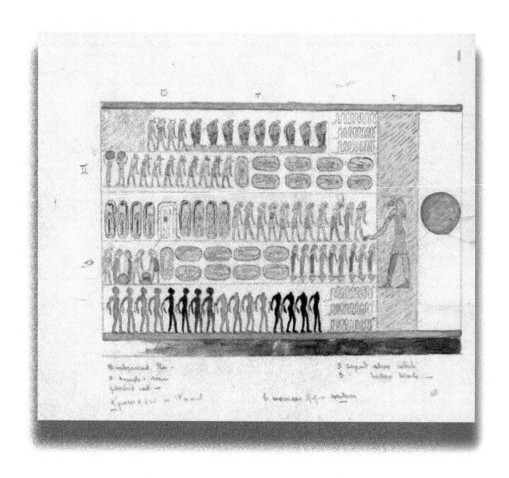

Fig. 233

Natacha Rambova's handwritten notations on a watercolor from a detail of the First Division of the
Book of Caverns from the tomb of Ramesses VI

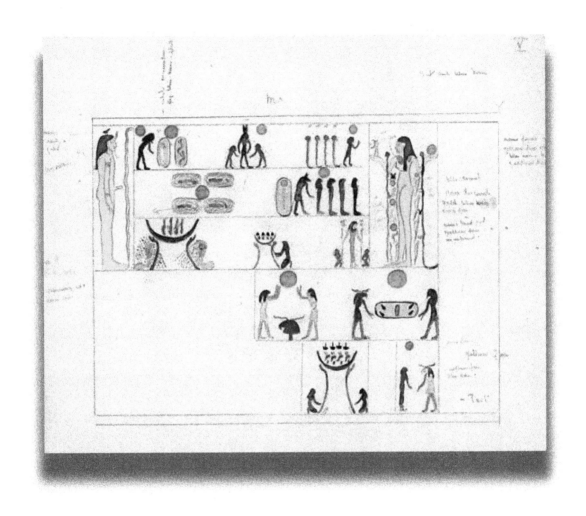

Fig. 234

Handwritten notations on a watercolor from a detail of the Fifth Division of the *Book of Caverns*

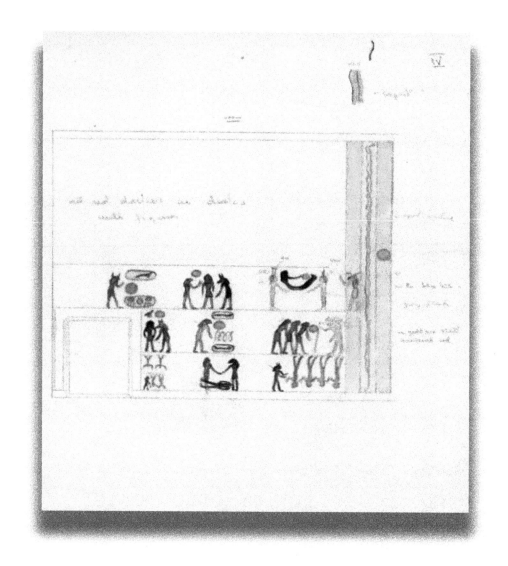

Fig. 235

Handwritten notations on a watercolor from a detail of the Fourth Division of the *Book of Caverns* from the tomb of Ramesses VI.

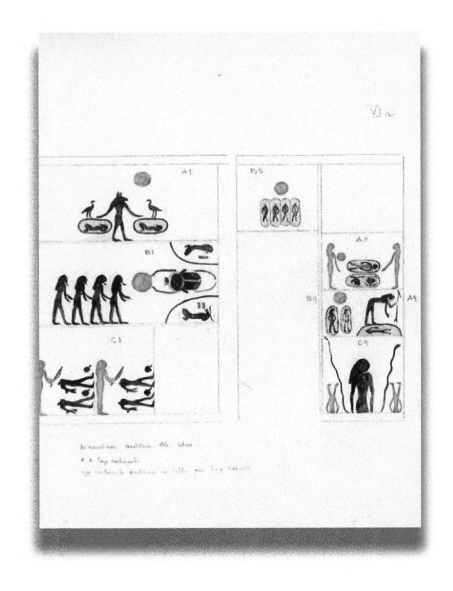

Fig. 236

Handwritten notations on a watercolor from a detail of the Sixth Division (Part A) of the *Book of Caverns* from the tomb of Ramesses VI.

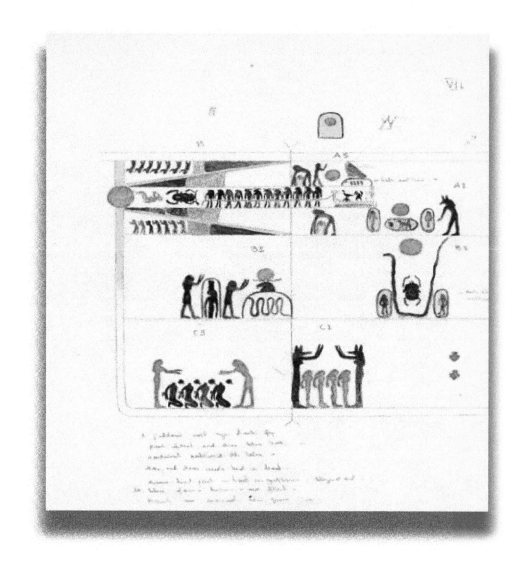

Fig. 237

Handwritten notations on a watercolor from a detail of the Sixth Division (Part B) of the *Book of Caverns* from the tomb of Ramesses VI

Fig. 238

Column Detail of Thumose III and Mut from the Temple of Luxor

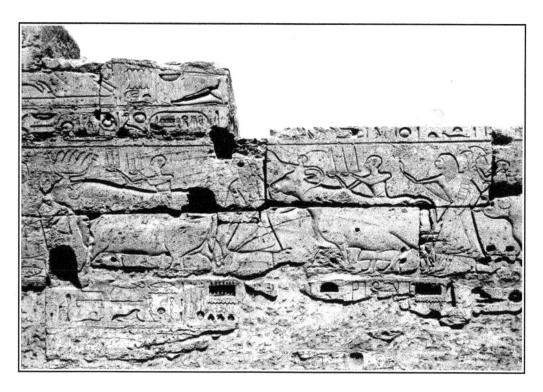

Fig. 239 Broken Stone Cattle – Cattle offering from the Temple of Luxor.

Fig. 240 Detail from Mortuary Chapel of Ramose (18th Dynasty), Western Thebes

Fig. 241

Bronze Ibex Divinity ca. 900 B.C.E.

Natacha Rambova Object Collection gifted to the Philadelphia Museum of Art

Dear Jack Barrett:

Although not connected specifically with my work here on the design scarab, and the psychological and religious significance of these early design patterns, here are a few notes which have psychological bearing which I would like to send on. It is always interesting to me to study the various racial tendencies and characteristics and to trace their roots.

There are probably few places where so little has changed from the past as in Egypt. There is something potently of the eternal and ever-enduring about this place. Even the swaying palms seem to be the same as those which looked down on all the changing fortunes of those long and deeply buried in the Tombs of the Kings.

To pass quickly over the last weeks in Luxor, I became great friends with the Arab dealer of antiquities mentioned before — a sheik of his village of Kourna, whose inhabitants have been digging in the tombs for buried treasure since the time of the Pharaohs themselves. His father was Petrie's head man in his excavations in Thebes and he was trained and grew up in association with the archaeological work which supplied his small shop with an endless stream of antiquities. He has known all the outstanding men in Egyptology, both past and present — Petrie, Budge, Breastead, Maspero, Weighll; Carter etc. He thinks the older men were far more competent than those working today as they had more background in comparative knowledge.

One afternoon while I was going over material he told me that if I was willing he would like to take me somewhere and would I be ready the following morning at six a.m. In the car as dawn was lighing the sky we drove through the early morning mist and watched the sunrise through the palms and the awakening life of the villages — faces being uncovered and bodies stretching in pleasure on the ground as field workers began a new day. Camels complained loudly as is their custom, donkeys made their wheezy breath-catching noises, dogs barked and the pidgeons made the air hum with their myriad voices as we passed by their crowded pottery domed houses.

Purple foothills across the Nile came and went and at last we slowed down before a long stretch of white sand and reck rock with hills in back — very similar to the white necropolis of Helwan where I had seen the Zaki Saad excavations on First Dynasty tombs. Here after a few moments an armed guard joined us and got into the car, these guards from the Department of Antiquities are dotted all over the countryside to prevent illegal excavating or digging by the fellaheen. We went a little further and up rock covered mounds to the entrance of a few early tombs — well protected by grilled iron doors. It seems this place had been one of the main sources of predynastic material — before digging was stopped by the building of a railway station and the vigilence of the guard. They pointed out to me the indentations in the rocky ground where

Fig. 242

Letter from Natacha Rambova to Jack Barrett at the Bollingen Foundation

Fig. 243

"In general she wore suit-dresses (jacket, blouse and skirt) but she also wore dresses both in Egypt and New York. All her clothes, when I knew her, were conservative and often businesslike as she didn't want to stress any association with glamour or Hollywood, especially as she dealt with scholars and Egyptological people." [35]

---

35 M. Hasselriis writes M. Morris on Nov. 7, 1986.

Fig. 244

Collection of Egyptian Scarabs
Museo Egizio, Turin

"She bought antiques, jewels and furnishings at a time it was still possible to do so. Many of her scarabs cost no more that a few cents or a few dollars – although she bought a few of them for some hundreds of dollars. A typical Egyptian bronze might have cost her $100.00 and so it went. Her mother gave her money in the 40's and early 50's to buy scarabs, amulets and bronzes. I bought a few at the same time and some of mine came from the same "tombs" or sites as did hers. We often bought things at the same time in the same shop."[36]

---

36 M. Hasselriis writes to to William McQuire on January 25th, 1981.

CHAPTER EIGHT

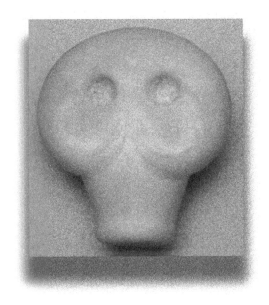

Fig. 245

Calcite ca. 4000-3200 B.C., Predynastic period
Bull's Head Amulet, from Natacha Rambova's Collection of Antiquities

THE COSMIC CIRCUIT

"To Mark Hasselriis, Metaphysician Extraordinaire, Companion on the Path and Fellow in the Work".

This dedication, appearing in *Your Psychic Potential* published in 1995 by M.J. Abadie, could also have been written to Mark Hasselriis by Natacha Rambova. Until Mark Hasselriis' passing in 1999, he lived his artistic and scholarly life as a practicing "disciple of Natacha Rambova's thought". [1]

His lifetime of artistry, epigraphic master work and passion for ancient cultures culminated in a remarkable archival legacy. Mark Hasselriis' life was defined by his artistic accomplishments and his nephew related how his uncle referred to himself as "an ancient man in a modern world." [2]

Throughout the last twenty years of Natacha Rambova's life, Mark Hasselriis was not only her disciple but her friend, confidant, companion, week-end housemate, artist, illustrator and oft secretary. Mark wrote,

"One friend thought I was in love with her. I wasn't, alas it was worship of a kind and worship can be wrong because it isn't the best kind of love." [3]

Hasselriis' trove of handwritten letters to Michael Morris comprise a fascinating glimpse into Natacha's personal and professional life during the Bollingen Egyptian expedition and the remaining years of her life. The letters are also revelatory regarding Mark and Natacha's relationship. One insight may be found in a comment he made concerning Natacha's reaction to Tony Dexter's portrayal of Rudolph Valentino in the 1951 biographic film, *Valentino*. Mark wrote how Natacha never spoke to him about that particular film yet added,

"...Eleanor Parker, however, played a part as a "Natacha" to Robert Taylor as a 'Mark' in a film called 'Valley of the Kings' where the lady is searching for the tomb of Joseph. Some of the props were from the film 'The Egyptian' by Mika Waltari and it was an intrigue and murder mystery. I thought the coincidental names odd to say the least...." [4]

The 1954 film, *Valley of the Kings*, which Mark Hasselriis felt to be Hollywood's accurate portrayal of Natacha Rambova and a film implying his role in her life, involves the lead female character's Egyptian expedition in search of the "confirmation of a unified religion". The members of the expedition convene at Mena House, as would Natacha's Bollingen Expedition, and the script involves ample dialogue about the "scientific versus the spiritual"; a prevalent dichotomy in Natacha's Egyptian work.

Despite the Hollywood invention in *The Valley of Kings*, Mark Hasselriis felt Eleanor Parker's character to be based on Natacha; a beautiful, aristocratic woman, leading an expedition of primarily men and Egyptians into the Valley of the Kings in search of a tomb and

---

1   Letter from William McQuire to Katherine Peterson, August 16, 1979, also letter from William McQuire to M. Morris, April 29, 1982.
2   Citation from John G. Rae III to E. Zumaya.
3   Mark Hasselriis letter to M. Morris.

4 M. Hasselriis letter to M. Morris, Nov. 7, 1989.

answers to esoteric enigmas. He believed the film to be a fictionalized treatment of the Bollingen expedition.

Mark Hasselriis was twenty-seven years younger than Natacha and remembered clearly the first time he saw her. He related the story of his first glimpse of Natacha when asked if she continued to wear her hair in a turban during her later years. Mark responded he saw her wearing a turban only once. He added that he realized he saw Natacha "turbaned" years after he began working with her. It was only when he and Natacha were discussing how they both attended the Thomas Wilfred Clavilux recital at the Graybar Building in 1938, that he made the connection. He says he had no idea who she was at the time and added that night she was memorably,

"One of the most beautiful woman I had ever seen...a goddess! Turbaned with make-up and dressed in silk and she was with a dumpy middle aged lady. I was afraid of beauty like that!" [5]

The "dumpy, middle-aged lady" attending the recital that night with Natacha was her friend Alice Bailey. [6]

When Mark and Natacha returned to New York in 1951, upon the termination of the Bollingen Foundation Egyptian expedition, he continued to be involved in her daily life while drawing most of the illustrations, or "diagrams", for the Bollingen Egyptian publications. Mark comments,

"For both of us 'art' was just as exacting a discipline as any text is for the scholar who only reads! She was something of a perfectionist, but while such a trait can be irksome in other people, it seemed to be a wholly justified quality in Natacha and one was at pains to fulfill her desire in every possible way." [7]

In 1957, Natacha's mother, "Muzzie" passed away. Upon receiving her inheritance, Natacha purchased a country home in New Milford, Connecticut. Shortly after she wrote Bollingen Foundation President Jack Barrett, reiterating that she no longer wished to edit Piankoff's work. She also requested the Bollingen Foundation inform Piankoff he should assume responsibility for his financial management. Natacha was adamant she devote her time in Connecticut to completing her two part life's work, *The Cosmic Circuit* and *The Mystery Pattern in Ancient Symbolism*.

On August 25, 1958 she wrote Jack Barrett,

"As you know, and as I have told Piankoff many times, I do not wish to do any more editing until I have finished my own work. I said this before and then did do the 'Mythological Papyri' which turned out well after things were straightened out in Cairo. But now I mean it. For the first time in over a year and a half my work is going well. It is a difficult book on the Religious Origins of the Zodiac, which has to take up all the calender problems, the religious feasts of the year, plus the animal and body-part symbols of the twelve divisions. It is a work that needs quiet and concentration. For the first time in over fifteen years, I have the peace and freedom from worry with which to work. My health is bad and I have not much more time or strength left and what I have I wish to use to finish at least this work I am on." [8]

With her health failing, she focused her waning energies on her own work while completing three manuscripts, *The Celestial Virgin*, *The Celestial Figure* and *Pantheos*. [9] Meanwhile, the Bollingen Egyptian publications, with Piankoff translating all texts and writing the introductions and with Natacha editing, achieved publication as the ambitious

5   M. Hasselriis letter to M. Morris, Nov. 7, 1989, p. 8.
6   M. Morris archival notes.
7   Ibid.

8   Rambova letter to Barrett on August 25, 1958.
9   M. Hasselriis interviews with M. Morris, saying he has copies of *The Celestial Virgin* and *The Celestial Figure* and Mai Mai Sze has a copy of *Pantheos*.

multi-volume, *Egyptian Religious Texts and Representations*.

In 1954, *The Tomb of Ramesses VI*, was published as Volume 1. *The Times Literary Supplement's* review expressed doubt whether the general reader had too much information to absorb while the specialist found too little. Natacha remained displeased with her lack of acknowledgment and this sparked further rancor with Piankoff. He wrote her in response,

"You accuse me of dark designs – the crafty Russian, Vishinsky trying to do in an honest American. Believe me, I never had the intention to get your name out of the title page. I only wanted to explain your part as editor...Not being an Egyptologist you will get all the blame for my religious speculations...I only wanted to stress in some way that I was the only one responsible for the translations and commentaries. So, please, forget the dark man with a beard and a bomb standing around the corner." [10]

Despite periodic tension, Natacha and Piankoff continued their work with the publication of Volume 2, *The Shrines of Tut-Ankh-Amon* in 1955. In 1957, Volume 3, *Mythological Papyri* was published, again edited by N. Rambova. However, this publication included a chapter she authored on the symbolism of the papyri.

During the late 1950's and early 1960's, Natacha resided primarily in her home in New Milford, Connecticut. Her Carmen Hill Road home was a tranquil retreat from life in Manhattan and a departure stylistically from her previously exotic dwellings[11] According to Mark Hasselriis, simplicity became her preferred décor. Scandinavian furniture and coordinated drapery reflected her increasingly Buddhist and zen aesthetic.

"Gilded bronzes from Tibet, Nepal or China stood on the mantle-piece or ledge and in her bedroom the Egyptian bronzes and faiences occupied a simple glass-fronted cabinet or rather, bookcase...Other treasures reposed in drawers, as she disliked clutter. She was very neat and everything went together in a natural and eclectic way stylistically...the red Chinese chair, the Swedish draperies in pastel colors with matching bedspreads, the plain good taste in fine woods with a decent piece or two from Bloomingdale's." [12]

As Mark spent many week-ends with Natacha in New Milford, it seemed logical he would remain home on Carmen Hill Road to care for the dogs, especially Natacha's beloved long-haired chihuahua, "Chicca", when she traveled to Egypt and the Middle East for a final time.

By then Natacha was suffering from liver problems and had been diagnosed with Scleroderma Esophageal Dysfunction. She was eating less as a result of her difficulty swallowing and was experiencing a dramatic weight loss. Despite this, she and Mark continued their work on the *Cosmic Circuit*. By 1963, Natacha's well-being had deteriorated drastically and she felt she had but a few months to live. [13]

In 1964, the Bollingen Foundation published Volume 4 of Piankoff's *Egyptian Religious Texts and Representations,* titled *Litany of Re*, which Piankoff dedicated to Natacha Rambova.

On September 29, 1965, Natacha was found delusional and semi-conscious in a hotel elevator in New York City. She was rushed to the hospital and there given a first electric shock treatment. According to Mark, previous to her collapse Natacha became convinced she was being *"attacked by demons from the netherworld"* and she often woke up screaming

10 Letter from Piankoff to Rambova, December 13, 1954.
11 Wehner, George, *A Curious Life*, p. 338. "When I entered Mrs. Valentino's apartment ..." (see Notes & Sources).
12 M. Morris archival notes of M. Hasselriis interviews.
13 Piankoff letter to Bollingen's Vaun Gillmor, July 1, 1963.

in the night. [14]

Mark visited Natacha in the hospital after her collapse where he tried and failed to prevent further shock treatments from being performed on her.

"She was as thin as a skeleton. It was a shock. She had been drinking milk and had a white mustache. She was too weak to even read." [15]

Natacha did not return to New Milford and was instead transported to Pasadena, California by relatives where she was placed in a nursing home. Hearing of Natacha's illness and her return to the west coast, Maud Oakes traveled from her home in Big Sur to Pasadena. As Natacha's condition grew more grave by the end of May 1966, Maud stayed in a small cottage on the facility's grounds; her view positioned to see Natacha's doorway.

While caring for the dogs at home in Connecticut, a stricken Mark Hasselriis mailed Natacha a ceramic tile he made for her, painted colorfully with an image of the Egyptian God, Anubis. Natacha kept this tile as her only personal possession in her room.

On the night of June 5, 1966, Maud woke to see the silhouette of a coyote trotting past Natacha's door. She knew coyotes frequently wandered down onto the streets and into the wooded neighborhoods of Pasadena from the Sierra Madre mountains. She called out to Natacha asking if she had just seen the animal. Natacha replied feebly, "That was no coyote, Maud." A few hours later Natacha Rambova passed away.

One month later, on July 20, 1966, Alexandre Piankoff died of a heart attack while visiting family in Brussels. As Piankoff had never transacted the transfer of his New York bank accounts, his wife, Helene was left without funds in Paris. A frantic search for Natacha's lawyer ensued, as she had been the only person in possession of Piankoff's *"Last Will and Testament"* and all documentation regarding his financial holdings. The details of Madam Piankoff's dire situation were revealed in a correspondence between Maud Oakes and Vaun Gillmor at the Bollingen Foundation. [16]

After Natacha's death, her "disciple" Mark Hasselriis continued to lecture and carry on her work, teaching at the School of Sacred Arts in New York and illustrating many books including the *The Mythic Image* by Joseph Campbell, *Isis and Osiris, Exploring the Goddess Myth* by Jonathan Cott, edited by Jacqueline Onassis and *The Hero: Myth/Image/Symbol* by Dorothy Norman. Mark's devotion to Natacha remained resolute and one of utmost respect and admiration for the remainder of his life.

Natacha Rambova's Egyptological contributions have just recently received acclaim. As a result of the research conducted by Egyptologists Rosalind M. Janssen and Barbara Lesko, Colleen Manassa Darnell, John Coleman Darnell and others, Natacha Rambova's years of Egyptological work are at last being recognized. In 2012, she was included for the first time in the *Who Was Who in Egyptology.*

As Natacha Rambova valued her work as an Egyptologist, so she devalued her former career in Hollywood as a designer. She threw many of her original sketches away and likewise, many of the twelve films on which she worked were lost.

As a result of the Museum of Modern Art in New York's efforts as well as those of other museum archives, the Utah Museum of Fine Arts, The Phoenix Art Museum and the Brooklyn Art Museum, a long overdue appreciation for her historical contributions is manifesting.

Her affiliation with Hollywood and its celebrity-driven notoriety surely kept her name vital. Yet, her life's work as an Egyptologist has not to date dominated her legacy despite her

---

14 M. Hasselriis to M. Morris. M. Morris archive.
15 Ibid.

16 Rambova managing Piankoff's finances and specifics of finances, *"...no one would be able to sort them out if she should die."* Letter to Dr. Piankoff from Vaun Gillmor dated July 16, 1963.

years of work and the scope of her accomplishments in this field. The recognition of her legacy has primarily been focused on her five years in Hollywood and fails to acknowledge the twenty years she devoted to her Egyptological work and writing.

It is thus an erroneous reflection of Natacha Rambova to ensconce her name so trenchantly in Hollywood iconography as the true body of her life's contributions found fruition on the sands of Egypt; where in the shadow of the great pyramids she left the imprint of her signature for posterity.

In 1926, Rudolph Valentino's business manager penned the following prophetic metaphor ten years before Natacha first traveled to Egpyt:

"Cleopatra is her greatest prototype in history. In fact, if I believed in reincarnation,I could very easily imagine that the soul of Natacha Rambova, with all of her physical perfections and her mysterious fascination, had once inhabited the body of Egypt's queen. And that the Nile and its desert sands had once been her natural habitat.." [17]

---

17 *The George Ullman Memoir*, p. 183

Fig. 246

Carmen Hill Road, New Milford, Connecticut

Fig. 247

The Thomas Wilfred recital in New York on the Clavilux

"I saw her with a turban only once in my life at the Thomas Wilfred Clavilux recital at the Graybar Building...but I did not realize that this fantastically beautiful woman was Natacha until she mentioned being there to me some years after I had already been working with her. I never made the connection." [18]

---

18 M. Hasselriis write M. Morris, Nov. 7, 1986.

Fig. 248

Hollywood's more accurate portrayal of Natacha Rambova
by Eleanor Parker in "The Valley of the Kings", 1954

Fig. 249

Eleanor Parker with Robert Taylor as the character of "Mark", in "The Valley of the Kings"

Filming started in November 1953. The film's world premiere took place simultaneously on July 21, 1954 in Cairo (as well as New York City). It marked the first time an American film held a world premiere in Egypt.

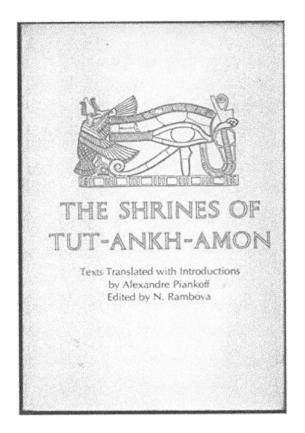

Fig. 250

Fig. 251

"This is the second of a series of publications on Egyptian religion which will include the complete photographic recording of hitherto unpublished royal tombs, important mythological papyri, and miscellaneous cosmological texts and symbolic representations. The series will include, where possible, the full translation of texts. The purpose of this series is to make available, both to scholars and to students of religion, essential religious materials that are either unrecorded or untranslated...Diagrams: Mark Hasselriis." [19]

"When they (Alexandre Piankoff & Natacha Rambova) talked it was animated interest. Natacha respected and liked Piankoff and he respected her. They did not always agree about the symbolism or Egyptian religious ideas. Late in their friendship (in the 1950's) Piankoff came to New York. Natacha held a reception or cocktail party for him at her house. I believe the Foundation also fêted him at a reception. He asked me if I knew where the Oyster Bar was, that was 'world famous'. Yes, I told him, so we went to Grand Central Station and the Oyster Bar and had pan roasted oysters." [20]

---

19 Editorial Note by Natacha Rambova in *The Shrines of Tut-Ankh-Amon*, by Alexandre Piankoff, The Bollingen Library, p. ix.

---

20 M. Hasselriis writes to M. Morris.

Fig. 252

"Natacha ate a variety of food until scleroderma made eating an agony. She liked Japanese food, Chinese food and old American food and Egyptian dishes – just about everything well-prepared....In 1960-1961, Natacha already had difficulty in swallowing (I was told after she died she had a tumor in her throat) and one day we sat in her enclosed porch and ate crushed caviar, the 'only' thing she said she could eat. At a sumptuous veal roast dinner I would have to force myself to eat in her presence, both to please her and Mrs. Riordan, her Norwegian cook.

After stuffing myself with food I did not want to eat, Natacha would then say, 'Well, perhaps I could eat just a little of it.' I quite consciously put on an act as if I thought it was delectable just to peak her appetite." [21]

21 M. Hasselriis writes M. Morris on Nov. 7, 1986.

Fig, 253

Fig. 254

"She was terribly earnest about her work or in conversations with authorities in art and archeology, but she was so poised and gracious that over a cocktail, (sweet martini or a sherry) she made anyone relax and feel at home and unhurried. She even got a television set in Connecticut and watched it briefly after dinner but she was not addicted to any new fad be it an idea or a technology. "[22]

22 M. Hasselriis writes M. Morris on Aug. 6, 1987.

Fig. 255

...."Books abounded, but in suitably sized bookcases or upon shelves of just the right size for the books which were there. Nothing appeared to be ill-fitting or made somehow to do; it was all measured and thought out carefully. It was the work of a designer, but the total effect was not in the least contrived or stiff." [23]

---

23 M. Hasselriis writes to William McQuire.

Fig. 256

Mark Hasselriis on the Long Island shore, 1958

"What would happen to society if everyone 'followed their bliss?' In other words if John Doe did follow his bliss when papa wanted him to be a lawyer, there might be fewer lawyers, etc. or more musicians; the remark simply means 'Follow your heart's desire, that's it!' [24]

---

24 M. Hasselriis letter to John G. Rae III.

Fig. 257

"It was in other words, through 'art' that I began to learn something of her philosophic excellence not only of the ancient mind at its best, but also of Natacha's quest for high achievement and quality in all that she did or was concerned with.

Working with such a woman and a human being, life acquired purpose. It was all not for nothing. It had meaning, it had a goal. The contradictions within the outer world such as loss of pride in one's labor or craftsmanship did not apply to one working for Natacha." [25]

---

25 M. Hasselriis interview notes. M. Morris archive.

Fig. 258

"...Natacha, as I have said, was clear about this matter between intellect and heart...We were in the kitchen in Connecticut I recall. She suggested I might write a little inspirational book about what I had learned and experienced by that time. I replied by saying, 'Oh no, Natacha, I couldn't; I haven't learned enough to write about such things!' She caught my meaning and said, 'Mark, don't confuse intellect with the spiritual. One doesn't have to be an intellectual to be spiritual!' She didn't mean I was accomplished in spiritual matters but that writing from the heart on the experience of making a spiritual quest was something I should attempt."[26]

---

26 M. Hasselriis writes M. Morris, Dec. 24, 1990. Photo: Mark Hasselriis, Forest Hills N.Y., 1958.

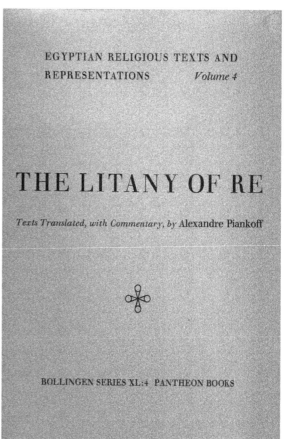

Fig. 259 The Bollingen Foundation publications of *The Shrines of Tut-Ankh-Amon*, edited by N. Rambova and *The Litany of Re*, dedicated to N. Rambova

"The 'peace offering' has been received and a letter of thanks reached me a few days ago. I still do not know what are the reactions to the frontispiece affair and hope that the tempest will not be directed at you...Speaking of the frontispiece, have you decided whether there will be one, or not? If yes, I suggest the Mentuemhat plate. I think your suggestion is excellent – let me dedicate *The Litany* to Miss Rambova."[27]

---

27 Alexandre Piankoff writes to Bollingen Foundation President on October 10, 1962.

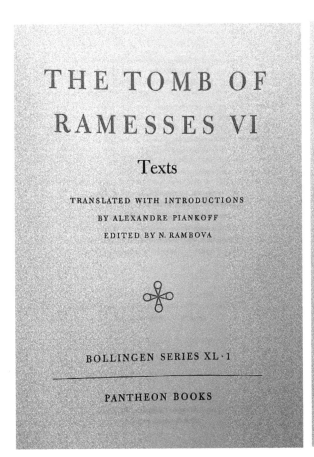

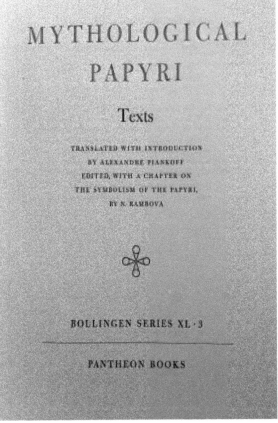

Fig. 260

Fig. 261

Volume I
of *The Egyptian Religious
Texts and Representations*

"Dear Natacha: I have just found time to read over the first part of the *Mythological Papyri* volume and I want to tell you that I think your chapter on the symbolism of the papyris illustrating the *Cosmic Circuit* and the Osirian Netherworld is excellent. Not only have you brought together a number of significant illustrations but your interpretation of them seems to me restrained and yet comprehensive and convincing."[28]

28 Natacha cites Egyptologist Dick Parker in a letter to Barrett, May 20, 1958.

Fig. 262

"Her humor was not confined to subtle intellectual points but included them. The behavior of an animal or pet could bring forth a chuckle, a smile and a subdued glee. Once I began to sing in her presence with her dog Chicca (a long-haired Chihuahua. The dog began to sing, howl, with head pointed up) and Natacha was genuinely laughing in her almost silent way."[29]

---

29 M. Hasselriis writes M. Morris on Aug. 6, 1987.

Fig. 263

Mark Hasselriis in the 1990's

"Natacha hated to be worshiped and I was, over the years subtle, I did not give that impression, but once I happened to sit on the floor at her feet and she complained to a friend; she hated 'the chela at the feet of the guru' image. The truth was I was not sitting at her feet as a tribute. I just wanted to sit on the floor!"[30]

---

30 M. Hasselriis writes M. Morris on Nov. 1, 1990.

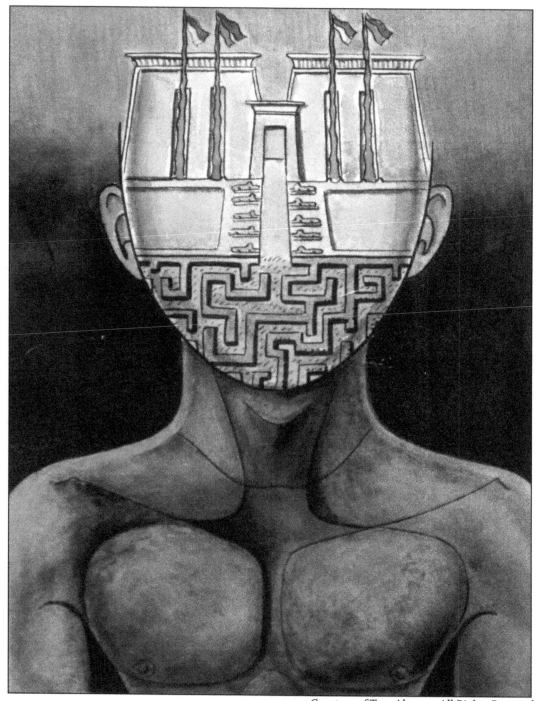

Fig. 264

Metaphysical & Symbolic oil painting by Mark Hasselriis

Fig. 265

Egyptian symbolic oil painting by Mark Hasselriis

Glyph drawn by M. Hasselriis on the back of a letter to Michael Morris

Fig. 266

Maud Oakes in her later years

Fig. 267
The last known photograph of
Natacha Rambova

"Now about poor Natacha - she is in an institute in Pasadena right near her three cousins. She never reads letters, she has no interest in T.V., radio, or the outside world. She is not interested in clothes, having her hair washed, or cut, etc. Her cousin writes me regularly and she says that N. (Natacha) now weighs 70 pounds.

Mentally she has her ups and downs. She remembers everything in the past and has a guilt complex in relation to her past life. Now, she does not want to see me, or anyone except these three cousins. Physically she is in bad shape and the doctors have no hope of improvement physically or mentally. Her address is "La Encinas 2900, East Del Mar Blvd., Pasadena, California.

I send her a post card every week and she loves these. Her step-sister, age 93, is in San Francisco and I see her every time I go up there."[31]

---

31 Vaun Gillmor writes to Piankoff, May 17, 1966.

Fig. 268

"There was magic just around the corner, and sometimes it burst forth when it was most needed, seemingly to contradict the outer world's impact, or some stultifying influence which otherwise would seem to deify pointlessness and justify criticism. " [32]

---

32 M. Hasselriis writes M. Morris on Jan. 25. 1981

Fig. 269

"On the Second Shrine of Tut-Ankh-Amon, the four aspects of birth or becoming are illustrated in the form of the four scarab-gods."[33]

33 *The Cosmic Circuit*, N. Rambova, p. 80. Drawing by M. Hasselriis.

Natacha Rambova's "Cosmic Circuit in Egypt"

Throughout the later 1950's and until her death in 1966, Natacha Rambova worked tirelessly on her life's thesis, *The Cosmic Circuit*. The extensive work was never published and exists today as fragile and incomplete copies in several archives: the Natacha Rambova Archive at Yale University, the Utah Museum of Fine Arts and the Library of Congress. Reviewing her typewritten manuscript, one notices she was still in an editing phase of her work as many footnotes are incomplete and the numbering of her images is at times in error.

The Cosmic Circuit is a synthesis of Natacha Rambova's decades of research, study and field work. The technical prose of her archaeological scientific paper is challenging for a general readership to comprehend as it is specifically oriented to Egyptological experts. This said, the importance of including an excerpt of Natacha's *Cosmic Circuit* remains unquestioned as it has never been published in any format and her scholarly contributions merit recognition. Egyptologist Colleen Manassa Darnell comments, "Although a lot of Egyptologists look at her work, it is under-appreciated and we are trying to bring her work to the forefront."[34]

Chosen for inclusion is an excerpt from her chapter on Egypt with illustrative drawings by Mark Hasselriis. The Table of Contents reads as follows:

The Cosmic Circuit

Part One: Cosmology

Part Two: The Creation of the Universe

Part Two Continued: The Cosmic Circuit in Egypt

Part Three: Symbols of the Cosmic Circuit, Body Parts

Part Four: Animal Symbols and the Twelve Months

Part Five: Religious Calenders

In the following introduction, Egyptologists Colleen Manassa Darnell and John Coleman Darnell elaborate on Natacha Rambova's *Cosmic Circuit* and contexualize her work within today's Egyptological métier.

---

34 "Egyptologists Celebrate Acquisitions with a Lecture", *Yale News*, Charlotte Wang, April 21, 2009.

Natacha Rambova's Syncopated Netherworld and The Cosmic Cycle

by

John Coleman Darnell and Colleen Manassa Darnell

One of the most important Egyptological works Natacha Rambova completed before her death[1] was an introduction to the solar imagery in a group of papyri with iconographic and limited textual material, all relating to the solar cycle and dating to the early first millennium BCE, primarily the Twenty-First Dynasty. The chapter Rambova contributed to her co-authored (with Alexandre Piankoff) volume on Egyptian religious papyri of the early first millennium BCE, represents a portion—and the only thus far published—of her well advanced but never completed manuscript on the "Cosmic Circuit."

The Mythological Papyri, as the documents that were one of the main sources for Rambova's work are now commonly known, combine images deriving from earlier compositions, such as the New Kingdom Netherworld Books, along with new representations normally involving a repetitious recasting of the union of the opposites of the two solar axes—east and west, south and north, diurnal and nocturnal, appear in meaningful, essentially quadripartite arrangements on the papyri. As Natacha Rambova observed regarding the Mythological Papyri: "In many instances Egyptian religious texts and representations appear contradictory until this cyclic concept of the renewal of life through the co-operation and fusion of opposites is understood. In this fusion ... the two widely separated geographic points of West and East, the sunset and sunrise mountains of Manu and Bakhu, become identified and joined, both in thought and in image. From geographic opposites they become associated symbols of the mysterious achievement of divine purpose."[2]

In popular imagination the funerary beliefs, imagery, and literature of the ancient Egyptians are to a greater or lesser degree bound to the treatise they called the "Book of Going Forth by Day"—better known to the modern world by the less accurate designation of "Book of the Dead."[3] The "Book of Going Forth by Day" originated during the period of political instability following the end of the Middle Kingdom (ca. 2055-1650 BCE),[4] and many of the best known and most elaborately

---

[1]   Already recognized to some extent in A. Niwinski, *Studies on the Illustrated Theban Funerary Papyri of the 11th and 10th Centuries B.C.*, OBO 81 (Fribourg and Göttingen: Academic Press and Vandenhoeck & Ruprecht, 1989), p. 67.

[2]   N. Rambova, "The Symbolism of the Papyri," in A. Piankoff and N. Rambova, *Mythological Papyri*, Ancient Egyptian Religious Texts and Representations 3 (New York: Pantheon Books, 1957) (quotation on p. 30).

[3]   E. Hornung, *Das Totenbuch der Ägypter* (Düsseldorf and Zurich: Artemis und Winkler Verlag, 1998); *idem, The Ancient Egyptian Books of the Afterlife*, trans. David Lorton (Ithaca and London: Cornell University Press, 1999), pp. 13-22 and 165-168.

[4]   R.B. Parkinson and S. Quirke, "The Coffin of Prince Herunefer and the Early History of the *Book of the Dead*," in A.B. Lloyd, ed., *Studies in Pharaonic Religion and Society in Honour of J. Gwyn Griffiths* (London: The Egypt Exploration Society, 1992), pp. 37-51; W. Grajetzki, "Another Early Source for the Book of the Dead: The Second Intermediate Period Burial D 25 at Abydos," *SAK* 34 (2006): 205-216; *idem, The Coffin of Zemathor and Other*

produced version of the composition date to the New Kingdom (ca. 1550-1069 BCE). Although the texts and vignettes of that treatise—itself containing some material originating with the first great surviving corpus of Egyptian funerary literature, the Pyramid Texts—would persist into the period of Roman domination of Egypt and the ultimate decline of the old religion, the New Kingdom Egyptians produced additional funerary literature that would be of great importance, both for their own religious productions of the first millennium BCE, and for the Egyptological work of Natacha Rambova.

The Netherworld Books of the New Kingdom and the Later Mythological Papyri

Although the compositions known as the Netherworld Books[5] may predate their first appearances during the Eighteenth and Nineteenth Dynasties,[6] they are best known as the dominant compositions decorating the walls of the royal tombs of the New Kingdom in the Valley of the Kings. Greatly expanding a tradition of otherworldly geography appearing in the Book of the Two Ways in the Middle Kingdom Coffin Texts, the Netherworld Books emphasize the totality of a solar-Osirian journey—itself with an excellent textual foreshadowing in Coffin Texts Spell 1068 within the Book of the Two Ways[7]—in which day and night, life and death, tomorrow and yesterday, meet and regenerate through the annihilating and recombining power of the solar deity Re and the mummiform god Osiris. The earliest of the books to appear—the Book of the Hidden Chamber (Amduat) and the Book of Gates—appear in twelve divisions (corresponding to the hours of the night), each division in three horizontal registers, the ram-headed form of the sun in his bark dominating the middle register. During the Ramesside Period a group of Netherworld Books appear without such strict divisions and registers, including the Book of Caverns and the Book of the Creation of the Solar Disk (Book of the Earth). Related treatises such as the Book of the Heavenly Cow and the Books of the Day and the Night are more concerned with cosmography than netherworldly topography.[8]

After the Ramesside Period, the Netherworld Books cease to be important elements in royal tombs, with the exceptions of excerpts from the Book of the Hidden Chamber and the Book of the Creation of the Solar Disk in royal tombs of the Twenty-First and Twenty-Second Dynasties at Tanis. Portions of the Netherworld Books become increasingly important, as seemingly disparate elements, within the corpora of non-royal tomb decoration, painted coffins, and funerary papyri during the early first millennium BCE.[9] Later in the first millennium BCE, the Netherworld Books appear in

Rectangular Coffins of the Late Middle Kingdom and Second Intermediate Period, GHP Egyptology 15 (London: Golden House Publications, 2010), pp. 103-104; C. Geisen, *Die Totentexte des verschollenen Sarges der Königin Mentuhotep aus der 13. Dynastie: ein Textzeuge aus der Übergangszeit von den Sargtexten zum Totenbuch* (Wiesbaden: Harrossowitz, 2004) (with S. Quirke, *Journal of Ancient Near Eastern Religions* 5 [2005]: 228-237); G. Miniaci *Rishi Coffins and the Funerary Culture of Second Intermediate Period Egypt*, GHP Egyptology 17 (London: Golden House Publications, 2011), pp. 149-153.

[5] Hornung, *The Ancient Egyptian Books of the Afterlife*, pp. 26-111 and 169-178.

[6] K. Jansen-Winkeln, "Sprachliche Bemerkungen zu den 'Unterweltsbüchern,'" *SAK* 32 (2012): 205-232; D. Werning, "Linguistic Dating of the Netherworld Books Attested in the New Kingdom: A Critical Review," in G. Moers, *et al.*, eds., *Dating Egyptian Literary Texts*, Lingua Aegyptia Studia Monographica 11 (Göttingen: Widmaier Verlag, 2013), pp. 237-281; J.A. Roberson, *The Ancient Egyptian Books of the Earth*, Wilbour Studies in Egypt and Ancient Western Asia 1 (Atlanta: Lockwood Press, 2012), pp. 457-459.

[7] J. Assmann, *Egyptian Solar Religion in the New Kingdom. Re, Amun and the Crisis of Polytheism*, trans. A. Alcock (London and New York: Kegan Paul International, 1995), pp. 57-58.

[8] Hornung, *The Ancient Egyptian Books of the Afterlife*, pp. 112-135 and 178-182.

[9] J. Lull, *Las tumbas reales egipcias del Tercer Periodo Intermedio (dinastias XXI-XXV): Tradicion y cambios*, BAR

"scholarly editions" on a series of elaborately decorated sarcophagi, being edited, having lacunae filled, with portions of one treatise augmenting and—by association—annotating other texts and depictions. The late first millennium use of extensive intercalations of larger elements of different treatises through application of a concept of "interchangeablity of parts"[10] develops out of the early first millennium BCE grouping of excerpts of various treatises—through application of the principle of *pars pro toto* substitution—to create a syncopated view of the Netherworld and the regenerative processes that occur there.

During the Third Intermediate Period, the Netherworld Books appear within the groups of papyri termed Amduat Papyri, Litany Papyri, Aker Papyri, and Mythological Papyri.[11] The Amduat papyri bear all or portions of the final four hours of that first attested of the New Kingdom Netherworld Books. The Litany Papyri depict forms of Re—some of these being innovations of the early first millennium BCE—with short descriptive texts. The uncommon Aker Papyri focus on the Book of the Earth/Book of Aker portion of the Book of the Creation of the Solar Disk,[12] although they can also incorporate elements from other treatises, such as the Book of the Hidden Chamber and the Book of Gates. The most expansive and varied source material, deriving material from all of the major New Kingdom Netherworld Books along with contemporaneous sources of early first millennium BCE date, is that of the Mythological Papyri.[13]

The Mythological Papyri and the Syncopated Netherworld

Within the major religious treatises of the early first millennium BCE, especially the Mythological Papyri, elements from longer works—hours of the Book of the Hidden Chamber, or even single deities—represent the corpus from which the extract in question derives. In particular, the Ninth through the Twelfth Hours of the Book of the Hidden Chamber can describe the entire nocturnal journey of the sun; the combined elements often stress the union of Re and Osiris.[14] In the Mythological Papyri, as Natacha Rambova first clearly demonstrated, combinations of descent and ascent, west and east, death and rebirth, reveal an emphasis on the cyclical aspects of the movement through time and space which is the ultimate focus of the ancient Egyptian Netherworld Books.

A linking of directional opposites appears in fact earlier, in both epithets of Osiris and the

---

International Series 1045 (Oxford: Archaeopress, 2002); J.H. Taylor Taylor, "Changes in the Afterlife," in W. Wendrich, ed., *Egyptian Archaeology* (Wiley-Blackwell: Malden, Oxford, and Chichester, 2010), pp. 223-226.

[10] C. Manassa, *The Late Egyptian Underworld: Sarcophagi and Related Texts from the Nectanebid Period*, Ägypten und Altes Testament 72 (Wiesbaden: Harrassowitz Verlag, 2007).

[11] A. Piankoff and N. Rambova, *Mythological Papyri*, Ancient Egyptian Religious Texts and Representations 3 (New York: Bollingen Foundation, 1957); A.-A.F. Sadek, *Contribution a l'etude de l'Amdouat*, Orbis Biblicus et Orientalis 65 (Fribourg and Gottingen: Academic Press and Vandenhoeck & Ruprecht Sadek, 1985); Niwinski, *Studies on the Illustrated Theban Funerary Papyri of the 11th and 10th Centuries B.C.*; É. Liptay, "Between Heaven and Earth II: the Iconography of a Funerary Papyrus from the Twenty-First Dynasty, Part 1," *Bulletin du Musée Hongrois des Beaux-Arts* 104 (2006): 35-61; idem, "Between Heaven and Earth II: the Iconography of a Funerary Papyrus from the Twenty-First Dynasty, Part 2." *Bulletin du Musée Hongrois des Beaux-Arts*, 105 (2006): 11-39.

[12] Roberson, *The Ancient Egyptian Books of the Earth*, pp. 295-299.

[13] C.Manassa, *The Late Egyptian Underworld*, pp. 438-439; A. Niwinski, "Iconography of the 21st dynasty: Its main features, levels of attestation, the media and their diffusion" in C. Uehlinger, ed., *Images as Media. Sources for the cultural history of the Near East and the Eastern Mediterranean (1st millennium BCE)*, OBO 175 (Fribourg and Gottingen: Academic Press and Vandenhoeck & Ruprecht, 2000), pp. 21-43.

[14] A. Niwinski, "The Solar-Osirian Unity as Principle of the Theology of the 'State of Amun' in Thebes in the 21st Dynasty," *JEOL* 30 (1987-1988): 89–106.

architectonic arrangements of Egyptian temple decoration. Although he normally bears an epithet such as lord of the West, Osiris may be associated with the eastern horizon, the place of repose for the mummy of Osiris at the end of the Twelfth Hour of the Book of the Hidden Chamber. This reversal of the west for the east as principal cardinal point for Osiris relates to the mixing of the normal south/east, and west/north associations of the south-north and east-west temple axes apparent in some religious texts and images. In a hymn to Re, the deity may be "Upper Egyptian (southern) king of the gods of the west, and Lower Egyptian (northern) king of the gods of the east."[15]

The Mythological Papyri focus on a repetitious recasting of the union of the opposites of the two solar axes—icons of the east-west daily journey, south-north annual solar cycle, images both diurnal and nocturnal, appear closely associated in meaningful, essentially quadripartite arrangements. The mountains of sunset and sunrise may appear fused, mated opposites combined like the images of the union of Re and Osiris also at the heart of Twenty-First Dynasty iconography. Vignettes may interact in a horizontal pairing within a single register of a treatise, and in vertical relationships connecting different registers.

One may expand upon Rambova's work, which she was unfortunately unable to complete, by seeking forerunners for her syncopated icons of the cycle of descent and ascent within the Mythological Papyri. A composition devoted to the Twelve Caverns,[16] usually known as chapter 168 of the Book of Going Forth by Day and occurring as a separate treatise in some royal tombs (on papyrus and later as wall decoration), is in its groupings of images a forerunner of the later Mythological Papyri. An extreme syncopation of the Netherworld, as a discrete treatise, appears in the version of the Book of the Solar-Osirian Unity in the Tomb of Ramesses IX[17]—the midday/midnight encounter of Re and the great chaos serpent Apep leads directly to a scene of the giant Re-Osiris that elaborates on the image of Osiris at the end of the Twelfth Hour of the Book of the Hidden Chamber. Such a linking of the middle and end phases of the nocturnal solar journey becomes common during the Third Intermediate Period, especially in the Mythological Papyri.

When one looks more carefully at the full range of religious iconography and textual sources from the first millennium BCE, the functioning of the concept of a combinatory syncopation of material is ever present. The combinations of excerpts from the Book of Going Forth by Day and the Netherworld Books, another characteristic mingling of different compositions occurring on many of the Mythological Papyri, continues a template appearing already during the reign of Tutankhamun in the first of the treatises belonging to the group of related compositions called the Books of the Solar-Osirian Unity.[18] Similar blending of elements of various Netherworld Books appears as well in the sarcophagus chamber of the tomb of Ramesses IV,[19] and resurfaces in the ancient scholarly concept of the interchangeability of parts on Late Period sarcophagi. Images such as that of the

---

[15] For temple axes, see C. Loeben, "Bemerkungen zum Horustempel des Neuen Reiches in Edfu," *BSEG* 14 (1990): 67; S. Cauville, "Une règle de la 'grammaire' du temple" *BIFAO* 83 (1983): 51-84. For the solar hymn associating south with west and north with east, see Assmann, *Ägyptische Hymnen und Gebete*, p. 110, no. 11 ll. 9-10.

[16] Hornung, *The Ancient Egyptian Books of the Afterlife*, pp. 54-55 and 173.

[17] J.C. Darnell, *The Enigmatic Netherworld Books of the Solar-Osirian Unity: Cryptographic Compositions in the Tombs of Tutankhamun, Ramesses VI, and Ramesses IX*, Orbis Biblicus et Orientalis 198 (Fribourg and Göttingen: Academic Press and Vandenhoeck & Ruprecht, 2004).

[18] Darnell, *The Enigmatic Netherworld Books of the Solar-Osirian Unity*, pp. 452-453; not the result of scribal ignorance, *contra* Niwinski *Studies on the Illustrated Theban Funerary Papyri of the 11th and 10th Centuries B.C.*, pp. 149-150

[19] E. Hornung *Zwei ramessidische Königsgräber: Ramses IV. Und Ramses VII*, Theben 11 (Mainz am Rhein: Philipp von Zabern, 1990), p. 88.

Hathoric cow emerging from the Western mountains, the well attested vignette to chapter 186 of the Book of Going Forth by Day, represents that composition in various new iconographic groupings on coffins of the period, emphasizing a reconciliation of chthonic and solar aspects of Amun theology.[20]

Excellent examples of Rambova's discovery of the syncopation of the Netherworld through pairings of the cardinal points appear in depictions of the emergence of images of East and West from a common mountain, opposing and balanced directions deriving ultimately from one another —and at the same time leading into each other. On the papyrus of Nespawtywtawy,[21] the forepart of the bovid Hathor—labeled "Hathor mistress of the West"—emerges from the mountains to the right, as though coming out of the western hills. On the left, the head and arms of a deity hold the rising sun, coming out of the eastern mountains. Papyri such as that of Gautsushen A and Djedamunefankh[22] reveal that these arms with head derive from the arms and head that emerge from the end of the underworld, the root of the eastern horizon, at the end of the Twelfth Hour of the night in the Book of the Hidden Chamber. According to the annotations to the Twelfth Hour, the arms are those of the deity Shu, who will bear the newborn sun into the luminous space of which Shu is himself the divine personification.

On the papyrus of Khonsumes A,[23] the syncopated Netherworld combines the dual up-down and side-to-side axes. A head with arms emerges to either side of a central "horizon" region; the arms of the deity are drawn such that the upper arms are essentially the silhouette of the hills, the head emerging between, and the forearms held out from the horizon, each pair grasping a solar disk. Between the heads and arms with disks are three divine standards; atop the first two are *heh*-deities, symbolizing years of cyclical time (as the labels above them indicate), followed by the orthography of *djet.t*-time atop the rightmost standard. To the left of this group is a slightly bowed, elderly Re-Horakhty, between the adoring figures of "his daughter," the goddess Maat, to the right, and the personification of *heka*-magic to the left. The iconography of this central group describes the intervening block of horizon-land between the heads and arms as an area of eternal renewal of the solar disk, and the propagation of order and the divine magical aura.

The facing directions of the heads emerging from the arms to each side of this horizon area reveal the common associations of north with west and south with east. Falcons on the appropriate standards label the arms to the right as the western horizon, and those to the left as the eastern horizon—the side-to-side motion of passage through the underworld and through the upper firmament. At the same time, the heads evoke the up-down motion of the solar cycle and the annual south to north progression of the sun, parallel to the side-to-side motion of the east to west and west to east cycles of day and night. The head of the western horizon faces down—to the north—and the head of the eastern horizon faces up—to the south. These images perfectly illustrate Rambova's complex initial statement on the iconography of the Mythological Papyri: "The root pattern illustrated in the scenes of these papyri is that of the eternally repeating cycle of the sun god: his emergence from the Watery Abyss at the dawn of each new creation, his descent in the West into the Necropolis of the Western Mountain, his passage through the night regions of Osiris, his rebirth from the horizon of the Eastern Mountain and renascent back into the heights of heaven."[24]

What Natacha Rambova recognized in the Mythological Papyri of the early first millennium

[20] É. Liptay, "Between Heaven and Earth. The Motif of the Cow Coming out of the Mountain," *Bulletin du Musée Hongrois des Beaux-Arts* 99 (2003): 11-30.

[21] Piankoff and Rambova, *Mythological Papyri,* pl. 3.

[22] Piankoff and Rambova, *Mythological Papyri,* pls. 24 and 27; *cf.* also pls. 28 and 29.

[23] Piankoff and Rambova, *Mythological Papyri,* pl. 16.

[24] Piankoff and Rambova, *Mythological Papyri,* p. 29.

BCE was an ever-recurring series of icons linking opposing elements, directions, and concepts in expressions of a cosmic cycle. This syncopation of the Netherworld and cosmic processes may in origin have formed part of the knowledge of the solar arcana expected of the Egyptian king as chief priest of the solar religion. A similar syncopation of the Netherworld Books already occurs within and even underpins the New Kingdom text known as the King as Solar Priest.[25] Allusions to such a focused and balanced syncopation of the solar cycle occur earlier, as in a self-presentation of the cosmic kingship of Hatshepsut in the Red Chapel, in which zoomorphic avatars and evocations of solar iconic imagery for both the diurnal and nocturnal worlds reveal the ruler as embodiment of the various elements of a syncopated solar cycle.[26]

Although her lengthy manuscript on the "Cosmic Circuit" remained unfinished at her death, Natacha Rambova's published Egyptological work represents a significant contribution to our understanding of netherworldly iconography.[27] In her published essay on the Mythological Papyri and her unpublished manuscript, she demonstrated that what might appear to be an illogical jumble of cosmic symbols within a funerary papyrus is a complex, yet internally consistent, representation of the cyclical nature of the solar journey. In the end, Rambova's unorthodox approach to Egyptology did not hamper—and indeed enhanced—her contributions to the study of an ancient set of beliefs that it is still important to remind ourselves was—as she most aptly stated in the Foreword to the "Cosmic Circuit"—"religion in its earliest form and deepest sense."

[25] J. Assmann, *Der König als Sonnenpriester*, ADAIK 7 (Glückstadt: J.J. Augustin, 1970).

[26] P. Lacau and H. Chevrier, with M.-A. Bonhème and M. Gitton, *Une chapelle d'Hatshepsout à Karnak* 1 (Cairo: Service des Antiquités de l'Égypte and the Institut Français d'Archéologie Orientale, 1977), pp. 149-153; Darnell, forthcoming.

[27] A summary of her Egyptological contributions, with references to earlier literature, appears in C. Manassa and T. Dobbin-Bennett, "The Natacha Rambova Archive, Yale University," *Göttinger Miszellen* 234 (2012): 85-100.

THE COSMIC CIRCUIT

NATACHA RAMBOVA

PP. 155 - 171, FROM *PART TWO, THE CREATION OF THE UNIVERSE, PART TWO, CONTINUED, THE COSMIC CIRCUIT IN EGYPT*

In an unusually complete symbolic form, the circuit is illustrated in two introductory vignettes of a Cairo Museum papyrus (Fig. 78), from the opposite perspectives of the sky goddess Nut and of the Osirian Netherworld. In the vignette on the left, the head, breasts and arms of the goddess are represented as she lowers and raises the disk. By turning the plate, the soul birds are seen to greet the sun in its descent, while its re-ascent is acclaimed by the four ape adorers of dawn.

Fig. 78.

In the vignette on the right, the arms of the <u>Ankh</u> surmounting the <u>Djed-pillar</u> are raised to both receive the disk into the region of death and to lift it again renewed in life, where it will enter the heavens through the horizon gates of Shu whose head and outstretched arms are seen above. [1] Greeting the sun are the two bearded soul birds with arms raised in worship, while below on either side kneel the sister goddesses Isis and Nephthys. Clarifying the circuit implications, the West sign is inscribed to the left, the East sign to the right.

It is obvious that a basic conception so commonly known as that of the cycle of solar descent in the West for rebirth in the East would not be continually reiterated in repetitious detail, hence the many abbreviated symbolic phrases in the texts, as well as the many synthesized representations in the tombs and on the coffins and papyri. In the Second Division of the *Book of What is in the Netherworld*, called in the introductory passage, "beginning of inscription facing West", we find the

---

1   For the horizon gates of Shu, see below section, *The Celestial Image.*

following abbreviated allusion to the cycle:

> *This is what they do: they cause the coming of*
> *darkness... It is they who keep guard over the*
> *day, (they) being the night in order that the*
> *Great God may enter the complete darkness, to*
> *rest in the Gate of the Eastern Horizon of Heaven.*[2]

Here, as in the synthesized symbolic representations of the death-birth cycle, the god enters into the Western Netherworld to achieve his purpose of renewal – and so comes to rest once more in the Eastern Horizon of the heaven-world.

On an anonymous papyrus in the Cairo Museum we are told:

> *The god circles in the sky in the direction of the*
> *Netherworld, he joins himself to the Mysterious*
> *Region of the Netherworld...The Netherworld is*
> *open to thee, the earth is thrown open to thee!*
>
> *Lo, thou proceedest in peace, those in the Evening*
> *Barge receive thee, thou art rowed by (those of*
> *the) Morning Barge. Thou proceedest, thou circlest*
> *towards the Netherworld...O hail! He who appears*
> *in the Eastern Mountain, Ruler of Creation...*

Beginning with the circling across the northern sky, the god descends into the West to join himself to the Mysterious Religion of renewal. In the next verse the entire cycle is described: the western descent in the Evening Barge, the eastern ascent in the Morning Barge, the circling across the northern sky for the re-descent, leading to the final birth in the Eastern Mountain.

As if in illustration of the above text, the various stages of the sun god's circuit are painted with significant details on a Twenty-first Dynasty coffin. (Fig. 79)

Fig. 79

---

2   *The Tomb of Ramesses VI*, p, 241.

Resting on the back of the sky goddess Nut in the cosmic heights, the ram-head of Amon, encircled by the uroboros, is shown in the solar barge of millions of years about to re-emerge from the darkness of the abyss, Nun.

Seated on a standard on the prow is the ape adorer ready to greet the northern dawn of the new cycle. Descending in the next stage into the West along the arms of Nut, the god, now in his form of Atum, is seated in the disk in the Evening Barge where he will be received into the earth's horizon of Geb by the arms of the waiting Netherworld divinity. Having passed through the night regions the god is next seen in the East as the disk of Khepri, mounting the legs of Nut in the Morning Barge.

Indicating the birth of a new cycle, the body of Shu is also represented in scarab form, as he separates day from night by lifting the sky body of Nut from her earth consort Geb.

Further in the text of the same anonymous papyrus, the circuit is again described:

> *They stay with Re in heaven in order to unite*
> *him with the Mysterious Region. They sail in the*
> *Evening Barge, they follow Re in the Morning Barge.*
>
> *Thou fly-est toward the sky as the Great Soul and those*
> *of the sky receive thee. Oh hail to thee in the Morning*
> *Barge, thou art received by the Evening Barge!*
>
> *Thou traverseth the sky, thou circlest toward the Netherworld.* [3]

On the shrines of Tut-Ankh-Amon, a text from Chapter 130 of *The Book of the Dead* again orients the entire circuit:

> *The sky and the earth are open! The East and the*
> *West are open! The Two Shrines are open! The doors*
> *are open for Re when he comes out of the horizon.*
> *The two doors of the Evening Barge are open, the*
> *gates of the Morning Barge are open.* [4]

To the modern, scientific mind, thinking in terms of precise definitions, the ancient love of synthesis, of enigmatic combinations, of seeing in terms of underlying unity, analogy, and over-lapping relationships, is often irritating and confusing. In discussing the almost endless forms and variants arising from this progressive association of ideas, Henri Frankfort says:

> "There is no denying that to us this spreading net of associations and identifications seems to destroy the significance of the symbols involved, and the limit of meaningfulness is well passed when we meet in the New Kingdom texts such compounds as 'Osiris-Apis-Atum-Horus in one, the Great God.' But if we disregard such extremes, we shall find that much that appears senseless at first sight is not

3   A. Piankoff, *Mythological Papyri,* pp. 196, 197.
4   A. Piankoff, *The Shrines of Tut-Ankh-Amon,* p. 111.

without meaning. Moreover, the primitives, far from sharing our passion for precise definition and distinction, appreciate each relationship which can be established between seemingly disparate phenomena as a strengthening of the fabric of understanding in which they attempt to comprehend the world." [5]

This fluidity in concept and identification through analogy is nowhere more obvious than in ancient cosmological orientation, where perspective, placement, and positions overlap and fuse to the point of apparent contradiction. In consequence the birth god Khepri, associated with the eastern horizon, is also found in the North, the West, and the South – all points of mysterious transference from life to death and death to life. In the North, as the innate power of self-creation, Khepri is identified with the creator Atum, the First God, as the one who first emerges from the primeval waters, Nun, at the dawn of creation – or by analogy at the beginning of each new cycle. This identification is described in the Pyramid Texts (§ 1652, 1655):

> *Atum-Khepri, thou wert high as (the) Hill.* [6]
> *Thou didst shine forth as Benben...*
> *Thou didst spit out Shu;*
> *Thou did spew out Tefnut.*
>
> *O Great Ennead who are in Heliopolis.*
> *Atum, Shu, Tefnut, Geb, Nut, Osiris, Isis, Seth, Nephthys,*
> *Children of Atum – his heart is broad because of his*
> *children, in your name of Nine.* [7]

In *The Book of the Becoming of Re*, the first principle declares: "I am he who came into being in the form of Khepri, and I was the creator of that which came into being." In the earlier version of Chapter XVII of the *Book of the Dead*, Khepri is called "the Primeval One, whose body is eternity." [8] As such the scarab god in the North represents the first stirring of creation on the new cycle, the re-beginning and re-emergence from the cosmic night of being into which the aged god had retired at the end of the prior great cycle. This is the birth from the Abyss described by the sun god in the *Book of What is in the Netherworld* when he says: "I approach the earth by day after having passed the (cosmic) night to rest my soul."[9] It was the coming out and coming down out of the interior of heaven [10] to re-descend into the Netherworld, likened to the first sunrise over the Primeval Hill:

> *Thou risest, thou risest, when thou comest forth*
> *from the Ocean of Heaven;*
> *Thou re-juvenatest thyself again on the place of*
> *yesterday*
> *Divine Youth, who came into being out of thyself.* [11]

---

5   *Kingship and the Gods*, p. 196.
6   The Primeval Hill likened to the pillar, the Ben-ben, which originated from a seed of Atum falling into the primeval ocean.
7   H. Frankfort, *Kingship and the Gods*, p. 153; *The Pyramid Texts*, trans. By Samuel A. B. Mercer, p. 253.
8   Coffin Text 335, A. de Buck, *The Egyptian Coffin Texts IV*, trans. A. Piankoff.
9   *The Tomb of Ramsesses VI*, p. 253.
10 A. Piankoff, *The Shrines of Tut-Ankh-Amon*, p. 34.
11 A, Scharff, *Aegyptische Sonnenlieder (1922)*, p. 31, quoted from H. Frankfort, *Kingship and the Gods*, p. 151.

This birth out of the cosmic night of Nun in the North – on the western side of the circuit (Fig. 79), was the descending western birth towards death in the night region below the western horizon. It was likewise the descending birth out of the arms of the sky goddess Nut (Fig.78) in the West – also symbolized by the birth into her mouth [12] – in contrast to the ascending birth from her vulva to the East. From certain descriptions of the goddess we learn that "Her mouth is the Western Horizon, her vulva is the Eastern Horizon." [13] In both positions we find the presence of Khepri and the disk. [14]

Placed in the West, Khepri as the Becoming One, denotes the "birth" of the god into the "darkness of the Region of Form," his earthly aspect as "Flesh": the point of transformation from the divine raiment of the solar realm into the death form of the lunar region in which the god becomes identified with the mummified figures of Osiris-man.(Figs. 65, 68a)

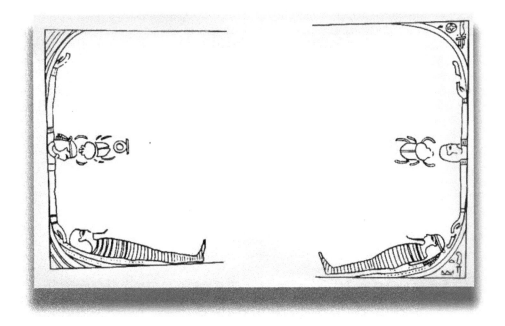

Fig. 65

---

12 Symbolically the goddess was said to "swallow" the disk to convey the image of its passage through the interior of her body in her aspect as the night sky.

13 *The Tomb of Ramsesses VI*, p. 39. Both the mouth and the arms of Nut are associated with the Western descent. The mouth symbol pertains to the symbolism of the Head, the arms to the Body-Part symbolism. See below section on the Head and the Arms.

14 CF. Figs. 59,63a,65,76, 81 and reference to the western side of the votive pyramid, p. 147. In *Pry. Texts* (§888): N. shines in the East like Re, he goes in the West like Khepri. *The Pyramid Texts*, trans. Samuel A.B. Mercer, p. 162.

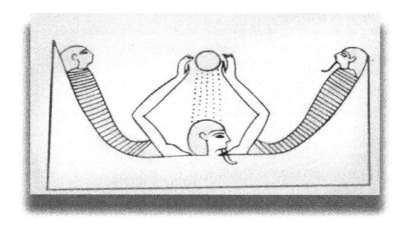

Fig. 68a

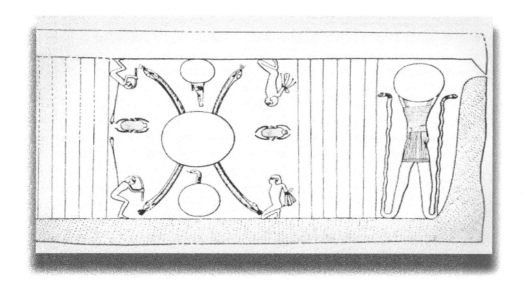

Fig. 80

In a unique cosmological mandala[15] centered between the West-East horizon "mountains" (Fig. 80) the scarabs flank the great disk in both West and East positions, while smaller disks mark the North and South. From the northern disk emerges the head of a crocodile,[16] from the southern a serpent head. Suggesting a descending and ascending division the enemies on the West side are unbound, while those on the eastern side kneel and are bound to indicate their subjugation.

---

15 *The Tombs of Ramesses VI*, Fig. 78.
16 See below section on the Crocodile.

458

The disk-headed divinity with the serpent legs standing in the curve of the eastern mountain is discussed below.

In the South, Khepri is seen emerging from the mountain of the night above Sokaris, the birth god of the Memphite necropolis, who symbolizes the revivification at the mysterious midpoint of the underworld passage where death first gives way to reawakening life.

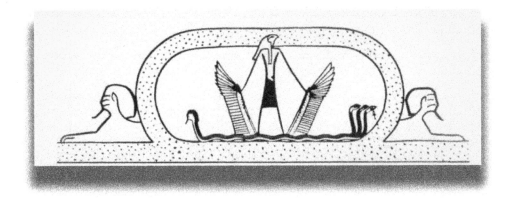

Fig. 82

On a wall representation in the tomb of Ramesses VI, (Fig. 82)this night passage from West to East is depicted by the solar barge with the ram-headed scarab traveling over the back of the double-lion god Aker. Denoting its entrance into and emergence from death in the pit of earth, at the central midpoint of the body, Aker's two arms lower and raise the disk. In the parallel conception represented in *The Book of What is in the Netherworld* (Fig. 82) the emergence of new life is symbolized by the hawk-headed Sokaris in his "egg" between the foreparts of Aker.[17]

In the East, Khepri appears at the sunrise resurrection which heralds the solar ascension back into the heights of heaven where the now aged god will once more enter the Abyss to "rest his soul" at the close of his circuit. A symbolic description of this aspect of the god is given in the *Book of the Divine Cow:*

> *Re had grown old, his bones became like silver.*
> *His flesh like gold, his hair like lapis lazuli.*

While more similar to the description give in the myth of Isis and Re[18] is the one of the god himself:

> *My limbs are feeble as in primeval times – I will*
> *not return until another (cycle) overtakes me.* [19]

---

17 The god Aker appears to be a lower symbolic aspect of the horizon lions Shu and Tefnut, hence joined to signify the West-East midpoint of union in the underworld.

18 See above pp. 35-39.

19 A. Piankoff, *The Shrines of Tut.Ankh-Amon*, pp. 27, 29.

In keeping with the traditional synthesizing of the death-birth concept associated with the West-East horizons, an even more subtle form of symbolic synthesis was also used in terminal texts and representations describing the sunrise birth. Here, together with the identification of West and East we find the fusion of the Netherworld sunrise out of the Abyss in the North[20] to suggest the return, completion, and re-beginning of the cycle.[21] This unified conception of sunrise is traditionally illustrated in a vignette from the papyrus of Qenna, by the disk lifted into new life by the arms of the personified <u>Ankh</u>. (Fig. 83).

Fig. 83

On either side the rising sun is worshiped by the Bentiu apes of dawn[22]- those on the right herald the eastern sunrise, those on the left the cosmic birth in the North-West. Another symbolic feature of interest are the four mountains of the four directions outlined in the background of the scene.[23]

---

20 In India the joining of these two points of Netherworld and cosmic birth is clearly described in a passage of the Atarva Veds (11.5.6.) : "The Brahmacari in a wink he goes from the Eastern to the Northern Sea – again and again joining in himself the Two Worlds." See also footnote p. 168.

21 As a religious form of presentation this enigmatic style of symbolic synthesis appears to have been develop during the Eighteenth and Nineteenth Dynasties in the tomb recordings of the epic mystery compositions: the *Book of What is in The Netherworld*, the *Book of Gates*, the Osirian *Book of Caverns* and the *Book of Night*. Although apparently a product of this period it flourished on the coffins and in the Mythological Papyri of the Twentieth and Twenty-first Dynasties and in the tomb representations of the later Ramessides.

22 In thus placing three ape worshipers on either side of the disk, the composition forms another version of the numerical tradition of the three-One-Three: here as a reverse higher world septenary to those illustrated above in Figs. 38B, 39, 44.

23 E.A. Wallis Budge, The Book of the Dead, p. 75; see also the similar version from the papyrus of Ani, p. 73.

Fig. 84

In the final scene of the *Book of Caverns* (Fig. 84) the birth from the Eastern Mountain is depicted by the disk passing through the mountain border,[24] the figure of the divine Child and the ram-headed scarab. Although serving primarily to illustrate the solar birth from the Netherworld, the symbolic context and structure of this terminal composition is so designed as to project the concept of cyclic wholeness and completion.[25] Hence twelve gods tow the barge containing the ram-headed sun god with a disk between his horns, a scarab, and a bird on a mound. Suggesting the yearly three seasons of four months, the first four towers are hawk-headed, the second are ram-headed, and the last four have bearded human heads.[26] Above the towers is a descriptive text:

> *Tow Re! We accompany the Unique Lord, Khepri*
> *of the attached head! Salutations to thee whose*
> *glory is great. You belong to the soul of the living*
> *forms, in peace in the interior of his disk! Re is in*
> *peace in the interior of his disk! This Great God*
> *enters into the Mountain of the East.*

---

24 See similar borders in the final scenes of the *Book of Gates* and the *Am-Duat, The Tomb of Ramesses VI*, Figs. 73, 87.

25 i.e. in that which terminates and completes lies the image of the whole. See above p. 137.

26 The first four figures represent the first four months of the descent from the western horizon (Thoth, Phaophi, Athyr, Choisk) ; the second four the four months of the ascent into the heavens (Tybi, Mechir, Phamenoth, Pharmuthi) ; the last four those of the return into the Abyss and re-descent (Pachons, Payni, Epiphi, Mesore). See below section on the twelve months of the Egyptian calender.

Above and below the last four towers is a bearded figure with elongated arms[27] bending over a mound containing a disk. Placed as they are these two groups symbolize the western and eastern mountains of sunset into and sunrise out of the lower world, between which the mysterious cyclic renewal takes place. The figure and the mound above, pertaining to the entrance into the vault of the heavens, are shown reversed.

Text above the upper mound:

> This god is like this. He bends (?) over the mysterious mound, in the interior of which is the great secret. This Great God speaks before this god when he passes (in) his boat. His bodies, his forms are at peace on (their) thrones.

Text above the lower mound:

> The One who presides the Mysteries. This god is like this, he bends (?) over the mysterious mound which contains the mystery in its interior. [28]

On a papyrus this passage through the Mysteries of the Netherworld transformations for the eastern rebirth is alluded to in an address to Re:

> Hail to thee Re! We cause thee to pass by the Mysteries, we cause thee to take a seat in the East. [29]

Of a similar symbolic tradition to the seven male and seven female towers of the barge in the *Book of What is in the Netherworld*[30] are the seven hawk-headed and seven human-headed worshipers in the triangular divisions made by the lines drawn from the mountains to the disk. The seven hawk-headed figures worship the western descent, the seven human-headed figures the eastern ascent. [31]

Preceding this final representation is a litany in which the god states that he has come forth from the two mounds of the horizon, or in other words he has completed his decent into and ascent from the Netherworld and has thus achieved the fashioning of this forms:

> This Great God comes forth from the two mounds which are in the Netherworld. This god becomes a form of forms of Exalted Earth.[32] This god speaks to the gods who are in his cavern...

---

27 The extension of the arms to form the two pillars or pylons of the horizon, see below section on the Celestial Image, pp. 215-218.

28 *The Tomb of Ramsesses VI*, pp. 133. 134.

29 A. Piankoff, *Mythological Papyri*, p. (uncited).

30 See above Fig. 38.

31 The hawk-headed figures of the West are in the form of Horus of the Horizon (see Fig. 92); those with the human heads represent those who have attained the divine head on the eastern horizon. Symbolic of attainment and completion they are also identified with the North. See below p. 183, Fig. 93. Also section on the month Phamenoth below pp. (uncited).

32 The god Tatunen or Exalted Earth represents the revivified or resurrected earth as the divine manifestation – the divinity made manifest.

462

O gods...behold, I come forth from my mounds!
I am born, my disk is established by the members
of the council who are in the following of He at
the Head of the West. They extend their arms to me.
I become! My forms are fashioned! Praise me,
because I have cared for you, inhabitants of the
Netherworld of mysterious forms!

O these my bodies of Atum, his members are his images..
O this soul of He of the Mound, his members, his images...
O this soul of Khepri, his members, his images..
O this soul of Shu...
O this soul of Geb....
O this soul of Osiris...
O this soul of Seth. [33]

After having come forth from his western and eastern horizon mounds, having achieved his rebirth and ascension into the heavens, the naming in the litany of the series of gods associated with the pattern of the original descending creation from the Abyss [34] serves textually to contribute the same picture of cyclic termination and re-beginning [35] suggested in the structural symbolism of the representation. Another unusual but similar conception of the circuit pattern is represented on the wall of the sarcophagus chamber of the tomb of Queen Tausert. (Fig. 85)

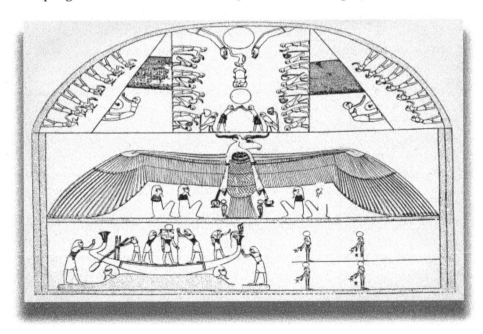

Fig. 85

---

33 *The Tomb of Ramesses VI*, p. 131.
34 Celestial Image, pp. 105-107.
35 "O thou who risest and settest in the Nun..." *Hieratic Papyri in the British Museum:Beatty Gift*, ed. By Alan Gardiner, Vol. I, text p. 76, trans. By A Piankoff.

Here again, in the upper register, are the seven worshipers on either side of the central birth composition (see Fig. 66);

Fig. 66

the seven hawk-headed figures on the right denoting those who greet the descent into the Western Mountain; the seven on the left in the ram-headed form of Re, being those who greet the ascent from the Eastern mountains. Placed within the border triangles are the two gods bending over the mounds, this time containing the head symbol rather than the disk. [36]

Suggesting the waters of the northern Abyss, into which the young god in the form of the birth Child will ascend before his re-descent into the West on the new cycle, the triangles are appropriately divided by a band of water lines.

In the middle register the great ram-headed solar hawk with outspread wings represents the divine form of the gods as Amon-Re in his circuit, holding in each claw the <u>shen</u> with two disk-crowned uraei emerging from his spread tail. To complete the circuit theme in the lower register the solar boat is shown at rest in the Netherworld on the back of the double-lion Aker (Fig. 82).

Probably the most complete symbolic conception of the ever-recurring cycle is that of the terminal scene from the *Book of Gates* [37] on a papyrus in the Bibliotheque National (fig. 86). [38] Here the solar barge with the new-born life depicted by the scarab is being held aloft by the arms of Nun, the Abyss. From above, the disk raised by the scarab is received by Nut who stands on the head of the reversed encircled body of Osiris: who thus symbolizes the recurrent cycle of the greater Netherworld creation that begins and returns into itself to begin anew. [39]

---

36 By reversing Fig. 85 the reader will see that the ram-headed figures, now on the right, are worshiping the large disk, birth Child, and ram-headed scarab which have arisen from the eastern mound to ascend between the arms of Nut; the hawk-headed figures on the left are worshiping the new disk which will descend into the western mound.

37 See below section on the Celestial Image, Fig. 97.

38 Papyrus of Khonsu-mes. See A. Piankoff, *Mythological Papyri*, No. 32.

39 See above, p. 163-164.

Fig. 86

Unifying the two opposite conceptions of life and death – the sun god Re, who descends into the darkness of the Western Necropolis to become identified with Osiris, Lord of the Dead – this scene is found to illustrate a text in the shrines of Tut-Ankh-Amon describing this moment of cyclic renewal:

> *The barge circles in the sky and the light appears.*
> *Osiris circles in the sky towards the West.* [40]

In a further text it is written:

> *The King, Lord of the Two Lands, will take all*
> *the forms he likes following Re in the Evening*
> *Barge, going to rest in the Morning Barge.*
>
> *Thou makest the transformations in heaven like Re,*
> *thou are born in the morning like him, thou sailest*
> *on high in the Evening Barge.* [41]

In the Eleventh Division of the *Book of Gates* the midpoint of the heavens in the North of the cycle is referred to in a text over eight goddesses called Those of the Morning:

---

40 See above the texts from the Anonymous papyrus, pp. 156-157.
41 A. Piankoff, *The Shrines of Tut-Ankh-Amon*, p. 112.

They come out from the Two Chapels of this Great
God, four to the East, four to the West. It is
they who call the spirits of the East and praise
this god. They adore him after he has come out,
when the child has appeared in his forms...They
cause to rise before this god when he turns toward
his gate to come out and stand in peace in the porch of the west.

The two chapels alluded to here appear to be those of the entrance into the Abyss from the East side, and the exit from the Abyss on the West side; so that the god enters into the heights and comes out on "the porch of the West" for his re-descent towards the Netherworld. [42] Alluding to the final scene (Fig. 86) the text continues:

This god enters the heights of heaven, he opens the
Netherworld toward the heights of heaven by his
forms which are in the Abyss. As to what opens the
Netherworld towards the Abyss it is the two arms of
the One Whose Name is Hidden. He is in complete
darkness when Re enters it (the heights of heaven)
at dawn. [43]

In less abstract illustrations the midpoint of the North, where the cycle returns into itself, is often symbolized by the transference of the god in his disk from the Morning Barge in which he ascends to the Evening Barge in which he re-descends (Fig 87). This act of transference is usually made by Isis and Nephthys. In our example, however, the god is passed by the goddess of the East to the goddess of the West.

Fig. 87

42 Confirming this allusion to the new creation to come forth from the porch of the West, the two pillars shown in the gateway of the Twelfth Division (below Fig. 87) are topped by the bearded human heads of two gods, given the names of creators Atum-Khepri. See *Pyr. Text* quotation p, 159.

43 *The Tomb of Ramsesses VI*, p. 218.

APPENDICES

468

IN MEMORIAM

FATHER MICHAEL MORRIS, O.P.
1949-2016

"Non hoc praecipuum amicorum munus est, prosequi defunctum
ignavo questu, sed quod voluerit meminisse, quae mandaverit exequi."
P. Cornelius Tacitus-Annnales Liber Secundus

ACKNOWLEDGMENTS

The completion of *Beyond Valentino* was accomplished only through the kind assistance of those who gave generously of their time and materials. I wish to acknowledge and extend my most sincere thank-you to:

William James for his support, historical insight, editorial assistance and valuable creative contributions, for his authoring the introduction contexualizing *Arriba España* and for sharing his remarkable photographic archive.

Maria Salomé Juaneda Pujol for her Natacha Rambova guardianship and for sharing her family history and her collection of Rambova's photographs and artifacts.

Tonina Matamalas, Catalina Ruiz and Sebastià Mascaró for their contributions in developing Ms. Maria Salomé Juaneda Pujol's story.

John Coleman Darnell and Colleen Manassa Darnell for authoring "*Natacha Rambova's Syncopated Netherworld and the Cosmic Cycle*", for imparting their insights into the Natacha Rambova Archive at Yale University and for the colorful inspiration on their Instagram account @vintage_egyptologist.

The Epigraphic Survey, based at Chicago House in Luxor, Egypt, Director W. Raymond Johnson, Research Associate and Associate Professor at the Oriental Institute, Sue Lezon, Photographer and Photo Archivist, Chicago House, Oriental Institute, Alain Arnaudies, Photo Archives Staff, Chicago House, Oriental Institute and J. Brett McClain.

Dr. Vladimir Rosov, for contributing his article of his 1999 interview with Michael Morris, for granting permission to publish Natacha Rambova's sketch titled, "The Egyptian Woman" and for confirming the engagement of Svetoslav Roerich and Natacha Rambova.

Gvido Trespa, Executive Director of the Nicholas Roerich Museum and Daniel Entin, Director Emeritus of the Nicholas Roerich Museum for granting permission to use a collection of photographs and for their prompt forwarding of the files.

Rosalind M. Janssen of University College London for forwarding her two ground-breaking articles on Natacha Rambova as the Egyptologist.

John G. Rae III, Susan Rae and Tove Abrams, for sharing their family archives including photographs, personal correspondence and personal information about their uncle, Mark Hasselriis.

Luke Kelly, Curator of Antiquities, Utah Museum of Fine Arts and Christina Samore, Registrar at the Utah Museum of Fine Arts for their assistance in granting permission to use the Joanovitch portraits and for expediting the scanning of Natacha Rambova's "*The Cosmic Circuit*", Adelaide Ryder, Collections Photographer and Digital Media Producer and Sandra Jones, accountant, for assisting in transacting the procurement of these documents.

Heather Vaughan Lee for sharing her copy of the Museum of Religion and Philosophy brochure with Michael Morris and for her consultation regarding Natacha Rambova's make-up line.

Dennita Sewell, Curator of Fashion Design, Phoenix Art Museum and Brian Jennings, Curatorial Assistant, Fashion, Phoenix Art Museum for permission to reproduce their photographs of Natacha Rambova's gowns and dress designs and for forwarding the files.

Agnès Macquin, Librarian, Institut Français Archéologie Orientale in Cairo for conducting a photographic search of their archives for images.

Carlos Lazurtegui for his artistry in the restoration of the cover image of Natacha Rambova.

Nello Rassu, Director of the Quazza Multi-Media Laboratory at the University of Turin for editing and retrieving the Convegno Valentino archival video of Michael Morris' speech delivered in 2009.

Fr. Michael Carey, O.P., for his support and faith in me and this project, also thank-you to Fr. Chris Renz O.P., Fr. Mark Padrez O.P. and Fr. Peter Rogers O.P., of the Western Dominican Province.

Pat and Paul Chamberlain for their continued support and for sharing Michael Morris' archive with me for use in completing this book.

Renato Floris, publisher of *Beyond Valentino* and sage overseer from the day of its inception, Diva Zumaya, Doctoral Candidate, School of Art and Architecture, University of Santa Barbara for her editorial assistance and art consultancy and Lucero Rabaudi, for his artistry in creating the cover design and endless patience with me in executing the final layout.

Thank-you for all!

The Authors & Contributors

Michael Morris-

Fr. Michael Morris, O.P., entered the Order of Friars Preachers for the Western Dominican Province and was ordained a priest on April 23, 1977. He was awarded his M.A. in Art History from the University of California, Berkeley in 1981 and studied at the Courtauld Institute of Art, London, in 1982 and he earned his PhD in Art History from UC Berkeley in 1986.

In 1991, his highly acclaimed biography *Madam Valentino: The Many Lives of Natacha Rambova* was published by Abbeville Press. Since 1998, his widely-read articles on religious art and iconography have been published by *Magnificat*. He taught at the Dominican School of Philosophy & Theology, Berkeley, and served as Director of the Santa Fe Institute, Berkeley, until his death on July 15, 2016.

Evelyn Zumaya -

Evelyn Zumaya has authored and edited a niche catalog of Rudolph Valentino books including *Affairs Valentino*, *The Affairs Valentino Companion Guide*, *The Lost Court Documents of Rudolph Valentino*, *The S. George Ullman Memoir* and *L'Affare Valentino*. She also edited *The Infancy of the Myth* by Aurelio Miccoli. She is a partner in the Turin based publishing firm of Viale Industria Pubblicazioni and contributed to the Kaplan Edizioni publication, *Rodolfo Valentino, Cinema, Cultura, Società tra Italia é Stati Uniti Negli Anni Venti*.

In addition to her authoring and editing these publications, she has worked as a fine artist with a professional focus on art conservation in her studios in Turin, Buenos Aires and Los Angeles.

William James -

William James is an English visual artist living and working in Spain. He designs installations conceived for specific contexts based upon free-form documentary research. These installations have explored the interplay between urban (public) spaces and spaces of intimacy as well as the physical and cultural constituents of spaces, locations and situations, and how they interact with individuals to modify actions and relations. His most recent project, *Las Ahijadas*, is a double-projection audiovisual installation utilizing oral history, video footage and archival materials to relate two histories presided over by two exceptional individuals who have shared the same *faux* Russian name: Natacha Rambova.

Dr. Vladimir Rosov -

Dr. Vladimir Rosov is an historian, orientalist and Doctor of Historical Sciences. He is a renowned scholar of Russian emigré history and the heritage of the Russian painter Nicholas Roerich and his family. He has authored numerous publications which comprise more than three hundred articles, brochures, monographs and albums. He holds the position of Head of The Roerichs' Heritage

Department at the State Museum of Oriental Art in Moscow and is also a member of the Union of Writers of Russia.

CARLOS LAZURTEGUI -

Carlos Lazurtegui is a photographer and digital restoration artist working in Madrid. His technical process of photographic conservation digitally preserves destabilizing photographs electronically while enhancing the appearance of the original. As an artist he appreciates motifs for their simplicity and composition and recognizes old photographs as "those frozen moments of a past era long gone".

When he first found the photograph of Natacha Rambova, appearing on the cover of this book, he did not know who she was but " fell in love with the pose, the gesture and the look". He then began the laborious process of restoring the photograph from its state of decay, pixel by pixel. His restorations and art are available @ www.lazurtegui.com

COLLEEN MANASSA DARNELL -

Colleen Manassa Darnell is an Egyptologist who teaches art history and studies ancient Egyptian Hieroglyphic texts as well as the impact of ancient Egypt on cultures throughout the world, including 1920's Egyptomania. Her exploration of the region of Moalla in Upper Egypt has led to the discovery of many tombs and a large late Roman settlement. She has published works on Egyptian military and literary texts as well as the survival of the Netherworld Books in the Late Period. In addition to her scholarly interest in Natacha Rambova, she is inspired by the exotic fashions and costumes which Rambova designed.

JOHN DARNELL -

John Coleman Darnell is Professor of Egyptology at Yale University and director of the Elkab Desert Survey Project. He is one of the founders of desert road archaeology in Egypt and has published myriads of rock inscriptions that he has discovered as well as books and articles on Egyptian historical and religious texts. One of the foci of his research is the ancient Egyptian Netherworld Books, including cryptographic compositions of the New Kingdom. Among his current projects is a discussion of the Third Intermediate Period Mythological Papyri based on the important essay by Natacha Rambova.

Notes & Sources

Introduction

1. "A questing woman..." *Kirkus Reviews*, review of *Madam Valentino, The Many Lives of Natacha Rambova*, by Michael Morris, August 1, 1991.

2. http://www.russiantearoomnyc.com/

3. *"Exotic Motions..."* Jennifer Dunning, *The Times Book Review*, April 18, 1990.

4. E-mail sent on March 23, 2014 from Michael Morris to Evelyn Zumaya, *"...I will say that we are presenting here ancillary material ..."*

5. Convegno Valentino, (Valentino Conference) *Rodolfo Valentino, La Seduzione Del Mito, Mostra, Film, Convegno, Seminari, Incontri, Omaggi, Recital,* Febbraio – Maggio 2009.

6. Convegno Valentino, *"Intorno a Rodolfo Valentino"*, February, 24, 2009.

7. E-mail from Michael Morris to Evelyn Zumaya, excerpt, May 2016.

8. Joseph Campbell, *The Mythic Image*, assisted by M.J. Abadie, Bollingen Series C, Princeton University Press, 1974. p. xi.

Note:
Additional Sources-

Account of Michael Morris' dinner interview and general correspondence with Flower Hujer, M. Morris archival materials including:

Christmas card & thank-you note from Flower Hujer to Michael Morris, dated December 15, 1989.

Press release issued for Flower Hujer's dance recitals at the Theater of the Riverside Church, May 22 and 23, 1990.

Promotional poster, *"Three Faces of Dance at Nikolais/Louis Chorespace Theater"* and cover of *Arabesque Magazine*, Volume XV, No. 3, September-October, 1989.

Written permission was granted to Michael Morris for use of their correspondence and quotes from various interviews by Flower Hujer.

Flower Hujer's Obituary, *The New York Times*, June 13, 1999. Ms. Hujer died May 1, 1999.

Prelude 1897-1925

1. The Artist as a Young Girl

1. "She was a stunning child." *Madam Valentino*, by M. Morris, p.31.

Note:

Opening chapter narratives excerpted from Michael Morris lecture delivered in Turin, February, 2009, titled, *"La Donna Dietro Il Mito. Il Ruolo di Natacha Rambova Nella Construzione del Divo", "The Woman Behind the Myth, Natacha Rambova's Role in the Creation of the Icon".*

2. "My interest in mythology and legend..." Undated letter from Natacha Rambova to Mary Mellon at the Bollingen Foundation, Library of Congress, Manuscript Division, Bollingen File.

3. *Madam Valentino*, p. 15-17.

4. "Her father was an Irish Catholic..." M. Morris archival notes.

Note:

Captions, "M. Morris archival notes" are cited from his hand-written, unpublished commentary.

5. "It was Aunt Elsie who..." M. Morris archival notes.

6. M. Morris, *Madam Valentino*, p.34 – 35.

7-8. Elsie DeWolfe commentary.

9. "She became a great fan of Pavlova..." M. Morris archival notes.

2. DANCE & DESIGN

Note:

Narrative excerpted from the Michael Morris lecture in Turin, February, 2009.

1. "Kosloff told Wink she had the potential.." *Madam Valentino*, p.43.

2. Origin of the name Natacha Rambova, "*By the way, the origin of her pseudonym is attributed to Kosloff. He was originally from Oranienbaum, a small town on the Gulf of Finland near St. Petersburg. Local residents called their city, "Rambov".* Cited from *Michael Morris, "I Was Fascinated by My Rambova",* by Dr. Vladimir Rosov, *The Ariavarta Journal, 2001.*

3. "Love comes and goes..." *Madam Valentino*, p. 50.

4. George Ullman, *The George Ullman Memoir*, p. 137.

5. "Kosloff was a dedicated..." Flower Hujer interviews with M. Morris.

6. "When Kosloff was mad at his students..." Ibid.

7. "The Aztec number was choreographed..." Ibid.

8. "When Rambova went to Kosloff's studio..." Vera Fredova correspondence with M. Morris.

9. "Supreme grace is represented..." Inscription on reverse side of original photograph, M. Morris Collection.

10. "Rambova was not so good at..." Vera Fredova.

11. "Her designs for *Salomé*..." Mark Hasselriis letter to M. Morris, October 6, 1987.

12."Kosloff was actually prudish..."Vera Fredova correspondence with M. Morris.

3. THE CREATION OF A HOLLYWOOD ICON

1. "She was gorgeous..." Notes from Mark Hasselriis telephone interview with M. Morris.

Note:

The Mark Hasselriis information in the Michael Morris archive consists of the letters Hasselriis wrote and hand-written notes Michael Morris transcribed during their telephone interviews.

Narrative excerpted from the M. Morris lecture in Turin, February, 2009.

2. "...the lure of Valentino.." *Madam Valentino*, p.152.

3. "Some of the farmer's of God's country..." Ibid., p. 152.

4. George Wehner, *A Curious Life*, p. 372.

5. "It was a hillside house..." *The George Ullman Memoir*, p. 173.

6. Ibid.

7. "The photos of Valentino posing as Nijinky's faun..." M. Morris archival notes.

8. "Valentino's most popular movie roles..." Ibid.

9. "Rudy's heightened psychic senses made it possible..." Natacha Rambova, *Rudy: An Intimate Portrait of Rudolph Valentino By His Wife Natacha Rambova*, p. 121.

10. "Rudy and Natacha's story is Pygmalion in reverse.." M. Morris archival notes.

11. "I do not hesitate to assert that..." *The George Ullman Memoir*, p. 184.

12. "Today you read about women who have taken commanding roles..." M. Morris interview with Susannah Hunnewell, *The New York Times Book Review*, October 27, 1991.

13. "Hollywood, which has made a fortune..." M. Morris archival notes.

14. "Despite the fact that the prestigious home..." E. Zumaya, *Affairs Valentino*, p. 130-131.

15. "The sun, sea and seclusion of Juan les Pins..." Ibid., p. 195.

Note:

"The Egyptian Woman" costume sketch by Natacha Rambova was contributed to this publication by Dr. Vladimir Rosov.

Michael Morris believed this sketch to have been destroyed: "*I have never seen the original drawing of the Cobra costume. It has been destroyed or belongs to some private collector.*"

16. "The Hudnut chateau is filled with..." Wehner, *A Curious Life*, p. 367-368.

17. "*What Price Beauty* ought to be called *The Divorce Picture*..." *The George Ullman Memoir*, p. 183.

18. "Upon our return to Hollywood plans were set into motion..." Ibid., p. 168.

19. "During the first few weeks of July, Natacha's nocturnal absences..." *Affairs Valentino*, p. 262.

Note:

The Star Sainty Gallery in London exhibits many paintings by Beltran-Masses. Beltran-Masses' painting of Rudolph Valentino as the Caballero Jerezano is currently housed in the Utah Museum of Fine Arts and was donated to the museum in 1951 by Mrs. Richard Hudnut.

20. "The agenda for the remaining of that day included..." Ibid., p. 266.

21. "Nevertheless she was sped in her labor of love..." *The George Ullman Memoir*, p. 184.

Note:
"*Mrs. Valentino on Graft*", is reprinted from *The Movie Weekly*, June 7, 1923.

Beyond Valentino 1925-1966

4. Venturing Solo

1. Letter from Mark Hasselriis to M. Morris, August 6, 1987.

2. Rudolph Valentino on United Artists studio lot in bungalow... *"His enjoyment of his 'restoration to bachelorhood' was apparently not solely a European activity..."* Affairs Valentino, p. 309.

3. Uncited newspaper article in M. Morris archive, *"Rambova Sees Fight of Wits"*, New York, April 23, 1926.

4. *"Rambova Busy with Theater and Writings"*, Portland Express, March 26, 1027.

5. George Wehner, *A Curious Life*, p. 360.

6. Ibid., p. 340.

7. *Variety, "Mystery Play a Hit", 1927, undated.*

8. *The New York Times, Sunday, February 7, 1926 and February 10, 1926, Variety,* Review titled, *"Natacha Rambova and Co. The Purple Vial (Sketch).*

9. Uncited newspaper article, *"Gowns? Natacha's Best Bet!"*, June 28, 1928.

10. George Wehner, *A Curious Life*, p. 13.

11. "She was no Pollyanna..." Mark Hasselriis correspondence.

12. *International Newsreel* photo and press release, August 24, 1925.

13. Ibid.

14. *"Miss Rambova in Hamilton Show, Valentino's First Wife Comes Here in 'When Love Grows Cold' "*, Lancaster News, March 20, 1927.

15. Uncited newspaper article in M. Morris archive.

16. "To achieve success..." *The George Ullman Memoir*, p. 160.

17. "Tuesday morning came..." George Wehner, *A Curious Life*, p. 373

18. *Photoplay* magazine, April 1926, published under column, *"Brickbats and Bouquets"*.

Additional reviewers comments regarding *The Purple Vial*, newspaper clippings from *The New York Times*, Sunday, February 7, 1926 and February 10, 1926, and *Variety*, review titled, *"Natacha Rambova and Co. The Purple Vial (Sketch).*

5. The Museum of Religion and Philosophy

Note: Michael Morris explains why he did not mention the engagement of Natacha Rambova and Svetoslav Roerich in *Madam Valentino*: *"At the time of my book's publication the Roerich Museum requested I not mentioned the affair between Svetoslav Roerich and Natacha Rambova. Upon the death in 1993 of board member Frances Grant, that restriction was apparently lifted. I thank the curator of the Roerich Museum, Daniel Entin, for his wise counsel during this period and for directing me toward materials that call for further research."*

M. Morris archival notes.

Note:

Francis Grant was the Executive Director of the Master Institute of United Arts, in 1929 she served as the Director of the Roerich Museum Press and Vice President of the Roerich Museum.

1. Roerich.org

2. Dr. Rosov, confirmation of engagement

between Svetoslav Roerich and Natacha Rambova and place of residence, move into the Master Building in 1929 cited in e-mail to E. Zumaya.

3. "Séances would typically begin..." Brian Taves, *Talbot Mundy, Philosopher of Adventure, A Critical Biography*, p. 175.

4. "It was then she was elected to serve..." *New York Times*, (1923-current file), August 18, 1929, *"Roerich Museum Elects: Theophile Schneider Is Made President of American Branch".*

5. "Natacha took the theosophical perspective..." Brian Taves, *Talbot Mundy, Philosopher of Adventure, A Critical Biography*, p. 168.

6. "Natacha never once engaged..." Letter from Mark Hasselriis to M. Morris, November 7, 1989.

7. "The circle of his scientific interests..." http://en.agnivesti.ru/the-roerichs/svetoslav-roerich/

8. "The cross-fertilization of the arts..." Roerich.org

9. "Since the mid-1920's..:" *From Synarchy to Shambhala*, by Markus Osterrieder, p. 101.

10. "I was very interested in ornithology..:" From S. Roerich, *Striving for the Beautiful*, p. 54, The Roerich Small Library.

11. "Dostoevsky said, 'Beauty will save the world'..." Agnivesti, *We Can not Linger*, by Svetoslav Roerich, Bangalore, July 3, 1989 and Sovetskaya Kultura, July 29, 1989.

12. "Roerich's ambition was no less than to prepare..." *From Synarchy to Shambhala*, by Markus Osterrieder, p. 101.

13. "Svetoslav was convinced that beauty...

"http://en.agnivesti.ru/the-roerichs/svetoslav-roerich

Note:

Michael Morris notes, "I am indebted to Rambova costume and fashion scholar, Heather Vaughan, for bringing the museum's printed pamphlet to my attention."

14. "The new era of enlightenment is awaited..:" Roerich.org, *Altai-Himalaya, Part XII, Tibet (1927-1928).*

15. Obituary of Devika Rani, *Independent*, March 26, 1994.

16. *The New Age of Russia, Occult and Esoteric Dimensions,* edited by Birgit Menzel, Kubon & Sagner, 2012, p. 25.

17. "The museum sustains an ongoing effort..." roerich.org.

"Michael Morris: I was Fascinated by My Rambova", Courtesy of Dr. Vladimir Rosov. All Rights Reserved. This article was first published in *The Ariavarta Journal in 2001.*

Note: The English version of Dr. Rosov's article was transcribed by Alexandra Andreeva. The text was translated by Oleg Albedil.

Note:

Michael Morris comments upon "defamatory" remarks by Colleen Moore in, *Silent Star,* by Colleen Moore, Doubleday & Co., Inc., Garden City, New York, 1968.

p. 98. " *Every night Natasha (sic) would hold a séance, calling forth help from the spirit world in her creative undertaking. Then, pencil and paper in hand, she would go into a trance and start writing. After her outpourings were typed up they were brought onto the set the next day and given to the director..."*

p.99. Ibid., *"The problem for Rudy's director, however, was not what to do with the blank pages if there were any, but what to do with the others. The script made no sense at all, inspiring one comment that Natasha's (sic) 'control' must be the now deceased Laura Jean Libby bent on proving she wasn't the world's worst writer after all. (A writer of potboilers about the working girl, such as When Love Grows Cold and Miss Middleton's Lover, people used to say of her that Laura Jean Libbey was to literature what the Cherry Sisters were to vaudeville.*

The Cherry Sisters were so bad people in the audience threw vegetables at them -and derived such pleasure out of doing it that the Cherry Sisters became a great attraction, but had to perform behind a net to ensure continuing this attraction.)

Word finally reached Valentino's New York financiers that the only thing Natasha's efforts were adding was to the mounting production cost, so Natasha was ordered off the set and a screenwriter brought in the straighten out the tangle."

Note:

Dr. Vladimir Rosov, confirms Svetoslav Roerich painted several portraits of Natacha Rambova.

Note:

Commentary on Svetoslav Roerich's portrait of Natacha Rambova, Fig. 131, sourced in part from consultation with Diva Zumaya, PhD., Candidate, History of Art and Architecture, University of California, Santa Barbara, California.

6. BETWEEN THE THUNDER AND THE LIGHTNING

Note: Arriba España, Up Spain reproduced through copyright permission granted to Michael Morris by Ann Wollen as, *"...Dear Bill (William McQuire) Michael wanted a copy of this. It is Frank's but he said it was OK for you two to have copies....he (Michael) plans to use the material...I am sure this is want Natacha would want."*

Also as cited: Reproduced under the authority of Ms. Wollen's permission granted to *"authorize Michael Morris to use the information and materials I have given him since 1980, including photographs, oral history, manuscripts and letters, as he sees fit in the preparation and publication of his work on Natacha Rambova."*

1. "Cleopatra is her greatest prototype in history." *The George Ullman Memoir,* p. 183.

2. Interview notes, Mark Hasselriis tells M. Morris, *"Howard Carter refused a lot of people who came in droves. How could he refuse Natacha Rambova?"*

3. Letter from Natacha Rambova to Ann Wollen, March 1, 1965.

4. Battle for Mallorca, August 16 – September 12, 1936.

5. Account of Natacha Rambova's support of Antonio Espina by William James.

6. "...a gathering of Alvaro and Natacha..." cited from an e-mail from M. Morris to William James.

7. "Natacha Rambova wrote she had moved..." Brian Taves, *Talbot Mundy,* p.199-200.

8. "The villa was noted for its simple planes..." Note written on reverse of photograph by Ann Wollen.

9...."the heads on the columns..." M. Morris archival notes.

10. "Nearly ten years after Valentino had expressed..." *Madam Valentino*, p. 204.

11. "The photo of Natacha with Beltran-Masses..." M. Morris archival notes.

12. "She was not one for smiling in front of the camera..." William James commentary.

13. "One could swim in the numerous rocky coves..." *Madam Valentino*, p. 202.

14. "Natacha was particularly excited..." Ibid., p. 207.

15. Mark Hasselriis correspondence with M. Morris.

16. "Now I realize that Natacha was at times..." Letter from Mark Hasselriis to M. Morris, September 16, 1989.

17. "To help lure tourists..." *Madam Valentino*, p. 202.

18. "It is possible Natacha designed this jewelry herself...." Heather A. (Vaughan) Lee, "*Natacha Rambova, Dress Designer (1928 – 1931), Dress, The Annual Journal of the Costume Society of America*, Volume 33, 2006, p. 34.

Notes and Citations for, *Arriba España, Up Spain, Introduction* by William James:

I. Ed. Carlos Jerez-Farrán, Samuel Amago, *Unearthing Franco's Legacy: Mass Graves and the Recovery of Historical Memory in Spain.* 2010, Notre Dame University Press, p. 62.

II. Note: Espina's wife was not the only person to seek assistance of this sort from the Bishop. Their pleas fell on deaf ears. In a letter to The Vatican's Secretariat of State in 1938, Bishop Miralles denied all knowledge of executions in Mallorca, thereby refusing to acknowlege what everyone else on the island knew.

III. William James also cites as sources:

Interviews with Mallorcan historian David Ginard i Féron.

Interviews with Natacha Rambova's goddaughter, María Salomé Juaneda Pujol.

Anthony Beevor, *The Battle for Spain*, Phoenix, London, 2007.

Georges Bernanos, *A Diary of my Times*, Borriswood, London, 1938.

David Ginard i Féron:,*El moviment obrer de Mallorca i la Guerra Civil (1936-1939)* (The Majorcan Worker's Movement and the Civil War [1936-39]), Publicacions de l'Abadia de Montserrat, Barcelona, 1999.

Paul Preston, *The Coming of the Spanish Civil War. Reform, reaction and revolution in the Second Republic*, Routledge, London, 1994.

Jean Schalekamp, *De una isla no se puede escapar* (From an Island there is No Escape), self-published, Palma de Mallorca, 1987.

7. ENVELOPED BY THE MYTH OF THE AGES

1. "In Egypt, the local people of Luxor..." comment by Mark Hasselriis, letter to M. Morris, Nov, 7, 1986, p. 7.

2. "My assessment, at the age of 23..." letter from Fred Husson to M. Morris dated August

20, 1990.

3. Oracular Technique as related to Mark Hasselriis, M. Morris archival notes.

4. Information on Natacha's students, Maud Oakes information and Old Dominion Foundation and Bollingen references; *Bollingen, An Adventure in Collecting the Past* by William McQuire, Bollingen Series, Copyright 1982, by Princeton University Press.

5. Oakes, Maud, *The Two Crosses of Todos Santos*, Introduction by Paul Radin, p. 5.

6. Natacha requests assistance from Bollingen Foundation to expedite her passport for trip to Guatemala stating her legal name as Natacha Rambova de Urzaiz, letter from Natacha to Donald D. Shepard, May 22, 1945.

Also: letter to Natacha Rambova from D.D. Shepard, Vice-President of the Bollingen Foundation, December 29, 1945, informing her of the transference of her grant from the Old Dominion Foundation to the Bollingen Foundation. Bollingen Foundation Container 12, Natacha Rambova, 470.3.

7. "By 1946, Natacha pressed on..." McQuire, *Bollingen*, p. 159.

8. Information regarding Natacha's first Bollingen grant: Letter from Natacha to A.W. Schmidt, June 15, 1946, *"I believe it will interest the Foundation to know that the research work made possible by the grant..."*

9. Information on Piankoff, *"Alexandre Piankoff (1897–1966),"* Extrait Du Bulletin De L'Institut Français D'Archèologie Orientale, T. LXV.

10. Initial meeting of Natacha Rambova and Alexandre Piankoff, Rosalind M. Janssen, *"Rambova and Piankoff: Tying up Loose Ends",* Göttinger Miszellen, 156 (1997) p. 67.

11. "At dawn the next morning..." Letter written from Natacha Rambova to Jack Barrett at the Bollingen Foundation, February 1947 from Luxor, Upper Egypt.

12. Mark Hasselriis information taken from his handwritten "Resumé", courtesy of John G. Rae III and Susan Rae.

13. "Convening at the Mena House.." M. Morris archival notes from interview with L. Fred Husson, also Bernard Bothmer, *Egypt 1950, My First Visit*, "Husson's darkroom at Chicago House.." p. 33.

14. In Luxor, Mark would stay at the Oriental Institute..."*I had a room and a drafting room. Natacha Rambova stayed at the Luxor Hotel."* M. Morris notes from Mark Hasselriis interviews.

15. Natacha's small dog in tow, Bernard V. Bothmer, *Egypt 1950, My First Visit*, edited by Emma Swan Hall, Oxbow Books, 2003.

16. "In addition to the above mentioned assignments..." Husson interview with M. Morris, April 9, 1990.

17. Mark Hasselriis writes, *"I was lonely in Chicago House after Fred Husson left. She (Natacha) had a disagreement with Fred and he decided to leave. I was lonely and she was picky and testy. A blow up occurred and she sent me a box of chocolates. Piankoff said calm down. 'She's temperamental – She's Irish!'* "

18. Natacha upset over Husson's afternoon tea showing of expedition photographs, Letter from L. Fred Husson to M. Morris dated, August 20, 1990.

19. Address of Alexandre Piankoff in Cairo, letter from Vaun Gillmor at Bollingen Foundation to Piankoff notifying him of Natacha Rambova's death, dated June 6, 1966.

20. Natacha assumes control over Piankoff's personal business affairs, letter from Vaun Gillmor to Maud Oakes, August 25, 1966, stating Natacha was in possession of only copy of Piankoff's will and banking information both in Paris and New York.

21. "Dear Miss Rambova..." Library of Congress, Bollingen Foundation file, Piankoff and Rambova letters, M. Morris archival references. Reproduced from the Collections of the Manuscript Division.

22. Natacha Rambova's letters to Bollingen Foundation... *"As you know, and as I have told Piankoff many times, I do not wish to do any more editing until I have finished my own work..."* letter dated, August 25, 1958.

Note: The following sources were also referenced:

Maud Oakes Obituary–*San Francisco Chronicle*, June 14, 1990.

Photograph of Maud Oakes and her quote cited from, *Dona Matilda of Todos Santos*, by Lanfranco Rasponi as published in *Vogue*, Dec. 1946.

23. "From Jung in Zurich..." Letter from Maud Oakes to Mima (Mary Mellon), 1943, McQuire, *Bollingen*, p. 71.

24. Ibid., p. 10, painting by Gerald L. Brockhurst, 1938.

25. "On my passport application..." Letter from Natacha Rambova to Donald D. Shepard, Vice President of The Bollingen Foundation, May 22nd, 1945.

26. "I have no degree to my name..." "*Dona Matilda of Todos Santos*" by Lanfranco Rasponi, *Vogue*, Dec. 1946.

27. "Natacha did not get along with..." M. Morris archive, M. Hasselriis interview notes.

28. "About Egypt, I do not know what to say..." Letter from Natacha to Ann Wollen, January 19, 1964.

29. "I had been told the only hotel in Aswan... Natacha Rambova writes to Bollingen Foundation President Jack Barrett from Luxor, Egypt, February 1947.

30. "Natacha didn't want to be photographed..." M. Hasselriis writes to M. Morris, September 16, 1989.

31. "Last evening I drove back from Karnak..." Natacha writes Jack Barrett at Bollingen Foundation.

32. "After watching the evening sunset..." Ibid.

33. "The material I was able to gather here..." Ibid.

34. "She was always pointing out details..." M. Hasselriis writes to M. Morris on October, 6, 1987.

35. "In general she wore suit-dresses..." M. Hasselriis writes M. Morris on Nov. 7, 1986.

36. "She bought antiques..." M. Hasselriis writes to to William McQuire on January 25th, 1981.

Note:

Handwritten notations on watercolor are from the *Book of Caverns*, from the Tomb of Ramesses VI, Courtesy of The Natacha Rambova Archive, Yale University, Gift of Edward L Ochsenschlager in memory of Donald P. Hansen.

8. THE COSMIC CIRCUIT

Your Psychic Potential, by M. J. Abadie, Illustrations by Mark Hasselriis, Adams Media Corporations, 1995.

1. "A disciple of Natacha's thought", cited letter from William McQuire written to Katherine Peterson dated, August 16, 1979, *"Mark is a disciple of Natacha's thought."* Also letter from William McQuire to M. Morris dated April 29, 1982.

2. "...An ancient man in a modern world", Mark Hasselriis' nephew, John G. Rae III to E. Zumaya.

Note: Letter from Mark Hasselriis to Michael Morris dated September 16, 1989, *"You have my full permission to use the letters and tapes of our conversations for the book.*

3. M. Hasselriis letter to M. Morris.

4. Ibid.

5. M. Hasselriis letter to M. Morris, Nov. 7, 1989, p. 8.

6. "The dumpy, middle-aged lady"... M. Morris notes.

7. "For both of us art..." Ibid.

8. Rambova letter to Barrett on August 25, 1958.

9. M. Hasselriis interviews with M. Morris, saying he has copies of *The Celestial Virgin* and *The Celestial Figure* and Mai Mai Sze has a copy of *Pantheos.*

10 Piankoff writes Natacha about the problems with review criticism, " You accuse me of dark designs...", December 13, 1954.

11. Wehner, George, *A Curious Life,* p. 338. "When I entered Mrs. Valentino's apartment ..."

"When I entered Mrs. Valentino's apartment on the top floor at 9 West 81st Street, I was at once charmed by its colorful atmosphere. The floors were carpeted in jet black. The walls were a soft gray and the woodwork, silver. Across the front of the large living room a long step led up through vermilion curtained French windows into a glass veranda from which the myriad lights of Central Park and the city beyond could be seen.

The furniture was of the modern art and was in Chinese red and black. Above the table hung a silver chandelier of exquisite workmanship representing a huge flower cup like a morning-glory's, with around it vine leaves, curling tendrils, and bunches of little silver grapes. A few pictures, extraordinary in coloring glowed from the walls."

12. "Gilded bronzes from Tibet..." M. Hasselriis to M. Morris.

13. "...she felt she had but a few months to live..." Natacha fears she will not live past the winter of 1963, letter from Dr. Piankoff to Vaun Gillmor, July 1, 1963, *"...I have received, when in Cairo, a distressing and morbid letter from Miss Rambova, she wrote me that she thinks to last only until the winter..."*

14. ..."She often woke up screaming in the night..." Mark Hasselriis correspondence with M. Morris.

15. "She was as thin as a skeleton..." Ibid.

16. Rambova managing Piankoff's finances and specifics of finances, *"...no one would be able to sort them out if she should die."* Letter to Dr. Piankoff from Vaun Gillmor, July 16, 1963.

Note:
Account of Natacha Rambova's death and final

months, Mark Hasselriis letters and Bollingen letter to Alexandre Piankoff dated May 17, 1966, citing letter from Maud Oakes including information regarding La Encinas, 2900 East Del Mar Blvd., Pasadena, Ca.

Note:
Also referenced-

Letter from Alexandre Piankoff to Natacha Rambova, November 16, 1964.

Letter from Piankoff to Jack Barrett, upset over Natacha's not editing the Litany of Re, Nov. 7, 1959.

Letter from Alexandre Piankoff to Natacha Rambova, January 13, 1965.

Letter dated August 25, 1958 from Natacha Rambova to Jack Barrett, ..."As you know, and as I have told Piankoff..."

Reference to Natacha Rambova's recognition as Egyptologist, *The Natacha Rambova Archive*, Yale University by Colleen Manassa and Tasha Dobbin-Bennett.

Natacha Rambova, in M. Joukowsky and B. Lesko, eds., *Breaking Ground: Women in Old World Archaeology*

Also, M.L. Bierbrier, *Who Was Who in Egyptology*, 4th ed., (London, 2012)

Also: Rosalind M. Janssen, *From Hollywood to Thebes: In Quest of Natacha Rambova (1987-1966)*, Gottinger Miszellen, 153, (1996).

17. *The George Ullman Memoir.*

18. "I saw her with a turban only once in my life..." M. Hasselriis writes M. Morris, Nov. 7, 1986.

19. Editorial Note by Natacha Rambova to *The Shrines of Tut-Ankh-Amon,* by Alexandre Piankoff, The Bollingen Library, p. ix.

20. "When they talked it was animated interest..." M. Hasselriis writes to M. Morris.

21. "Natacha ate a variety of food..." M. Hasselriis writes M. Morris on Nov. 7, 1986.

22. "She was terribly earnest about her work.." M. Hasselriis writes M. Morris on Aug. 6, 1987.

23. "Books abounded..." M. Hasselriis writes to William McQuire.

24. "What would happen to society..." M. Hasselriis letter to John G. Rae III.

25. "It was in other words..." M. Hasselriis interview notes, M. Morris archive.

26. "Natacha, as I have said, was clear..." M. Hasselriis writes M. Morris, Dec.24, 1990.

27. "The peace offering has been received..." Alexandre Piankoff writes to Bollingen Foundation President on October 10, 1962.

28. "Dear Natacha, I have just found time..." Natacha cites Egyptologist Dick Parker in a letter to Barrett, May 20, 1958.

29. "Her humor was not confined to..." M. Hasselriis writes M. Morris on Aug. 6, 1987

30. "Natacha hated to be worshiped..." M. Hasselriis writes M. Morris on Nov. 1, 1990.

31. "Now about poor Natacha..." Vaun Gillmor writes to Piankoff, May 17, 1966.

32. "There was magic just around the corner..." M. Hasselriis writes M. Morris on Jan. 25. 1981

33. "On the Second Shrine of..." *The Cosmic Circuit,* N. Rambova, p. 80.

APPENDICES

Note:

In Memoriam Latin translation: "It is not the chief duty of friends to follow the dead with unprofitable laments, but to remember his wishes, to fulfill his commands "

Other Sources:
www.beyondvalentino.com
www.affairsvalentino.com/
www.viplibri.net
aureliomiccoli.blogspot.it/
theinfancyofthemyth.blogspot.it/

List of Plates

Opening

Fig. 1. Michael Morris Collection.

Fig. 2. *Madam Valentino, The Many Lives of Natacha Rambova,* by Michael Morris, Abbeville Press, 1991.

Fig. 3. M. Morris Collection. Inscription on the 1989 original photograph of Flower Hujer by Jack Mitchell.

Fig. 4. *Neb-Kheperu-Re,* Diagram by Mark Hasselriis from *The Shrines of Tut-Ankh-Amon,* Second Volume of *The Egyptian Religious Texts and Representations.* Texts Translated with Introductions by Alexandre Piankoff, Edited by N. Rambova, Bollingen Foundation, Inc., New York, 1955.

1. The Artist as a Young Child

Fig. 5-7. M. Morris Collection. Photographs cited as "Courtesy of Ann Wollen" are reproduced under the authority of Ms. Wollen's permission granted to *"authorize Michael Morris to use the information and materials I have given him since 1980, including photographs, oral history, manuscripts and letters, as he sees fit in the preparation and publication of his work on Natacha Rambova."*

Fig. 8. M. Morris Collection, Courtesy of Philip S. O'Shaughnessy.

Fig. 9. M. Morris Collection, Courtesy of Ann Wollen.

Fig. 10-11. M. Morris Collection.

Fig. 12- 15. M. Morris Collection, Courtesy of Ann Wollen.

Fig. 16–25. M. Morris Collection.

Fig. 26. M. Morris Collection, Courtesy of Ann Wollen.

2. The Aztec Dance

Fig. 27. M. Morris Collection, Courtesy of Ann Wollen.

Fig. 28-29. M. Morris Collection, Courtesy of Leslie Flint.

Fig. 30–33. Courtesy of Vera Fredova.

Fig. 34-37A. M. Morris Collection, Courtesy of Ann Wollen.

Fig. 38. Courtesy of Vera Fredova.

Fig. 39. Courtesy of The Academy of Motion Picture Arts and Sciences.

Fig. 40. R.R. Stuart Collection, Hollywood, California.

Fig. 41-43. Courtesy of The Academy of Motion Picture Arts and Sciences.

Fig. 44. M. Morris Collection

3. The Creation of a Hollywood Icon

Fig. 45. Courtesy of The Academy of Motion Picture Arts and Sciences.

Fig. 46-51. M. Morris Collection, Courtesy of Leslie Flint.

Fig. 52-52A. Courtesy of Leslie Flint. Photographs by Helen MacGregor with credit given to her partner, Maurice Beck when first published in *Vanity Fair,* c. 1924.

Fig. 53-56. Courtesy of The Academy of Motion Picture Arts and Sciences.

Fig. 57. M. Morris Collection.

Fig. 58-61. Courtesy of the National Film Archives and Stills Library of the British Film Institute, London.

Fig. 62. M. Morris Collection.

Fig. 63-67. Courtesy of Elizabeth Hudnut Clarkson, Hudnut Family Archivist.

Fig. 68-75. Courtesy of Ann Wollen.

Fig. 76. Paul Joanowitch, Austrian, *Richard Alexander Hudnut Portrait,* 1925, Oil on canvas. Gift of Mrs. Richard A. Hudnut, from the Permanent Collection of the Utah Museum of Fine Arts.

Fig. 77. Paul Joanowitch, Austrian, *Winifred Kimball Hudnut Portrait,* 1925, Oil on canvas. Gift of Mrs. Richard A. Hudnut, from the Permanent Collection of the Utah Museum of Fine Arts.

Fig. 78. Paul Joanowitch, Austrian, *Natacha Rambova,* 1925, Oil on canvas. Gift of Mrs. Richard A. Hudnut, from the Permanent Collection of the Utah Museum of Fine Arts.

Fig. 79. Courtesy of Dr. Vladimir Rosov, All Rights Reserved.

Fig. 80-83. Courtesy of The Museum of Modern Art/Film Stills Archive, New York City.

Fig. 84. M. Morris Collection.

4. VENTURING SOLO

Fig. 85 - 90. M. Morris Collection.

Fig. 91 - 92. The New York Public Library at Lincoln Center, Performing Arts Research Center.

Fig. 93-94. E. Zumaya Collection.

Fig. 95-100. M. Morris Collection.

Fig. 101. Natacha Rambova, American, (1897-1966). Dinner Gown with Belt, 1928-1931, gold braid embroidery on silk velvet. Collection of Phoenix Art Museum, Gift of Mrs. Philip Markert. Photo by Ken Howie.

Fig. 102. Natacha Rambova, American, (1897-1966). Afternoon Ensemble, 1928-1931, printed silk chiffon and crepe. Collection of Phoenix Art Museum, Gift of Mrs. Philip Markert. Photo by Ken Howie. Natacha Rambova, American, (1897-1966). Afternoon Dress, 1928-1929, printed silk satin. Collection of Phoenix Art Museum, Gift of Mrs. Philip Markert. Photo by Ken Howie.

Fig. 103. Natacha Rambova, American, (1897-1966). Dress and Jacket, 1928-1931, silk velvet and brocade. Collection of Phoenix Art Museum, Gift of Mrs. Philip Markert. Photo by Ken Howie.

Fig. 104. Natacha Rambova, American, (1897-1966). Evening Dress, 1928-1931, silk chiffon. Collection of Phoenix Art Museum, Gift of Mrs. Philip Markert. Photo by Ken Howie.

Fig. 105. M. Morris Collection.

5. MUSEUM OF RELIGION & PHILOSOPHY

Fig. 106-120. Courtesy of the Nicholas Roerich Museum, All Rights Reserved.

Fig. 121. Courtesy of Heather A. (Vaughan) Lee.

6. BETWEEN THE THUNDER & THE LIGHTNING

7. ENVELOPED BY THE MYTH OF THE AGES

Fig. 228. Natacha Rambova Archive, Yale University, Gift of Edward L Ochsenschlager in memory of Donald P. Hansen.

Fig. 229-230. M. Hasselriis illustrations in *The Shrines of Tut-Ankh-Amon,* by A. Piankoff.

Fig. 231-241. Natacha Rambova Archive, Yale University, Gift of Edward L Ochsenschlager in memory of Donald P. Hansen.

Fig. 242-243. M. Morris Collection, Courtesy of Ann Wollen.

Fig. 244. E. Zumaya Collection.

8. THE COSMIC CIRCUIT

Fig. 245. Bull's Head Amulet, Natacha Rambova's Collection of Antiquities, Courtesy of the Yale University Art Gallery.

Fig. 246-251. M. Morris Collection.

Fig. 252-255. M. Morris Collection, Courtesy of Ann Wollen.

Fig. 256. Courtesy of Tove Abrams. All Rights Reserved.

Fig. 257. M. Morris Collection.

Fig. 258. Courtesy of Tove Abrams. All Rights Reserved.

Fig. 259-262. M. Morris Collection.

Fig. 263. Courtesy of John G. Rae III & Susan Rae. All Rights Reserved.

Fig. 264-265. Courtesy of Tove Abrams. All Rights Reserved.

Fig. 266-268. M. Morris Collection.

Fig. 269. *The Cosmic Circuit,* N. Rambova, Illustration by Mark Hasselriis.

APPENDICES

"In Memoriam" photograph of Michael Morris, Courtesy of the Western Dominican Province. All Rights Reserved.

WHO'S WHO IN *BEYOND VALENTINO*

ALEXANDRE PIANKOFF-

Alexandre Piankoff (1897–1966) was born in St. Petersburg, Russia and died in Brussels, Belgium. Having graduated just prior to the beginning of the First World War, he enlisted in the Russian Army. After the war he left Russia to continue his Egyptological studies in Berlin. In 1926, he entered the Sorbonne in Paris and by 1930, he received his doctoral degree after presenting his thesis, "Le Coeur' Dans les Textes Egyptiens". He was fluent in Russian, French, English, Turkish, Arabic and Farsi and became a French citizen in 1936. In 1940, he moved to Cairo.

There, as a member of the Institut Français d'Archéologie Orientale of Cairo, he began his extensive field work which included the recording of several ancient Egyptian tombs, most notably the tomb of Ramesses VI. His work, funded by the Bollingen Foundation, resulted in the publication of the prestigious *Egyptian Religious Texts and Representations,* which includes the individual volumes: *The Tomb of Ramesses VI* published in 1954, *The Shrines of Tut-Ankh-Amon* published in 1955, *Mythological Papyri* published in 1957, *The Litany of Re* published in 1964 and *The Pyramid of Unas* published posthumously in 1968.

ALVARO DE URZAIZ Y SILVA-

Alvaro de Ursaiz y Silva (1900?-1961) was the second born son of the Countess del Puerto. His royal lineage granted him aristocratic status in Spain throughout his lifetime. Alvaro and Natacha Rambova remained legally married until he planned to remarry in 1956. He then traveled to New York City to seek an official annulment of his first marriage. The annulment was granted based on the grounds Natacha had no intention to have children when she married him. Alvaro then married a Spanish aristocrat, the daughter of a count, Esperanza Maldonado y Chavarri. Because of his conservative leanings as revealed in Natacha's essay, *Arriba España,* he became known as a Pro-Franco Fascist sympathizer.

ELSIE DEWOLFE-

Elsie DeWolfe (1859 – 1950) continued to be a noted name in interior design until the 1930's. She died in her home in Versailles, France. Although she began her career as an actress, she is best remembered as a cutting edge designer utilizing 18th century French furniture to embellish her light and airy pastel interiors. In 1926 she married Sir Charles Mendl although she did not live with him. She maintained her address and residence with Miss Elizabeth Marbury until her death in 1950.

MAUD OAKES

Maud Oakes (1903 - 1990) was born in Seattle, Washington. As a child, her family moved to New York City. There she became a writer, an accomplished artist and ethnologist; eventually studying, documenting and recording the ceremonies, myths and art and the Mam of Guatemala and the Navajo of Arizona. Her research was funded initially by the Old Dominion Foundation which later became the Bollingen Foundation.

After a trip to Egypt in 1947-1948, she moved to Big Sur, California. In 1950, she organized an expedition to India to study the Nagas, however political strife there at the time forced her to abandon this research. Instead, she traveled to Peru with a goal to study the Incan culture.

While in the Andes, her Jeep rolled down a mountainside during a rain storm, resulting in serious injuries including a broken neck. She returned to Big Sur to recover where she immersed herself in Jungian analysis and her publication on Jung which she titled, *The Stone Speaks*. Her entire archive of research papers, manuscripts and artwork was destroyed when her Big Sur home burned to the ground. Maud died of Alheizmers in 1990. Her publications include *Where the Two Came to Their Father: A Navaho War Ceremony*, *The Two Crosses of Todos Santos: Survivals of Mayan Religious Ritual* and *Beyond the Windy Place – Life in the Guatemalan Highlands*.

MARK HASSELRIIS-

Mark Hasselriis (1924–1999) was born and raised in New York City. He lived most of his life in Forest Hills, Queens, New York and Bayport, Long Island. He served with Dwight David Eisenhower in Paris during World War Two and visited the island of Mallorca in the 1980s. His extensive world travels included trips to Saudi Arabia and the Middle East.

Mark Hasselriis illustrated many books throughout his prolific career including, *The Mythic Image* by Joseph Campbell, *The Hero: Myth/Image/Symbol* by Dorothy Norman, *Isis and Osiris – Exploring the Goddess Myth*, by Jonathan Cott, edited by Jacqueline Onassis and *Your Psychic Potential*, by M.J. Abadie. Mark lectured and taught at the School of Sacred Arts in New York City on West Fourth Street, where he was known for his classes on Egyptian Heiroglyphic painting.

A brochure for the School of Sacred Arts states that Mark Hasselriis, "...served as artist-draftsman for the epigraphic survey at Khonsu and Medinet Habu Temples for the Oriental Institute of the University of Chicago. As an artist with the Bollingen Foundation expedition, he recorded the great tomb of Ramesses VI and the shrines of Tut-ankh-amon." As art adviser to the Bollingen Foundation, Mark Hasselriis illustrated such works as, *Mythological Papyri of the 21th Dynasty*, *The Great Litany of Re*, Dale Saunders' *Mudra* (on Japanese rituals and hand gestures) and Joseph Campbell's *The Mythic Image*s. He also lectured on the Survey of Sacred Arts.

SVETOSLAV ROERICH-

After leaving New York City in 1931, Svetoslav Roerich (1904–1993) lived the remainder of his life in India where he was recognized as a celebrated artist. In 1936-1937, a first exhibition of his art was held at the State Exhibition of the United Provinces in Lucknow. Continuous annual exhibitions of his work were subsequently organized and in 1941, Svetoslav was commissioned to paint several official portraits of India's Prime Minister, Jawaharlal Nehru. In 1945, he married Indian film star, Devika Rani Chaudhuri, known as Devika Rani. At the time she was acting administrator of the film studio, "Bombay Talkies".

After their marriage, Svetoslav and Devika lived outside of Bangalore on an estate they christened, "Tataguni." In addition to collecting local folk items and studying flora, Svetoslav continued his work as an accomplished artist with his paintings being showcased throughout India, Europe and in Russia. In 1960, a comprehensive retrospective of his work was held in Delhi. The same year Svetoslav returned to Russia for an exhibition of his art in the State Pushkin Museum of Fine Arts in Moscow.

Svetoslav painted primarily landscapes and portraits in the Russian Academist style, utilizing his signature bold colors. He received prestigious honors and awards during his lifetime including being named *Honorary Doctor of Veliko Tarnovo* by the University in Bulgaria, *Cavalier of the Order of Cyril and Methodius* in Bulgaria and an *Academician of the Academy of Fine Arts of India*. He and Devika devoted much of their lives in India to the funding and management of the cultural center, Karnataka Chitrakala Parishrath in Bangalore. In the late 1980's, several organizations were founded in honor of Svetoslav Roerich including "Peace Through Culture", "The Soviet Roerich Fund" and "The International Center of the Roerichs".

Svetoslav Roerich is buried on his estate Tataguni in Bangalore. Upon the death of Devika Rani, Tataguni was brought under the governing body, the Svetoslav Roerich and Devika Rani Roerich Estate Board.

THEODORE KOSLOFF-

After Theodore Kosloff's (1882–1956) relationship with Natacha Rambova ended, he continued to work in the motion picture industry, appearing with co-stars including Nita Naldi, Bebe Daniels and Gloria Swanson. However, with the advent of sound in cinema his heavy Russian accent brought an early end to his acting career. His final movie, made with DeMille was *Madam Satan*. Kosloff continued to teach and manage his ballet schools until his death. He is buried in Valhalla Memorial Cemetery in North Hollywood with his star on the Hollywood Walk of Fame being located at 1617 Vine Street in Hollywood.

VERA FREDOVA-

Vera Fredova, Winifred Edwards (1894–1989) was born in London and first danced with Anna Pavlova. She joined Kosloff's troupe in 1916 and performed with Kosloff until 1919. She remained a partner in his dance schools in San Francisco and Dallas until 1934. She returned to England where during the Second World War she volunteered with the Red Cross. After the war, she did not return to ballet as a dancer but as a teacher at the age of fifty-three. She taught at the Valois school, Sadler Well's and at the Royal Ballet School where she was a revered instructor until 1955. Among her well-known students are Deanne Bergsma, Anthony Dowell, Lynn Seymour, Antoinette Sibley, David Wall and Monica Mason.

FLOWER HUJER-

The Hollywood-born dancer, Flower Hujer (1907-1999) moved to New York City after leaving Theodore Kosloff's dance troupe. During the 1940's, she set out on her own professionally by securing roles in various Broadway musicals and off-Broadway productions. She founded her own dance company in New York and produced many dance recitals primarily of a religious nature. She danced well into her eighties and died in her home in Astoria, New York on May 1, 1999.

MARY MELLON-

Mary Mellon, (1909-1946) affectionately referred to as, "Mima", named her Bollingen Foundation after Carl Jung's Swiss retreat outside of Zurich. She infamously commented after hearing Jung lecture for the first time that she had no idea what he was talking about but knew it involved her. She then made it her life's goal to publish his works in English.

She was married to the wealthy Paul Mellon, the son of Andrew Mellon, Secretary of the Treasury under three U.S. Presidents. With this fortune at her disposal, Mary Mellon funded what has been referred to as the salvation of the world's cultural soul. Her Bollingen Foundation was initially founded to publish Carl Jung's work in English, but soon evolved into supporting many scholars and their work in art historical research, archaeology, literature and other culturally vital endeavors.

The many photos of Mary Mellon smoking a cigarette are in hindsight distressing as she suffered from asthma from childhood. It would be during the throes of one asthma attack that she died in 1946. With many scholars dependent upon her patronage, her husband Paul continued to fund the Bollingen Foundation projects, scholars, editors and scientists and anthropologists who all revered Mima and her dedication to their work.

Mai Mai Sze-

Mai Mai Sze (1909-1992) was born in China and moved to London as her father was the Chinese ambassador. In 1921, she and her family moved to the U.S. where she would graduate from Wellesley College in 1931. Initially she devoted her artistic talents to illustrating, advertising graphic design and fashion magazine illustration while earning herself a loyal readership by penning a column in the *New York Post* titled, "East-West". Upon the encouragement of her friend Dorothy Norman, she acted as an advocate for war relief in China.

Mai Mai Sze was a devoted student of Natacha Rambova and attended her classes and lectures for many years in New York. Her affiliation with Rambova would result in her illustrating some of *The Egyptian Texts and Representations*. As a Bollingen Fellow, Mai Mai Sze authored the Bollingen publication, *The Tao of Painting: A Study of the Ritual Disposition of Chinese Painting*," published in 1956. At the time of her death, Mai Mai was living with designer Irene Sharaff and it is presumed they were partners.

BIBLIOGRAPHY

Note: This bibliography itemizes publications referenced in addition to those cited in the complete *Madam Valentino* bibliography.

BOOKS-

Alovisio, Silvio and Giulia Carluccio, with Preface by David Robinson, *Rodolfo Valentino, Cinema, Cultura, Società tra Italia é Stati Uniti Negli Anni Venti,* Kaplan Edizioni, 2010, Torino.

Andreyev, Alexandre, *The Myth of the Masters Revived, The Occult Lives of Nikolai and Elena Roerich,* Koninklijke Brill, Leiden and Boston, Netherlands, 2014.

Bothmer, Bernard V., *Egypt 1950, My First Visit,* Edited by Emma Swan Hall, Oxbow Books, 2003.

Cott, Jonathan, Is*is and Osiris, Exploring the Goddess Myth,* Doubleday, 1994.

Drayer, Ruth A., *Nicholas and Helena Roerich: The Spiritual Journey of Two Great Artist*s, Quest Books, Revised Edition, 2005.

McQuire, William, *Bollingen, An Adventure in Collecting the Past,* Princeton University Press, 1982.

Miccoli, Aurelio, *The Infancy of the Myth*, Translated into English by Angelo Perrone, Viale Industria Pubblicazioni, Torino, 2014.

Moore, Colleen, *Silent Star,* Doubleday & Co., Inc., Garden City, New York, 1968.

Morris, Michael, *Madam Valentino, The Many Lives of Natacha Rambova,* Abbeville Press, 1991.

Norman, Dorothy, *The Hero: Myth/Image/Symbol,* The World Publishing Company, 1969.

Oakes, Maud, *The Two Crosses of Todos Santos,* Introduction by Paul Radin, Bollingen Series XXVII, Princeton University Press, 1951.

Oakes, Maud, *The Stone Speaks, The Memoir of a Personal Transformation*, Chiron Publications, 1987.

Piankoff, Alexandre, T*he Shrines of Tut-Ankh-Amon,* Bollingen Foundation, 1955.

Prophet, Mark L. and Elizabeth Clare Prophet, *The Masters and Their Retreats,* Summit University Press.

Roerich, Nicholas, *Altai-Himalaya, A Travel Diary,* roerich.org.

Roerich, Svetoslav, *Art and Life*, International Center of the Roerichs, Moscow, 2004.

Taves, Brian, *Talbot Mundy, Philosopher of Adventure, A Critical Biography*, McFarland & Company, Inc., 2006.

Ullman, George, *The S. George Ullman Memoir, The Real Rudolph Valentino by the Man Who Knew Him Best*, Viale Industria Pubblicazioni, Torino, 2014.

Wehner, George, Introduction by Talbot Mundy, *A Curious Life*, 1929, Horace Liveright, New York, 1929.

Zumaya, Evelyn, *Affairs Valentino, Special Edition*, Viale Industria Pubblicazioni, Torino, 2015.

ARTICLES AND ESSAYS-

*"Alexandre Piankoff" (1897–1966) "*Extrait Du Bulletin De L'Institut Français D'Archèologie Orientale, T. LXV.

Altai-Himalaya, Part XII, Tibet (1927-1928), Roerich.org

Bender, Thomas, *"With Love and Money"*, *The New York Times*, November 14, 1982. Review of William McQuire's, *Bollingen, An Adventure in Collecting the Past*.

Crandell, Stephen, *"Mary Mellon–The Woman Who Decided to Save the History of the World's Soul"*, *The Huffington Post*, 11, 26, 2014.

Janssen, Rosalind M., *From Hollywood to Thebes: In Quest of Natacha Rambova (1987-1966)*, Gottinger Miszellen, 153, (1996).

Janssen, Rosalind M., *Rambova and Piankoff: Tying up Loose Ends*, Gottinger Miszellen, 156, (1997).

Kenneth Archer International, Interviews on Nicholas Roerich, 1982 – 1983, roerichjournal.com.

Manassa, Colleen and Tasha Dobbin-Bennett, *The Natacha Rambova Archive, Yale University*, Gottinger Miszellen, 234, (2012).

Manassa, Colleen, *Echoes of Egypt: Conjuring the Land of the Pharaohs*, Exhibition at the Yale Peabody Museum of Natural History, April 13, 2013-January 4, 2014, Catalog of Exhibition.

Osterrieder, Markus, Agni Yoga, *"From Synarchy to Shambhala: The Role of Political Occultism and Social Messianism in the Activities of Nicholas Roerich"*.

Rasponi, Lanfranco, *Dona Matilda of Todos Santos*, *Vogue* magazine, Dec. 1946.

Roerich, Svetoslav,*"We Can not Linger"*, Agnivesti, Bangalore, July 3, 1989, Sovetskaya Kultura, July

29, 1989.

Roerich, Svetoslav, *Striving for the Beautiful*, The Roerich Small Library.

Tulskaya, A., *Agni Yogi Quarterly/International*, "*The Teachings: Francis Grant, A Life Dedicated to the Roerich Pact*", 2016, Vol. XXXVIII, no.3.

Vaughan, Heather A., "*Natacha Rambova, Dress Designer (1928 – 1931)*", Dress, *The Annual Journal of the Costume Society of America*, Volume 33, 2006.

Literary Vitae of Natacha Rambova

Books

Rudy: An Intimate Portrait of Rudolph Valentino By His Wife Natacha Rambova
Hutchinson & Co. (Publishers) LTD.
Paternoster Row, London, E.C.
December, 1926

Technique for Living
by
James Henry Smith, Natacha Rambova and illustrated by Mildred Orrick
Essential Books, 1944

The Road Back : A Program of Rehabilitation
by
James Henry Smith and Natacha Rambova
Creative Age Press, 1945

Screenplays

The Hooded Falcon
What Price Beauty
All That Glitters

Articles

Harper's Bazaar
Town and Country Magazine
Vogue Magazine
American Astrology Magazine,
Serial articles on the philosophy and the psychology of zodiacal symbolism
from February 1942 – June 1943

ESSAYS

Arriba España, "Up Spain"
The Symbolism of the Papyri

UNPUBLISHED MANUSCRIPTS

The Cosmic Circuit
The Mystery Pattern in Ancient Symbolism
Pantheos
The Celestial Virgin
The Celestial Figure

EDITORIAL WORK

1954 - *The Tomb of Ramesses VI*

1955 – *The Shrines of Tut-Anhk-Amon*

1957 – *Mythological Papyri*

WORKS DEDICATED TO NATACHA RAMBOVA

1965 – *The Litany of Re*

FILMOGRAPHY OF NATACHA RAMBOVA

1917 *The Woman God Forgot* (costumes)

1920 *Billions* (costumes & sets)

1921 *Forbidden Fruit* (costumes and sets with Mitchell Leisen)

1921 *Aphrodite* (costumes & sets)

1921 *Camille* (costumes & sets)

1922 *A Doll's House* (costume & sets)

1922 *Beyond the Rocks* (costumes)

1922 *The Young Rajah* (costumes & sets)

1923 *Salomé* (costumes & sets)

1924 *Monsieur Beaucaire* (costumes & sets with Georges Barbier)

1924 *The Hooded Falcon* (screenplay writer & costumes with Adrian)

1924 *The Sainted Devil* (costumes with Adrian)

1925 *The Cobra* (costumes with Adrian)

1925 *What Price Beauty* (producer & design consultant)

1926 *When Love Grows Cold* (actress)

Note: Neither *Aphrodite* or *The Hooded Falcon* were realized as films. *Billions, A Doll's House, The Sainted Devil* and *What Price Beauty* are lost films. Fragments of footage exist of *The Young Rajah* and *When Love Grows Cold*. What are considered Rambova's masterpieces have survived, *Camille, Salomé* and *Monsieur Beaucaire* with photographic stills available in film archives.

Index